FRENCH LITERATURE
In The Twentieth Century

COMPARATIVE LITERATURE series

Italian Literature
by Christopher Cairns

The English Novel: Defoe to the Victorians
by David Skilton

American Literature Vol I: Nineteenth and Early Twentieth Centuries
by Ann Massa and Scott Donaldson

American Literature Vol II: The American Novel in the Twentieth Century
by Miles Donald

French Literature In The Nineteenth Century
by Christopher Robinson

Comparative Literature

FRENCH LITERATURE
IN THE TWENTIETH CENTURY

Christopher Robinson

DAVID & CHARLES
Newton Abbot   London

BARNES & NOBLE
Totowa, New Jersey

For Luke, Dorcas and Patience

The quotation from Poetry of Departures *by Philip Larkin is reprinted from* The Less Deceived *by permission of The Marvell Press, England.*

British Library Cataloguing in Publication Data
Robinson, Christopher
  French literature in the twentieth century —
(Comparative literature).
  1. French literature — 20th century — History and Criticism
  I. Title   II Series
  840'9'00912   PQ305
  ISBN   0-7153-8076-1
  ISBN   0-389-20121-9 (United States)

© Christopher Robinson 1980

All rights reserved. No part of this publication may be reproduced, stored in a retrieval system, or transmitted, in any form or by any means, electronic, mechanical, photocopying, recording or otherwise, without the prior permission of David & Charles (Publishers) Limited

and printed in Great Britain
by
Redwood Burn Ltd Trowbridge
for David & Charles (Publishers) Limited
Brunel House Newton Abbot Devon

First published in the USA 1980 by
Barnes & Noble Books
81 Adams Drive
Totawa, New Jersey, 07512

Contents

Preface 6

1 NEW PERCEPTIONS 7
Emotion, intellect and the creative act · Poetry of travel ·
The inter-relation of the arts · Order and adventure ·
A modern sensibility

2 LITERATURE AND THE SELF 52
Gide · Proust · Céline · Experimental autobiography

3 THE CULT OF YOUTH 82
Childhood as a lost paradise · The otherness of adolescence

4 THE CULT OF MANLINESS 109
Adventurers · Man and nature

5 PHILOSOPHICAL DILEMMAS 132
Surrealism · Essentialists in the theatre · The absurdity
of life · Playing at meaning · New mythologies

6 CHRISTIAN CONVICTIONS 178
The rejection of reason · A world without God ·
Sexuality as evil · Good and evil: the novels of Bernanos ·
The aesthetic dilemma

7 ACTION AND SOCIETY 201
Commitment and the novel · Commitment and poetry ·
Commitment in the theatre · Realism versus stylisation

8 NATIONAL CONSCIOUSNESS 227
Africa and the Caribbean · Algeria · Switzerland ·
Quebec

9 THE LITERATURE OF LITERATURE 258
The self-conscious novel · The *nouveau roman* ·
New mythologies expanded

Epilogue 281

Further Reading 284

Index 286

Preface

One has only to look at studies of nineteenth-century French literature published in the 1880s to see how rash a project it is to attempt to assess the relative achievements of the writers of one's own century. How ill-judged the criticisms of morbid M. Baudelaire and immoral M. Flaubert now seem. The phenomenon is not restricted to critics of the Belle Epoque; when drawing up a list of the best French novels in the period 1900-50 a distinguished committee contrived to omit *Le Grand Meaulnes*, while including Jacques de Lacretelle's *Silberman*. The fact is that Time imposes an orthodoxy of value judgments with which the prudent concur and against which the bold revolt. Like a man trying to judge the proportions of a Palladian mansion when standing at its very entrance the contemporary critic cannot for certain determine the relative significance of the parts of the literary edifice. Deprived of a temporal perspective he has no orthodoxy to guide his vision and can therefore construct no heterodoxy.

The analysis of twentieth-century French literature which follows will be a somewhat personal attempt to detect patterns of development, indicate links between authors not always considered together, and suggest the limitation of types of writing still fashionable. I have made every effort to take into account shifting French evaluations of their own achievements. That is, however, no reason for not making Anglo-Saxon judgments in a book intended for a largely Anglo-Saxon audience. One cannot suppose the French deficient in aesthetic sensibility because they value Poe highly; there must be qualities in Poe which speak more readily to a Frenchman than to an Englishman. The development of literature on the two sides of the Channel since the 1920s has been so divergent that some writers well thought of in France will inevitably find little favour in England or America. If my prejudices show, I hope they can at least be said to be well defended.

CHAPTER I
New Perceptions

> See! on the cumber'd plain
> Clearing a stage,
> Scattering the past about,
> Comes the new age.
> Bards make new poems,
> Thinkers new schools,
> Statesmen new systems,
> Critics new rules.
> All things begin again . . .
>
> (Matthew Arnold, 'Bacchanalia or The New Age')

Cultural change does not, unfortunately for critics, occur so neatly as Matthew Arnold's words might seem to suggest. It would be naïve to suppose that a significant modification in intellectual values or literary forms took place precisely at the beginning of the present century, or even that so substantial an agent for social upheaval as World War I miraculously engendered a cultural revolution. The intellectual heritage of the nineteenth century so clearly moulds the chief preoccupations of the twentieth that it is tempting to see the whole of post-Revolutionary French literature as an extended Romantic agony, in which Victor Hugo begat Baudelaire, Baudelaire Rimbaud, and Rimbaud the surrealists, whilst on a co-lateral line Baudelaire fathers the symbolists, the symbolists Proust and Gide, and they in their turn the 'new novel' and existentialism respectively. Yet such an approach has distinct disadvantages. It glosses over the extent to which the nineteenth-century preoccupation with the tensions between metaphysical and materialist ideals, the individual and society, liberty and order, has been developed along distinctively twentieth-century lines. More disturbingly, it lends authority to the semi-official myth that contemporary French literature consists principally in writers and groups such as those named above, who can all be fitted into a family tree. Any account which relegates Radiguet, Cocteau, Giono, Montherlant or Saint-John Perse to the status of exceptions, outside some main literary current, is plainly inadequate. Yet a tendency to think along such lines persists among literary historians. Let us therefore begin our investigation by looking at what the new century itself considered to be modern, in the hope that thereby we may pick up some ideas for a less conventional approach to the disparate, but in many ways complementary, strands of cultural activity which have created a distinctively twentieth-century French sensibility.

Modernism can be seen as a redefinition, a development of Romanticism, designed firstly to move away from abstractions and ideals and turn man's attention to new experience of the physical world around him, and secondly to return to art the sense that its value lay precisely in its being art. Neither of these ideas is in itself a twentieth-century development: the emphasis on living for the experience of the moment was central to the art of the decadents, and the value of art in itself can be found quite separately expounded in Gautier and Mallarmé. If, however, you put the two strands together, you arrive at a concept of art in which its function is to alert men to the possibilities of the world by offering new perspectives on it. Individualism, subjectivism and liberation from convention of any kind are prerequisites for such an approach, and any attempt to re-impose a metaphysical dimension must take the existence of all these responses to the world into account. But the art which evolves must not simply be the bi-product of an individual viewpoint. It must contain sufficient structure, sufficient rules of its own to be independent of the personality of its creator.

Emotion, intellect and the creative act
A philosophical basis for these new twists to old concepts can be found in the writings of Henry Bergson (1859-1941), of whom André Gide very accurately observed: 'In times to come his influence on our period will be detected everywhere, simply because he is of his time and always swims with the tide. That is the reason for his representative importance.' Bergson, in his major works *Essai sur les données immédiates de la conscience* (1889), *Matière et mémoire* (1896) and *Le Rire* (1900), defines a view of man's perceptions, and his translation of those perceptions into art, which gives the prime role in experience to instinct and intuition, making the intellect an instrument that deforms our vision, and language the means of reducing our perceptions to a lowest common denominator. Here is to be found a philosophical justification for that reduction of the outer world to a contingent status and that raising of individual perceptions to the status of true reality, which characterised a major part of French poetry from Nerval to Mallarmé. For Bergson, the external world can be defined only spatially, the mental world only temporally. Habits of language have obscured this difference by lending the illusion of temporal duration to the material world (the idea of succession being a synthesis of observations by a conscious observer) and by breaking up the stream of consciousness into 'states of mind' which appear to be distinct from one another only because of the spatial images in which we express them. Intellect, an essentially analytical process, can cope with the successive sensations that link the self with the outer world, but can only distort the stream of consciousness which these sensations feed in the individual, by reducing his unique experiences to a series of symbolically stylised states, stylised,

that is, by the reductive symbolism of language itself. As he puts it in *Le Rire*: 'We only grasp the impersonal aspect of our feelings, the aspect which language has been able to codify permanently, because it is more or less the same, in the same conditions, for all men.' Literature, then, becomes the attempt to break down the 'practical' essence of language — its use as a notation for the shared practical element in experience — in order to communicate the private experience of the individual. Artists 'will struggle to get us to see something of their own visions: by rhythmic arrangements of words, which thus contrive to form a structure of their own and to animate themselves with an original life of their own, they tell us, or rather suggest to us, things that language is not designed to express.'

Bergson's views on art can also be seen as encouraging turn-of-the-century artists to throw off social and literary constraints: 'The only aim of art is to sweep aside ... generalities which are conventionally and socially accepted, in other words, everything that hides reality from us.' His concept of *élan vital*, proposed in *L'évolution créatrice* (1907), although one might agree with Paul Valéry in dismissing it as 'poetry', concords with the movement towards the cult of energy and action in literature. The value he placed on intuition and the concealed inner self gives weight to the cult of a new form of subjectivity, consisting in the value given to the artist's instantaneous responses to the immediate sensations of the contingent world. His view of the absence of conventional duration within the inner self justifies the theory of simultaneity which gained favour in painting and poetry just prior to World War I. Of course, not all the parallels with Bergson's ideas are 'modern'. There are links between his philosophy and the ideas of some symbolists, even with the anti-intellectualism of the Catholic revival and the Nationalists. But there are more striking connections with the insistence on life as a process of *becoming* which is basic to the thought of André Gide, the portrayal of life's disconnected moments and of the mobility of consciousness which is characteristic of the poetry of Paul Valéry, the special status given to memory and art by Marcel Proust or the concern with the renewal of literary expression which is manifested quite differently in Gide and Apollinaire. Going beyond these one perceives the paradoxical connection between Bergson, destroyer of abstract systems, and Sartre, promoter of them, in the former's insistence on the primacy of the present and on the gap between man and the physical world, concepts essential to Sartrean existentialism. In a looser way it is obvious that Bergson's ideas could also prepare the way for an interest in the subconscious or in the process of *becoming* inherent in the states of childhood and adolescence. They could equally co-exist with new attempts to synthesize the various branches of art into total effects or to use art to change accepted categories of reality. After all, Bergson's lecture 'La perception du changement', with its emphasis on the mental change wrought in the spectator by the special perceptions embodied in a painting, could stand in itself as a justification for the development of the visual arts from Cézanne to the cubists, and for the influence of that development upon French poetry 1910-25. Once one is talking of new perceptions, of intermittence, of *becoming*, then the work of writers such as Valery Larbaud, Cocteau, Radiguet, Blaise Cendrars, even Alfred Jarry or André Breton — none of them in any technical sense Bergsonian — begins to seem compatible with many elements in the Bergsonian world-view.

Let us try to piece together a pattern of distinctively twentieth-century ideas basic to French 'modernity', drawing our examples from some of the writers listed above. Gide and Valéry, whose formative years were in both cases lived entirely in the previous century, offer a good starting place. Their literary roots are in symbolism — both belonged, with Odilon Redon, Yeats and Gauguin, to the younger group who attended Mallarmé's 'Tuesdays'. Yet neither wrote anything exclusively consignable to a symbolist aesthetic. Of the two, Valéry (1871-1945) is the less representative of a specifically French modernity, although his work had a considerable influence on poets in other countries, notably T.S. Eliot and George Seferis. His poetry concerns itself primarily with the exploration of the nature of consciousness and of the creative process, but it is abstract only in the sense that he seeks to go beyond his own individuality to a perception of something universally valid. As he expresses it in 'Le Rameur' (*Charmes* 1922) *'Je remonte à la source où cesse même un nom'* (I am going back to the spring where there ceases to be even a name.). Like Bergson, Valéry rejects abstract systematisation. The basis of his art lies in the transmutation of sense impressions of the visual world: 'I find what I need in the perception, and then in the imaginative recreation, of the *matter* of things — water, rock, a soft mass of leaves, very fine sand, flesh.' Like Bergson, he sees this transmutation as an inevitably personal process, because the independent reality of external objects cannot be perceived. Each man sees his own reality:

> The world is dependent on our senses. To transpose the world into thought without acknowledging the human element in the thought process (or at least to transpose the visible world into thought without taking into account the role of the observer) is nonsensical.

The act of thought is an act of choice, a necessary act which leads Valéry to give a weight to intellect hardly found again in French poetry before Yves Bonnefoy. But Valéry's understanding of the term *intellect* needs defining, since, as he expresses it, in a modification of Pascal's famous maxim, *'L'esprit aussi a ses raisons que la raison ne connaît pas'* (The mind too has its reasons unknown to reason). Intellect for Valéry is the conceptual counterpart of feeling, and does not stand in opposition to it. On the contrary, he sees creativity as an activity of the entire mind, with no separation of the functions of intellect and emotion. As he puts it in 'Aurore' (*Charmes*):

*[Je] vais cherchant
Dans ma forêt sensuelle
Les prémisses de mon chant.
Etre! . . . Universelle oreille!
Toute l'âme s'appareille
A l'extrême du désir . . .
Elle s'écoute qui tremble
Et parfois ma lèvre semble
Son frémissement saisir.*

[[I] go in search of the premises of my song in my sensory/sensual forest. The act of being! . . . Ear to the Universal! The whole mind strives to equate itself with the ultimate point of desire . . . It hears itself trembling and sometimes my lips seems to catch its *frisson*].

Clearly Valéry would have found quite acceptable Ezra Pound's definition of an image as 'that which presents an intellectual and emotional complex in an instance of time'.

In *La Jeune Parque* (1917) and *Charmes* the apparent antithesis of sense and mind is really part of a synthetic process in which both elements retain their independent identities but function in unison. In *La Jeune Parque*, originally intended as a 'farewell to poetry', the tension between body and mind is symbolised in the figure of the young virgin awakening to her physical possibilities under the stimulus of a religio-sexual dream (the Serpent's bite) and bringing to bear on her experience, and the flow of memories released in her, a conscious intelligence which gives her the power to be of the natural world while retaining her independence from it. The meaning of the poem is multivalent, offering symbols for a series of possible antitheses within the human condition, for example, the submission of purity to action, or the passage from an instinctive to a conscious mode of perception, but it is difficult not to see it as ending in a synthesis of the value of sensuality to mind, an assertion of physical experience as the force from which the mind can gain new stimulus:

> *Alors, malgré moi-même, il le faut, ô Soleil,*
> *Que j'adore mon coeur où tu te viens connaître,*
> *Doux et puissant retour du délice de naître*

[So, despite myself, I must, O Sun, adore my heart where you come and know yourself, a gentle and powerful repetition of the intense pleasure of being born].

The dangerous and destructive power of sensuality can be absorbed into a creative function.

La Jeune Parque retains an intangibility of meaning akin to that of some symbolist poetry, for example, Mallarmé's *L'Après-midi d'un faune*, because Valéry himself was interested, clearly, more in the process of composition than in communicating a defined concept or concepts. As early as his two long essays, 'Introduction à la méthode de Léonard de Vinci' (1895) and 'Une Soirée avec Monsieur Teste' (1896), this preference for the act of creation over the thing created is apparent in his thought. In a letter written in 1922 he makes the applicability of this attitude to *La Jeune Parque* explicit when he writes:

> Sensuality, memories, emotions, awareness of the body, depth of the memory and previous lights or skies seen again etc. From this web, which has no beginning or end, only intersections, I made a monologue on which I had imposed, before undertaking it, conditions of form as strict as the conditions of content were light.

The often lighter and consciously more fragmentary poems of *Charmes*, though they depend on ambiguity within the individual image, are more precisely directed towards the single end of interpreting the synthesis between the inner forces of the self. This does not mean that the creation of form loses its pre-eminence in Valéry's eyes. Of one of the major poems of the collection, 'Le Cimetière marin', he observed that he started writing with, as his only intention, 'a rhythmic pattern, empty, or rather filled with meaningless syllables, which came and obsessed me for while', a remark whose implausibility is lessened if put in the context of T.S. Eliot's statement in 'The music of poetry' (*On Poetry and Poets*):

> I know that a poem, or a passage of a poem, may tend to realize itself first as a particular rhythm before it reaches expression in words, and that this rhythm may bring to birth the idea and the image; and I do not believe that this is an experience peculiar to myself.

It is easy to go on from this to show how Valéry consciously varied metre, rhyme scheme and stanza shape to give a unique form, within the collection, to all but two of the twenty-two poems (the two exceptions, 'Aurore' and 'Palme' being, significantly, placed first and last when Valéry altered the order of the poems for the 1926 edition). But differences of form are matched by thematic similarities, shared images, and the consistent application of certain effects of poetic diction. Several of the poems are overtly turned towards the subject of poetic creation. 'Aurore' expresses the poet's response to the challenge of a new day: the growth of intellectual perception, the resistance to the potentially stifling effect of excessive intellectualism in the form of the '*Maîtresses de l'âme, Idées/Courtisanes par ennui*' (Mistresses of the soul, Ideas/grown courtesan through boredom) and the stimulus of contact with the physical world where

> *Toute feuille me présente*
> *Une source complaisante*
> *Où je bois ce frêle bruit . . .*
> *Tout m'est pulpe, tout amande,*
> *Tout calice me demande*
> *Que j'attende pour son fruit.*

[Each leaf offers me a willing spring at which to drink in this frail sound . . . To me everything is fruit-flesh, everything is kernel, every calyx asks me to wait while its fruit forms.]

'La Pythie' expresses the poet's ambiguous attitude to the disruptive irrational forces of emotion and inspiration, symbolised in the figure of the Pythia, whom Valéry initially reduces to a manic animal figure, but whose ravings are suddenly transformed into a communication of inner truth. In the 1926 edition Valéry followed this poem by the almost frivolous sonnet on the same theme, 'Le Sylphe', in which inspiration is cast as a swiftly fading scent, indefinable and (a maliciously witty touch) destined to cause confusion among literary critics:

> *Ni lu ni compris?*
> *Aux meilleurs esprits*
> *Que d'erreurs promises!*

[Neither read nor understood? What future errors in store for the great minds!]

'Poésie,' more seriously, expresses the danger to the poet of excessive intellectualising, whilst 'Palme' embodies the sense of the slow and mysterious process of artistic creation itself.

To say that these poems are 'overtly turned towards the subject of poetic creation' is not to limit them specifically to that, because their images, like those of the other poems, are founded on the contrasts of stasis and motion, dark and light, languor and vigour, purity and sensuality, death and life. The most accessible and possibly the most satisfying of all Valéry's poems, 'Le Cimetière marin', synthesizes in its shifting perspectives the whole range of these oppositions. The man and the poet speak here with one voice. Valéry portrays himself as falling into the trap of contemplating the absolute, which is eternally static, and thus denying his own nature, whose mutability is its most positive quality. Yet eventually he breaks free, bidding his body to break the thought-process within which it is encaged and open itself to the immediacy of the sensual world:

> *Buvez, mon sein, la naissance du vent!*
> *Une fraîcheur, de la mer exhalée,*
> *Me rend mon âme*

[Drink in the birth of the wind, my breast! A freshness breathed from the sea gives me back my soul].

The oppressive tranquillity of a Mediterranean noontide (reminiscent of Leconte de Lisle's *Midi*) to which even the sea 'this tranquil roof where the doves walk' adhered, is finally broken, and nature, man, poet returned to the motion which is their essence. As the best-known line in the whole of Valéry's *oeuvre* puts it: '*Le vent se lève . . . il faut tenter de vivre*' (The wind is rising . . . an attempt at living must be made).

The images in which the idea of sensory stimulation is most constantly portrayed in *Charmes* are ones which the collection most obviously shares with *La Jeune Parque*, those of sexuality. Without any attempt at eroticism or even sexual precision, Valéry explores the possibilities of female sexuality, and male response to it, as a source for sensual images. In 'Dormeuse' and 'La Fausse Morte' the sexuality provides the primary image of the poem; in the former the poet contemplates the sleeping woman, in the latter the woman creates the 'false death' of orgasm for the poet. Elsewhere the woman provides a secondary image necessary to the communication of another level of thought; for example, in 'Abeille' the girl invites the bee to sting her breast, the sensuality of the image being overlaid with the poem's sustained reference to poetic inspiration. The complementary sexual orientation of images of the male can be found in the figure of Narcissus in 'Le Fragment du Narcisse', and in the plane tree, naked and white like a young Scythian, and the winged sperm of the other trees in 'Au Platane'. Throughout the majority of these poems the notion of sensual contact is balanced by a distance or even an hostility on the part of the male. In 'Dormeuse' he is detached from the woman as she sleeps, and refers slightingly to the absence of her soul 'busy in hell'; in 'Intérieur' the woman moves around the room without disturbing the poet's thought-processes. Even in 'La Fausse Morte', where the poet is wholly given over to sensuality, he focuses on the stimulus given to himself, rather than on any union. Finally, one must note the way in which the stylistic preciosity which gives an even patina to all the poems is itself part of the way in which sensuality is neutralised by intellect. The conceits of early seventeenth-century poetry, appropriate in any case to the highly antithetical thought-structure of Valéry's work, carry with them the advantage of being both traditionally associated with love poetry and, by their very contrivance, purely intellectual devices. The closing lines of 'La Fausse Morte', with their paradoxes of repeated death and death as more valuable than life, reduce the animality of the evocation of the sex act in the same way that the articifial word order, word play and visual stylisation of 'L'Abeille' help transfer the reader's attention from the sexual potential of the young girl/bee sting theme to the intellectual point of

> *Soit donc mon sens illuminé*
> *Par cette infime alerte d'or*

[So let my senses be fired by this tiny golden warning].

Manner and matter are in both harmony and counterpoint with one another.

Valéry is, then, a poet who, despite his affinities with Mallarmé, expresses himself through very tangible images. His exploration of the self is one in which the opposing forces of body and mind are held in some sort of equilibrium by the sheer momentum of the poetic act. One can define as 'modern' in his work the exploration of the self in strictly non-metaphysical terms, the desire to keep the basic dichotomies of the human experience in synthesis, and the constant preoccupation with the nature of the creative act itself. In all these respects he can be compared with his now more widely read contemporary, André Gide (1869-1951).

Gide's early works are similar in theme to some of Valéry's poetry, but much more tormented and unresolved in their handling of the problems. His first published work, *Les*

Cahiers d'André Walter, which appeared anonymously in 1891, already handles in parallel the difficulty of reconciling sensual and spiritual love and the exposition of a number of fundamental artistic principles.

In his next substantial work, *Le Voyage d'Urien* (1893), the same urge for constraint and purification is portrayed, but expressed in a more overtly ironic fashion. The narrative depends on a series of symbolic landscapes designed to be the visible expression of the abstract emotions around which the work is structured. The voyage of the title is an argosy undertaken by a group of young men whose reason for setting off together is simply that their 'virtues are similar'. The quest is an escape from study into action. As Tradelineau proclaims to his companions:

> What is the point of knowing how we come to be here? Why look for very mysterious motives for our presence on the *Orion*? We have left our books because we were beginning to get bored with them, because a memory, which we would not admit to ourselves, of the real sea and sky made us lose our faith in the value of study; something else existed; and when the mild and fragrant breezes came and ruffled the curtains at our windows, despite ourselves we descended to the plain and advanced. We were tired of thinking; we wanted action . . .

Yet from the start the reality of this action is thrown into doubt. As Nathanaël puts it, perhaps they are living in their dreams, while their real selves are asleep at home.

The journey becomes two things: at one level, as Gide put it in the edition of 1896, the dream of life itself 'from our astonished birth to our unconvinced death', at another a gentle mockery of a generation who seek in literature the heroism they cannot find in life. For the first part of the journey it is the sensual and exotic which dominate the companions' experience, in the second part the world of *ennui*, that soul-penetrating boredom which negates the whole significance of existing. The goal is the Sea of Ice, a great wall, and below it a frozen corpse holding in his hand not the secrets of the

Universe but a blank sheet of paper. It is indeed, as the pun in the title suggests, a *voyage du rien*, a non-journey, for not only does the sterility imposed by purity seem less attractive than even the more calamitous sorts of sensuality encountered, but the whole escapade is not a definition of life but an avoidance of it. The worlds of sensuality and intellect have not been brought together; the attraction of purity as an end in itself is fading; the sense that literature must retain contact with the outside world is growing.

Four years later, in *Les Nourritures terrestres*, the pendulum has almost swung to the opposite limit: total rejection of both intellect and art. It is a call to return to immediacy expressed in a form which itself rejects conventional constraints. Yet it is also the first of Gide's works to succeed in holding two inimical qualities, self-indulgence and self-denial, in balance. In a preface to the 1927 edition Gide wrote:

> Certain people are only able, or are only prepared, to see in this book a glorification of desire and instinct. I find this a short-sighted interpretation. Personally, when I re-read it, I find it more an apologia for *divestment*.

In fact, the glorification of desire and instinct and the divestment go hand in hand, creating in the book (it is difficult to give it a category, composed as it is of a lyrical framework of exhortations and ecstatic exclamations, interlarded with maxims, anecdotes, descriptions and even poems) an identification of the longings of the body with the aspirations of the soul. It is not a hymn to hedonism, for physical and spiritual longings are both directed to the same end: God, pantheistically defined as imminent in every object and every act. As the opening of Book I observes: 'Do not wish to find God other than everywhere.' This notion becomes the basis for the essential Gidean concept of *disponibilité* (availability). In limiting ourselves to a single experience, idea or person, we are shutting ourselves off from new manifestations of the divine.

We are also cutting ourselves off from the development of our own possibilities (just as the river banks in Valéry's 'Le Rameur' represent the restriction placed by a linear life on the potential development of the poet). Gide proclaims a Bergsonian sloughing-off of knowledge and convention, leaving the individual the frightening but rewarding freedom to learn and to create himself anew with each and every fresh experience. What is important is experience itself and not anything obtained through it. To put it in more precise Gidean terms, desire enriches more than the possession of what is desired, to the point at which self-restraint, the deferring of the immediate gratification of desire, creates a more intense experience than indulgence. The resultant fervid state Gide identifies with love. These ideas are posed very early in the book, then illustrated, developed and re-expressed in a quasi-religious torrent of words. Many of the images are, in the broadest sense, erotic, hymning the physicality of the moment through hunger, thirst, desire for sensation and evocations of intense Mediterranean landscapes. In the figure of Ménalque in Book IV the exhortations of the narrator to Nathanaël are embodied in a sustained illustration of how such a liberty can (but not *should*) be fitted into a life-style — an anti-social one in conventional terms, for Ménalque, earlier portrayed as the narrator's own mentor, is a man who teaches children to leave their families and 'makes their hearts sick with desire for bitter wild fruits, and apprehensively curious for strange love'. In the fifth book the evocation of pleasures achieved passes into a pastoral mode in the voice of the narrator himself. The scenery here is all French, but in the following two books the places instanced range over Europe, north, east, but above all south, culminating in the descriptions of the Mediterranean coast of Africa:

> You cannot imagine, Nathanaël, what this deluge of light can eventually become; and the sensual ecstasy brought about by this

persistent heat . . . A branch of olive against the sky; the sky above the hills; the song of a flute in a café doorway.

Mobility: each setting bringing its lessons to the man ever sensible to the sensations of the moment; banished the intellect, even the lesson of the book itself only an initial stimulus: 'Nathanaël, now you must throw away my book. Emancipate yourself from it. Leave me . . . leave me . . .' Here is the completely 'modern' man, body and mind united in the ecstasy of the sensual present. The reinstatement of immediacy which Valéry will achieve by the delicately nuanced tensions of form, image and language is conservative in comparison with this rich, often over-ripe, poetry, an extended, deliberately fragmented hymn to man's potential for significant experience.

Poetry of travel
Gide's development does not, of course, stop with this work, which neither faces up to the radical psychological discontinuity to which it inadvertently condemns man, nor considers how the kind of liberty which it extols can be made compatible with existence within the framework of society. But Gide's answers to these problems will be discussed in another context. It is the Gide of *Les Nourritures* who most readily connects with another contemporary manifestation of Bergsonian values, early twentieth-century experimental poetry. One could quite easily apply the precept to be found in *Les Nourritures* — 'Multiply one's emotions. Don't shut oneself up in one's own life, one's own body; open the hospitality of one's soul to others' — to the life and works of Blaise Cendrars (1887-1961), in the same way that many of Cendrars' phrases, 'The simple fact of being alive is real happiness', 'Live, oh just live, and forget about what comes next! Don't feel remorse. It's not your job to pass judgments!', would not be out of place in Gide's work. Similarly, the theme of mobility which Gide

proposes provides the central images of much of Cendrars' poetry, where travel both staves off that stasis which is the death of artistic stimulation and offers the opportunity to explore reality more fully, providing a constantly renewed series of sensations.

Cendrars was not, of course, the first poet of his period to take up the theme of exotic travel. In 1908 Valery Larbaud (1881-1957) published anonymously his *Poèmes d'un riche amateur*, destined to reappear under his own name (in a slightly amended form) in *A.O. Barnabooth, ses Oeuvres complètes, c'est-à-dire un Conte, ses Poésies et son Journal intime* (1913). Adopting a way of excluding irrelevant subjectivity very different from that of, say, the English imagists, Larbaud projects himself into a third-person character, an objective vehicle for the poet's own responses to the world. This is the young South-American-born millionaire, Barnabooth, the embodiment of a complete freedom from material want and social convention, eager to absorb every new experience from his travels and yet endowed with a critical irony. (Gide noted in his *Journal*: 'Amusing, these poems of Valery Larbaud. On reading them I can see that I should have been more cynical in my *Nourritures terrestres*.') The poetry itself is a curious mixture of the lyricism of Walt Whitman, whose work Larbaud greatly admired, and the irony of Laforgue. The verse form is varied *vers libre*, whose conventions Larbaud treats somewhat tongue-in-cheek:

> *Mes amis reconnaissent ma voix, ses intonations*
> *Familières d'après dîner, dans mes poèmes.*
> *(Il suffit de savoir mettre l'accent où il faut.)*
> *Je suis agi par les lois invincibles du rythme,*
> *Je ne les comprends pas moi-même: elles sont là.*

[My friends recognise in my poems my voice, its familiar after-dinner intonations. (It's all just a matter of getting the stress right.) I am in the power of the invincible laws of rhythm, I don't understand them myself: they're just there.]

The diction is sometimes relaxed, often exotic and full of foreign names, yet also easily admitting the everyday, in a conscious rejection of the hermetic language of much symbolist poetry:

> Après avoir aimé des yeux dans Burlington Arcade,
> Je redescends Picadilly à pied, doucement.
> O bouffées de printemps melées à des odeurs d'urine,
> Entre les grilles du Green Park et la station des cabs,
> Combien vous êtes émouvantes!

[After making love with my eyes in Burlington Arcade, I stroll back down Picadilly. O whiffs of spring mixed with smells of urine, between the railings of Green Park and the cab rank, how you do stir me!]

This kind of contemporary reference can of course degenerate into a frivolous *chic*, as in the early poetry of Cocteau (eg, *Le Prince frivole*) with its references to 'in' places and people, like the Ritz, Charvet, Guerlain. In Larbaud it is all part of the wide-eyed openness to experience of his young hero, and the desire to record it in its most raw and striking form.

In Cendrars the effect is, deliberately, more dramatic. Larbaud's half-joke at the expense of disembodied rhythm finds itself taken up as seriously by Cendrars as by Valéry and Eliot. In Cendrars' case it is not merely poetry that is born as rhythm, but man himself:

> There is no science of man, man being in essence the carrier of a rhythm. The rhythm cannot be translated into visible terms . . . In the beginning was the rhythm and the rhythm was made flesh.
> (*Moravagine*, 1926)

This inner music — Cendrars saw music as the manifestation of the human spirit which is closest to its irrationality and spontaneity, and therefore capable of revealing the mind uncontaminated by the falsifying effect of reason — is translated into his poetry in the rhythm of travel itself. In his *Prose du Transsibérien et de la petite Jeanne de France* (1913), dedicated 'to musicians', he collages memories of his travels in Russia in 1905 as assistant to an agent in clocks and watches, with other experiences both biographical and imagined, suppressing the natural time structures so that, within the poem, travel and Paris are values simultaneously in tension with one another. Cendrars could almost take as his motto Barnabooth's lines:

> *J'ai senti pour la première fois toute la douceur de vivre*
> *Dans une cabine du Nord-Express, entre Wirballen et Pskow.*

> [The first time I felt to the full the sheer bliss of being alive was in a sleeping-car between Wirballen and Pskow.]

His first-person narrator (not as distinct, on the surface, from his creator as Larbaud's hero but very much a fictionalised projection nonetheless) has felt not the bliss of life but its violence. The images of Moscow as deliciously edible swiftly give way to the 'great Red Christ of the Russian revolution' — the abortive 1905 uprising. The adolescent excitement at crossing Russia by train — 'I thought I was playing at pirates' — and the laconic sketching of the merchants and women on the train are cut across with a starker picture:

> *En Sibérie tonnait le canon, c'était la guerre*
> *La faim le froid la peste le choléra*

> [In Siberia the cannon thundered, it was war famine cold plague cholera].

Into this framework are thrown scraps of the poet's relationships, his other travels, his childhood, things he has read, the public events of his day. The pathetic figure of the little French prostitute (the suggestion of Joan of Arc in the formulation Jeanne de France puts France into a curious perspective in the poet's inner world) punctuating the flow of images with her phrase 'Are we far from Montmartre, Blaise?' emphasises the clinging to the familiar of the adolescent faced by the horrors of war in an alien landscape. And, throughout, the rhythm of the verse gives the sense of onward impulsion, the rhythm of relentless travel:

> Maintenant, j'ai fait courir tous les trains tout le long de ma vie
> Madrid–Stockholm
> Et j'ai perdu tous mes paris
> Il n'y a plus que la Patagonie, la Patagonie, qui, convienne à mon immense tristesse, la Patagonie, et un voyage dans les mers du Sud
> Je suis en route
> J'ai toujours été en route
> Je suis en route avec la petite Jehanne de France
> Le train fait un saut périlleux et retombe sur toutes ses roues
> Le train retombe sur ses roues
> Le train retombe toujours sur toutes ses roues

[Now, I've run all the trains for the whole of my life / Madrid–Stockholm / And I've lost all my home draws / There's nowhere left but Patagonia, Patagonia, to suit my boundless sorrow, Patagonia and a voyage in the South Seas / I'm travelling / I've always been travelling / I'm travelling with little Jehanne of France / The train makes a dangerous leap and falls back on all four wheels / The train falls back on its wheels / The train always falls back on all four wheels].

The patterns of repeated rhythmic units, repeated sounds, repeated phrases, phrases that grow or shrink in repetition, all form a continuo against which the fragmented sense, itself complicated by various kinds of word play (*paris* suggesting both bets and Paris, the train apparently about to fall on all 'fours' rather than 'wheels'), conveys the simultaneity of past, present and future within the poet's mind.

Cendrars' other poetry is essentially similar in kind to the *Prose du Transsibérien*. 'Le Panama ou Les aventures de mes sept oncles' (1918) which, together with 'Prose' and Cendrars' first poem 'Les Pâques à New-York' (1912), was collected under the title *Du monde entier* (1919), extends the associative technique, image freely suggesting image, to a much more violent pitch, although never so randomly that the connective completely disappears. Exotic place names, rail and steamship companies, famous trains and their descriptions are piled up among images of the ascetic traveller, *'J'ai du pain et du fromage/Un col propre'* (I have bread and cheese/ a clean collar), and the creative artist, *'La poésie date d'aujourd'hui'* (Poetry dates from today).

The fascination with the listing of exotic names and with the recording of the artefacts of modern civilisation is, of course, not particular to Cendrars any more than the theme of travel. The (understandably) dreary urban landscapes of the Belgian poet Emile Verhaeren (1855-1916), particularly in his collection *Les Forces tumultueuses* (1902), and the poetry of the unanimists, led by Jules Romains, who sought to convey the underlying corporate identity of urban man, both emphasise the physical characteristics of the modern world. What Cendrars brings to this kind of material is a new perception of the relationship of man to his creations, achieved by re-ordering the normally successive presentation of reality. His association with the painter Robert Delaunay led in 1912 to his formulation of the doctrine of 'simultaneity' — the suppression of conventional time scale through the simultaneous presentation of events and thoughts separately experienced (ie, Bergsonian inner timelessness). Further, his contact with the cinema encouraged the formulation of a staccato series of intercut glimpses of the physical world, forming visual continuity without a linear theme. His later poetry, of which only the *Dix-neufs poèmes élastiques* (1919) and *Kodak* (1924 — the title had later to be changed to *Documentaires* because the camera firm complained!) are of much interest, treats these techniques in a more consciously experimental and fragmented way. It is in his prose writings, notably *Moravagine* (1926), *L'Or* (1928), *Les Confessions de Dan Yack* (1929) and *Emmène-moi au bout du monde* (1955), that he develops a world-view consequent upon his poetic practice. Man is shown as totally responsible for himself in the midst of an absurd universe. His aim should be to realise all that is virtual within himself, to drain each experience of its potential, then move on to something new. Through the will of the artist to construct his works out of his experience, the absurdity can in some degree be transcended. Such a 'morality', logically extending the openness to sensation on which the poetry is built, takes us into the world of Montherlant, Malraux and the existentialists. The parallels to Cendrars' *poetry* are better found in pre-war developments in painting and music, and in other poets of 1900-20, notably Apollinaire and Cocteau.

The inter-relation of the arts
Before embarking on an investigation of what these two poets add to our awareness of modern sensibility, one should, perhaps, glance briefly at the whole question of the inter-relation of art forms raised by the question of Cendrars' debt to Delaunay — for the give and take between literature, painting and music in the period 1900-25 is of great importance for the development of all three arts. In a sense to put a chronological limit of any precise kind on this inter-reaction is misleading. A case can be made for the existence of the same phenomenon at least a decade earlier, where Debussy, the impressionists and some symbolists have common ground. In the early years of this century, however, artistic sympathy became positive collaboration. A prime catalyst in this at one level was undoubtedly Diaghilev and his *Ballets russes*. Their French seasons, 1909-14 and 1917-29, not only revolutionised both the form and the status of ballet in western Europe, but also brought together for music, décor and scenario some of the most exciting talents of the day.

What Diaghilev demanded of his collaborators was *shock*. He seems to have appreciated artistic innovation for what it brought to the art concerned, but as an impresario, working initially with his experienced Parisian counterpart, Gabriel Astruc, he was just as interested in the drawing power of controversy among the wealthy élite on whom the ballet depended for the core of its audience. For the 1909 season (while the company was still that of the Russian Imperial Theatres) the sheer exoticism and lavishness of Bakst's sets and designs and the relatively unfamiliar music of Russian composers were enough in themselves. They were not entirely without preparation, however, in that Diaghilev had organised an exhibition of Russian art for the autumn *Salon* in 1906, and two seasons (1907-8) of Russian music, including works by all the leading composers. In 1910 and 1911 it was the turn of Stravinsky with *Firebird* and *Petrushka*. But by 1912 the emphasis was moving towards French works. The relatively unsuccessful *Le Dieu bleu* to a Cocteau scenario with music by the salon idol, Reynaldo Hahn (a friend of Marcel Proust), was followed by the first of the great scandals, *L'Après-midi d'un faune*, danced to Debussy's orchestral interpretation of Mallarmé's poem, with designs by Bakst. The uproar was largely caused by the young Nijinsky as the faun, seemingly all but naked in this skin-tight spotted leotard with a bunch of grapes swaying provocatively over his genitals, miming the sexual act as he made love to the nymph's scarf. The following year the tone of the ballet moved more sharply towards the innovatory with Stravinsky's then controversial *Rite of Spring*, which caused a near-riot on the first night by its unconventional discordancies and insistent primitive rhythms. The shift was even more marked with the staging in 1917 of *Parade*, scenario by Cocteau, designs by Picasso, music by Satie. After this, music by modern composers and designs by modern painters gradually became standard features of ballet — Cocteau's last collaboration with Diaghilev, *Le Train bleu* (1924), to music by Milhaud, a work designed to show off the acrobatic prowess and physical charm of the young English dancer, Anton Dolin, had a front curtain by Picasso (intended for the whole ballet season) so striking that Diaghilev adopted it as the official front-cloth for the company.

This account shows something of the gradual acclimatising of public taste to the new movements in the arts. Such a process necessarily depended upon a long period of communication between artists and writers behind the scene. There is no better way to get a sense of the inter-penetration of the avant-garde communities in Paris in the early years of the century than by browsing through the appropriate chapters of Gertrude Stein's *The Autobiography of Alice B. Toklas*, for all the significant figures of the period seem to have flocked to the rue de Fleurus: notably, among the painters, Matisse, Braque, Picasso and Juan Gris and among the poets, Apollinaire, André Salmon, Max Jacob and even Cocteau (brought by Picasso). The attention paid to artistic developments by the poets is well represented by Apollinaire's articles on cubist painting published in 1913 as *Méditations esthétiques: Les Peintres cubistes* (in the context of which Braque rather unkindly observed that Apollinaire could not tell the difference between a Raphael and a Rubens but did a handy job at keeping the public confused), by Cocteau's articles on art, music and poetry written in 1919 for the newspaper *Paris-Midi*, the majority of which appeared together in book form the following year under the title *Carte blanche*, and by Cendrars' writings on the aesthetics of painting and poetry collected later in *Aujourd'hui*.

Order and adventure
Although Cendrars' comments on light, depth and colour are certainly the more enlightening, it is Guillaume Apollinaire (1880-1918) whose name is the more frequently linked with the leading painters, particularly the cubists. Like André Salmon (1881-1969) and Max Jacob (1876-1944) he has been labelled a cubist poet, a dubiously meaningful tag also attached to utterly different poets such as William Carlos Williams. Apollinaire's poetry, charming though it often is, parades a tamed, tea-shop version of the modern. It constitutes a collage of contemporary

poetic practices rather than a source of new directions. In his first collection, *Alcools*, subtitled *Poèmes 1898-1913*, he presents a series of personal moments which fail to add up to a full fictional persona and depart too often from autobiography to constitute a real exploration of the self. We are offered neither a poetic transposition of a personal reality nor the creation of an independent identity, as in Baudelaire's *Les Fleurs du Mal* or Cendrars' *Prose du Transsibérien*. The innovations with which he is often unwisely accredited — the rejection of punctuation and of regular typography and set verse form, the introduction of townscapes and the bric-à-brac of modern living — are quite simply not new. He only suppressed the punctuation in *Alcools* at the proof stage, borrowing the idea from Cendrars or from Marinetti's futurist manifesto; in adopting the device of irregular printing (which he does not do until *Calligrammes* of 1918) he is following the immediate example of Mallarmé's *Un coup de dés*, not to mention, in reverse chronological order, the English baroque poets, the French *grands rhétoriqueurs*, and various Alexandrian and Hellenistic rhymesters; he writes in set verse forms far more widely than Larbaud or Cendrars (or even the Laforgue of the *Derniers vers*); and the use of the landscape of the city and the artefacts of modern society as fit matter for poetry had been, as we have seen, a commonplace of French poetry for at least a decade. In the context of an inquiry into the characteristics of twentieth-century literature, it is fairest to read Apollinaire, like Bergson, as an example of someone whose representative importance depends precisely on his swimming with the tide.

The most accessible, and as it happens the most conventional, poems in *Alcools* are the short elegiac lyrics celebrating loss — lost love, the evanescence of time, the general sense of sadness that can be evoked through a Laforguian use of autumn imagery. 'Le Pont Mirabeau', with its fluid rhythm, musical effects and folksily simple refrain —

> *Vienne la nuit sonne l'heure*
> *Les jours s'en vont je demeure*

[Let night come let the hours strike/days pass I stay]

— is a perfect example of the effective but conservative style of much of the collection. The nine poems grouped as *Rhénanes*, written 1901-2, and formerly intended for a volume to be called *Le Vent du Rhin*, extend the mood of the elegiac poems (many of which, 'Les Colchiques', 'Le Vent nocturne' 'Automne', 'Automne malade', also date from Apollinaire's stay in Germany), but they hardly introduce any extension of poetic form. Together they give the impression of a moodscape, a literary transcription of an inner state, compounded of subjective impressions of Germany, literary reminiscences, and glimpses of the poet's love life.

If one is looking for consciously experimental work, it is to some of the longer poems that one must turn — 'La Chanson du mal-aimé', 'Vendémiaire', 'Zone'. This is not a question of development: 'Zone' and 'Le Pont Mirabeau' were both written in 1912. 'Zone' is expressed in a curious mixture of self-address, 'In the end you are weary of this old world', and first-person assertion, 'I've lived like a madman and wasted my time'. It recreates what seems to be a walk from the centre of Paris out to Auteuil, where the poet was living, but the impressions of the moment are interleaved with memories of the past presented as simultaneous:

> *Il est neuf heures le gaz est baissé tout bleu vous sortez du*
> *   dortoir en cachette*
> *Vous priez toute la nuit dans la chapelle du collège*

[It's nine o'clock the gas-light is turned down all blue you sneak out of the dormitory/You pray all night in the college chapel].

The loose-rhythmed couplets are imitations of Cendrars'

first-published poem 'Les Pâques à New York', which had appeared earlier in 1912; the preoccupation with religion viewed from a very untraditional angle is reminiscent of the same poem. The overall attempt is to combine what has been called *adventure*, the exploration of new ways of looking at the world, and *order*, in this case the traditionalism represented by the Church. Through the imagery of the aeroplane and the Ascension of Christ, a genuine if somewhat crude synthesis of the two apparently contradictory tendencies is achieved. But the bulk of the poem wavers between autobiographical notes, gawky sentimentalism and opaque references. The over-indulgence of the authorial 'I' obscures the novel perceptions of the authorial eye.

'Zone', which stands first in the collection, can be taken as a key poem in the sense that it adumbrates the range of tone and topic to be explored by the poems that follow. But far and away the most exciting of the poems is 'La Chanson du mal-aimé', a sequence of seven sections written independently over the period 1902-4 and first published in 1909, which, like 'L'Emigrant de Landor Road', relates to an autobiographical episode. Apollinaire refashions this personal material into a myth of the poet as ill-starred lover, in a verse which is tightly ordered, with its five-line octosyllabic stanzas, but whose transitions of thought are conducted by the adventurous technique of lyrical juxtaposition. The initial narrative of the poet randomly following Londoners who vaguely recall his lost love gives way to a joyful *aubade* representing the lost love in its happy phase, and this in turn leads to verses evoking the intensity and sincerity of the poet's emotions. However, his attempt to dominate his beloved modulates into tyranny; hence the following three-stanza interlude, the reply of the Zaporogue Cossacks to the Sultan of Constantinople's demand for their submission, for the Cossacks' constancy in rejecting a tyrant stands symbol for the same constancy in the beloved. This episode is succeeded by a series of transpositions of the poet's unhappiness into black-and-white images interspersed with the standard themes of baroque love poetry — pain, fire, death. Through the introduction of the Catholic symbolism of the poet as pierced through the heart by seven swords like Our Lady of Sorrows, the pain motif generates the next section, seven verses describing the swords. But here, with a sharp application of the element of surprise, the tone changes from melancholy to a mischievous bawdiness, since, as Roger Little has neatly expressed it, 'each sword is given particular phallic overtones apparently to correspond to different states and capacities of the male organ'. The change of mood is only momentary. With the last section, the poet, victim of 'the demons of chance', is returned to the destiny of the wanderer, but this time across Paris 'without having the heart to die there'. Yet the final note of the poem is not one of aimlessness, since amid life's *ennui*, expressed in lines that could have been lifted straight out of Laforgue —

> *Les dimanches s'y éternisent*
> *Et les orgues de Barbarie*
> *Y sanglotent dans les cours grises*

[Sundays make themselves eternal there/and the barrel-organs/sob in the gray courtyards],

the poet retains his instinctive response to the creative stimulus of the city around him. His final words, turning away from personal mischance, repeat an earlier verse insisting on the range of his poetic talent:

> *Moi qui sais des lais pour les reines*
> *Les complaintes de mes années*
> *Des hymnes d'esclaves aux murènes*
> *La romance du mal-aimé*
> *Et des chansons pour les sirènes*

[I who know lays for queens/laments about my own life/ hymns like those sung by galley slaves/ the ballad of the man crossed in love/and songs for the Sirens].

Although the poem's concessions to a Romantic-symbolist aesthetic are obvious, its combination of a traditional concept of the poet and a self-consciously old-fashioned verse form, with a suppression of normal time structure and a juxtaposed presentation of such antithetical elements as the disembodied emotions of baroque love poetry and the humorously transposed symbols of sexuality, makes it a work both ordered and yet daring. There is, in the handling of such complex material, a hint of the intellectual manipulation of sense data and emotion within a deliberately restricted verse pattern which one associates with Valéry — not a quality found anywhere else in Apollinaire's poetry. If the definition of true originality, as T.S. Eliot proposed in an introduction to the poetry of Ezra Pound, is development, 'La Chanson du mal-aimé' has a better claim to the title than most of *Alcools*.

Calligrammes, the only other significant collection of Apollinaire's verse to appear during his lifetime, is more consistently innovatory, and shows well the strengths and weaknesses of his attempts in this direction. One can set aside the 'calligrammes' themselves, picture-poems which are clever stylisations of the objects to which the 'words' refer, as in the typical example 'Coeur Couronne et Miroir', shown overleaf on p36.

The idea of producing instant response to all aspects of a subject, equivalent to the analytic simultaneity of the cubists, presenting all surfaces equally, can only be reproduced faithfully in a poem at the expense of language itself. As 'Coeur Couronne Miroir' shows, the words are quite submerged by the design, and even the use of the poet's name 'reflected' in the mirror as the equivalent of his face is merely an amusing piece of ingenuity. Typographical games are meaningful only when

CŒUR COURONNE ET MIROIR

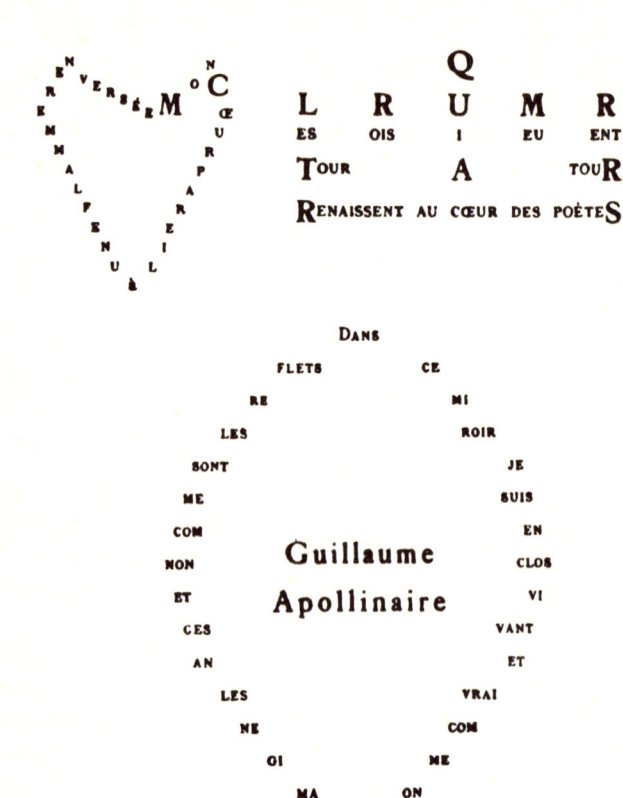

```
          M  C
     VERS E  Œ        L     R    Q    M    R
                     ES    OIS   U   EU   ENT
                                 I
                     TOUR         A       TOUR
                     RENAISSENT AU CŒUR DES POÈTES
```

```
                    DANS
            FLETS          CE
         RE                   MI
      LES                       ROIR
     SONT                         JE
     ME                           SUIS
     COM                          EN
     NON     Guillaume            CLOS
     ET                           VI
       CES  Apollinaire         VANT
         AN                    ET
           LES              VRAI
              NE         COM
                 OI   ME
                   MA ON
                     I
```

visually abstract as in Mallarmé's *Un Coup de dés*, when enforcing a satirical point as in Cendrars' 'OpOetic' sonnet dedicated to Cocteau (here is a sample from the opening —

     OpOetic quels crimes ne
à Jean COctO   cOmmet-On pas
         en tOn nOm!
Il y avait une fOis des pOètes qui parlaient la bOuche en rOnd

— the first line means 'There were Once sOme pOets whO talked with their mOuths all rOund'), or when providing a comic moment *within* a straightforward poem as is the case for some poems of *Calligrammes*, like 'Fumées' (Smoke) with its pipe shape for the line 'and I smoke Zone tobacco':

>   Et je fu
>   m
>   e
>   du
>   ta
>   bac
>   ^{de}NE.
>   _{Zo}

One can also treat with a fairly detached interest 'Les Fenêtres', 'Les Arbres' and 'Lundi rue Christine', the second two both pure conversation-poems, and all three so disconnected that, though the reader can appreciate them as curious associative games, they do not possess any independent aesthetic value. What of the rest of the collection? A clue to the work as a whole is offered by the opening poem 'Liens', in which, as the title suggests, semantic *links*, and sometimes more formal ones too, are established between a series of at first sight unconnected phrases. The first line, 'ropes made from cries', suggests the web of connections woven from the individual outbursts of the poet. From this grow images dependent on words indicating connection — across, tie up, shake hands, bind, rails, cables, bridges — within which the poet plays both with paradox — that three men can have links when all three are 'free of ties' — and with word form, 'Cordes et Concorde', the word for harmony containing the word for rope. This delicate net of images is followed by an outburst rejecting *in toto* the substance of *Alcools*:

> *J'écris seulement pour vous exalter*
> *O sens ô sens chéris*
> *Ennemis du souvenir*

> *Ennemis du désir*
> *Ennemis du regret*
> *Ennemis des larmes*
> *Ennemis de tout ce que j'aime encore*

[I write only to exalt you/ O senses O my darling senses/Enemies of memory/Enemies of desire/Enemies of regret/Enemies of tears/ Enemies of everything I still love].

The new poems are to be explorations of immediate sense impressions offering slight and disguised links with one another, and turning their backs on the themes of melancholy and of ill-starred love.

The poems of the first section, 'Ondes', fulfil this pattern admirably, given that it contains several calligrammes (linked by form), the three above-mentioned disjointed conversation-poems (meant for the reader to forge his own links) and poems picking up themes and images from 'Liens' itself. The subsequent five sections of war poetry offer more of a problem. Frivolity may be excused in a soldier as a source of relief from

> Batter of guns and shatter of flying muscles
> Carnage incomparable and human squander
> (Wilfred Owen, 'Mental Cases').

That does not make it admissible to introduce frivolity into war poetry — which should communicate the essentials of the situation itself. The use of the line *'Ah Dieu que la guerre est jolie'* from the poem 'L'Adieu du cavalier' to translate the title of the film *Oh What a Lovely War* is adequate comment on one whose poems too often exude an air of 'What do we want with eggs and ham/When we've got plum and apple jam'. Many images are in themselves forceful, but lack an appropriate context. The notion of treating night gunfire as *'Feu d'artifice en acier'* (steel fireworks) would be effective if used in an ironic structure, but in 'Fête', as the title betrays, it is part of a purely decorative development. It is not that Apollinaire is incapable of writing ironically. A rare example is 'Guerre', with its laconic blending of military diction and political phrase-making, and its ironic suggestion of the pointlessness of what men are going through. The fact is that Apollinaire's perceptions of life are generally so trivial that he is unable to comprehend the real experience of war. Only in the fifth section of the collection, *Obus couleur de lune*, are there a few poems which command attention by their attempt to achieve a communication of a new vision, rather than merely playing with words. 'Merveille de la guerre', 'Il y a', and 'Simultanéités' all get as close as is feasible in the linear structure of literature to being simultaneous, in the sense of suppressing the duration which the act of reading normally imposes upon the subject matter of a poem. Here, momentarily, innovation and experience seem genuinely to overlap, and hence to cause the reader a sensation of power and point generally lacking. Elsewhere his verse swithers between an embarrassing naïvety and an even more embarrassingly glutinous patriotism. If he was not paid for this stuff by the French propaganda agency, he certainly should have been.

Calligrammes, as I said earlier, encapsulates the vices and virtues of Apollinaire's attempts to be modern. Like his vastly over-rated lecture on 'L'esprit nouveau' given in 1917, his poetry is collaged from the avant-garde clichés of the day. Much of it is self-indulgent, shallow, tasteless, trivial and shapeless. But he explores with great gusto the possibilities of immediacy, of everyday images, the suppression of the logical connectives of practical language, the avoidance of conventional time-sequence; he carries out his exploration in the conscious attempt to make literature absorb the 'discoveries' of painting; and he does all this without a facile decrying and rejection of the poetic tradition which his generation had inherited. It is a limited achievement but one which he himself gets perfectly into perspective in 'La Jolie Rousse', the closing poem of *Calligrammes*, when asking, after the manner of Villon, for the indulgence of the partisans of Order towards those in search of Adventure, he says:

> *Nous ne sommes pas vos ennemis*
> *Nous voulons vous donner de vastes et d'étranges domaines . . .*
> *Nous voulons explorer la bonté contrée énorme où tout se tait*
> *Il y a aussi le temps qu'on peut chasser ou faire revenir*
> *Pitié pour nous qui combattons toujours aux frontières*
> *De l'illimité et de l'avenir*
> *Pitié pour nos erreurs pitié pour nos péchés*

[We are not your enemies/We want to give you vast and strange domains/. . . We want to explore goodness an enormous region where all is silent/There is also time which can be chased away or brought back/Have pity on us, ever fighting on the frontiers/Of the infinite and the future/Have pity on our errors pity on our sins].

Apollinaire's reputation as a poet has undoubtedly benefited from his early death two days before Armistice day, 1918. His work received a critical attention more lavish than that given to longer-lived contemporaries, and he was often unjustifiably accredited with all the achievements of the avant-garde of his day. Had the reputation of Jean Cocteau (1889-1963) rested entirely on what he wrote before 1918, he would certainly have received a great deal less critical attention than he has. However, setting aside the three sets of salon verse which he himself firmly repudiated later, the early collections of Cocteau's poetry, *Le Cap de Bonne-Espérance* (1919), *Discours du grand sommeil* (1920) and *Vocabulaire* (1922), together with his first essays at what he called 'poetry of the stage', namely *Parade* (1917), *Le Boeuf sur le toit* (1920) and *Les Mariés de la Tour Eiffel* (1921), are all very typical examples of experimental work of their period. *Le Cap de Bonne-Espérance*, dedicated to the pilot Roland Garros who was a prisoner of war in Germany, is based in theme and typography on the image of the aeroplane and its flight, one of the classic symbols of modern invention and of movement in the poetry of Cendrars and more especially of Apollinaire (eg, in 'Zone'). Garros had taken Cocteau for a flip; these poems are his own aerial journey as poet, with the aviator as his captive symbol:

> Je t'emporte à mon tour
> aviateur de l'encre
>   moi
>
> et voici mes loopings
> et mes records d'altitude

[I in my turn carry you off/pilot in ink/me/and here are my loops/and my altitude records].

The symbolism of the ten poems adds up to the poet's attempt to soar beyond visible reality and penetrate to a higher sphere of meaning. Poetry itself is the aeroplane, the method of escape. The tone moves between personal and objective, the images are sometimes closely related, sometimes as violently disjointed as a conversation-poem, especially in 'Préambule: d'un art poétique', and in 'Tentative d'evasion' where the language at one point collapses into combinations of vowels (admittedly sounding rather like an engine starting up). The glimpses of the modern world and the literary references are nonetheless mostly well blended into a comprehensible emotional continuity. It is particularly interesting to note how the only poem openly evoking the War, 'Géorgiques funèbres', attains both a more forceful communication of its subject and a greater variety of tone and verbal plasticity than does Apollinaire's war poetry. A poet's conscious exercise of his art on such a theme ceases to be offensive when it is both a critical exercise and one in which the horror is fully absorbed, however detached the expression of it. Thus the destruction of Reims, the figure of Joan of Arc implicitly set against the Apocalyptic vision of St John on Patmos, both put into the laconic context of —

> *Un jour peut-être ayant recul*
> *on chantera la grande guerre*

[One day perhaps with a bit of distance/the great war will be a subject for song],

give the precise sense of knowing how to balance the poetic vision of war with its grim realities, how to set 'the silken signature of a shell' against 'The horse is stumbling over its own entrails/"They're aiming at the gasometer, major"'. It is in the last poem, 'Parabole de l'Enfant Prodigue', that the intention declared in 'Préambule' to set aside eloquence is fully carried through in the simplicity of the diction, which combines with the expressive rhythms and typographical shapes to communicate a religious solemnity of attainment from which the vividness of immediate sensation is never excluded.

Discours du grand sommeil, another series of ten poems, with prologue, written between 1916 and 1918, is closer to the simplicity and strictness of Cocteau's later poetry. This time the war runs through the whole collection (or poem, if you prefer to see it as a continuum in ten episodes), sometimes evoked in starkly realistic images, at others forming the basis for expressing in an objective fashion the poet's feelings about friendship, death and the antithetical forces revealed in human nature by the pressures of wartime. It is here that there first appears the figure of the angel, important in later works from the critical essay *Le Secret professionel* (1922) onward. In *Le Rappel à l'ordre* (1926) Cocteau describes angelism in terms of a series of unifications of opposites, selfishness and disinterestedness, cruelty and pity, debauchery and purity, to which in *Journal d'un inconnu* he will add the opposition virile/androgynous. These qualities appear elsewhere in his work both as attributes of the adolescent heroes of certain plays and novels, and as fundamental to the poet himself. The significance of the association between angelism and youth I will discuss later (p98). When connected with the figure of the poet, the angel is a mystical force of inspiration, forcibly entering him and fomenting the painful creative process that leads to the work of art, as in 'L'Ange Heurtebise' (1925 — the poem can also be read as an extended sexual allegory, with the angel doubling as physical lover). But in *Discours* the angel is presented only as a force already within the poet, commanding his response to the physical world. It represents the creative impulse within the unconscious. By the time of *Vocabulaire* this type of private symbolism has expanded and become almost codified. Not merely angels, but bees, birds, images of metamorphosis abound. A typical poem is 'A force de plaisirs', a series of opaque images, angels slipping out of school, metamorphoses in reverse (marble to salt, salt to flesh), the short life and death of a rocket. The verse itself has a classical formality, returning to strict metres and rhyme, but within it surprise and sensual immediacy are retained. It is as though Valéry's conscious control has been crossed with the explosive subjectivism of Apollinaire.

This development within Cocteau's poetry makes more sense if put in the context of his theoretical writing and his stage work of the period. His aesthetic mentors were, as he stated in *D'un ordre considéré comme une anarchie* (1923), Picasso and Eric Satie. In his first critical work, *Le Coq et l'Arlequin*, he shows us what was important for him in the music of Satie: 'Satie teaches us the boldest lesson of our times — to be simple', the same quality that is praised, along with the related notion of economy, in the essay 'Picasso' in *Le Rappel à l'ordre* (1928). In these writings, and the articles collected in *Carte blanche*, there is a rejection of the over-facile imitation of the rhetoric of rebellion cultivated by writers in the Rimbaud–Lautréamont tradition, combined with an admiration for the value of shock in the poems of Cendrars and in the new techniques of Max Jacob, whose verbal acrobatics and flouting of logical connection in his main collection, *Le Cornet à dés* (1917), incorporate a large element of humour. In addition, Cocteau demands for poetry the intellectual control implicit in Picasso's analytical cubism and in the geometrical (as he saw it) style of Satie's music. He also wants to parallel in literature the way in which *Les Six* (Milhaud, Poulenc and co) were extending the range of conventional musical idiom by introducing into serious music the rhythms of jazz and the motifs of ragtime. And he seeks to emulate the cubist painters in making the act of creating art more important than the interpretation of purely physical reality. The blending of these many and different approaches to artistic renewal required a new approach, which can best be summed up in a phrase from *Le Coq et l'Arlequin*, as F. Steegmuller neatly translates it in his biography of Cocteau, 'To be daring with tact is to know how far we may go too far.' Cocteau's neo-classicism, if such it may legitimately be called, is 'daring with tact' and at the same time a natural manifestation of the desire to go beyond the fireworks of the 'new spirit' without degenerating into the anti-literary automatism of the surrealists.

The inter-relation of the various branches of art can be best seen in Cocteau's stage works. *Parade* was the first ballet to introduce realism of individual sights and sounds; Satie's *faux-naïf* score includes the aural illusion of typewriters, a dynamo, sirens, an express train and an aeroplane, Massine's choreography makes the characters mime their occupations, Picasso's costumes and set, for all their cubist stylisation, identify characters and place. The scene is a Sunday fair, with a travelling theatre outside which three 'acts' perform to draw an audience for the main show inside. The acts, a Chinese conjuror, an American girl and a pair of acrobats are taken by the crowd for the real show. No amount of persuasion to the contrary by the three managers or even by the members of the acts themselves can persuade people otherwise. As well as satirising such aspects of the modern world as advertising, and providing a genuine flash of visual and aural humour (which was the source of the work's success at its recent London revival) *Parade* transcends the representational by suggesting a deeper meaning fundamental to Cocteau's concept of the theatre and of the artist's relationship to the public. Life itself, and art in particular, are destined to be misunderstood by the majority, who take a surface bustle and glitter for the sole meaning, instead of penetrating beyond.

Le Boeuf sur le toit is another work of collaboration. Milhaud had returned from a trip to Brazil and composed a score full of echoes of popular tunes, sambas and tangos. Cocteau persuaded him to let him use this music for a show — it is difficult to find a more precise word — set in an American bar during 'prohibition'. It is a fantasy sequence, as 'real' as *Parade* in its presentation of an identifiable contemporary situation, but equally stylised, the characters wearing carnival heads, the set and costumes done by Dufy. There is no plot and no apparent meaning. Life is being re-structured into art, this time in a farcical way (all the performers were circus artists, the pretty barman and the two women being played by the Fratellini trio, well-known clowns).

This attempt to produce a humorous poetry of the real but exotic (even in American bars negro dwarfs must be moderately unusual) was followed, quite naturally, by an equally humorous poeticisation of the everyday, in *Les Mariés de la Tour Eiffel*. This was another ballet proper, commissioned by Rolf de Maré for performance in Paris by the Swedish Ballet in 1921, with music by no less than five of *Les Six* (Milhaud, Poulenc, Honnegger, Georges Auric and Germaine Taillefer) and designs by Jean and Valentine Hugo. There was also a text, a kind of running commentary on the action, spoken from backstage through two vast gramophone horns. The centre of the action is the Eiffel Tower itself (at that time topped with a telegraphic station, hence the Telegram Waltz which the ballet contains). An absurd wedding-party, straight out of a Labiche farce, is being photographed. Out of the camera come an ostrich, a bathing-beauty, a very large baby, a lion, and finally a dove. And that, with all the comic possibilities it provides, is that. But the consequences of it in Cocteau's art, and other people's, are clear. Musically, it leads to Diaghilev's commissioning of Poulenc's *Les Biches* (décor by Apollinaire's former mistress Marie Laurencin), to ballets by Auric, and to Milhaud's *Le Train Bleu*. Theatrically it created a lasting impression on the adolescent Jean Anouilh — he describes it as having determined his vocation as a dramatist. And, as the preface to the published text shows, it confirmed Cocteau in his view that the function of the theatre, like the function of poetry, was to suggest the deeper meaning of the familiar objects around us.

A modern sensibility
What, then, has this undoubtedly eclectic glance at the state of French literature in the approximate period 1895-1922 revealed? Bergson, Valéry, Gide, Larbaud, Cendrars, Apollinaire and Cocteau are at first sight a heterogeneous collection of writers. Can aspects of their work taken together really show the specifically twentieth-century lines of development which French literature was beginning to follow? I think they can. One can rapidly disregard either image or manner as indicators in themselves. As Eliot observed, 'one is not modern by writing about chimney pots or archaic by writing about oriflammes'. Thus, for all that it sounds like contemporary language in its rhythm and diction,

> Rome disappoints me much; I hardly as yet understand, but
> *Rubbishy* seems the word that most exactly would suit it

is in fact a couplet from Clough's *Amours de Voyage* of 1849. Theme is scarcely more helpful. What have the texts we have looked at been, in a deeper sense, *about*? Tensions between sensuality and spirituality, travel as liberation, the necessity of avoiding stasis, the complexity of the artist's craft? All true, but, put like that, it could be *Les Fleurs du Mal* one had been discussing. To have recourse to the Bergsonian doctrines with which I began might make the inquiry seem narrower and more circular than it has actually been, yet some of the points cannot but recur. John Middleton Murry's article on the connection between Bergson and avant-garde attitudes to art, published in the magazine *Rhythm* in 1911 under the title 'Art and Philosophy', gives an excellent idea of how apparently irreconcilable facets of the writers we have looked at could be shown to stem from common beliefs. Immediacy and rational control are no longer inimical if intuition is 'that point, as it were, at which the reason becomes most wholly itself'. The intensity of present experience and the possibility of learning from the past are reconcilable as parts of a single process if no art can be said to break entirely with the past in that *all* art expresses, however bizarrely, a present in which, of necessity, the past still exists. Putting these two sets of reconciled contrasts together, we reach the point at which art can be represented, in Murry's words, as turning

> ... to regard the things of daily life with the eyes of the heightened reason; and in the moment of intuition once more to behold and make actual, though for a moment, the great continuity.

This notion of a higher, but empirical, reason, expounded in France by Tancrède de Visan's *L'Attitude du lyrisme contemporain* (1911), and made influential in England via the interest of T.E. Hulme, and thus of the imagists, is precisely the justification for speaking in the same breath of Valéry's poetry (which is for that very reason *not* symbolist), Gide's early prose, the 'angelic' poetry of Cocteau on the one hand, and on the other the more obviously down-to-earth poetry of Larbaud, Cendrars and Apollinaire. All of them are seeking, like the cubist painters, to transcend superficial 'realism' but without ever losing contact with the intense sensual experiences provided by the material world. The immediacy of objects in the physical world and the sharpness of the sense impressions that convey them are present in the work of every writer considered and, with the possible exception of *André Walter*, in every work. It is equally true that the art that employs these sense impressions is not mimetic, even in an 'impressionist' way. For each of the writers, reality is a set of perceptions unique to himself, perceptions intensified into art. The assertion of man's need to be aware of his individual response to life had been strengthening in the late nineteenth century. It is typified by the observation of the Austrian poet and dramatist, Hugo von Hofmannsthal, in an essay of 1891 on Maurice Barrès, that by thinking the comfortable thoughts of others, we fail to notice what is best in ourselves. Earlier in the nineteenth century the cult of individual perception tends to be transcendental. The twentieth-century writer is not a visionary. There is no moral vision transcending reality in a Baudelairean sense, no nightmare creation of alternative reality in the manner of Rimbaud. The artist is a man with unusual power over words which allows him to transmute his intensified perceptions into the independent 'objects' of art. All the literature concerned is subjective in origin, some of it — and here comes the first of the divisions between our writers — achieves objective status. The key element in this transmutation is not a perceptual one such as, for example, the fragmentation of conventional time (important though that is for many twentieth-century writers), but the attempt to make language depart from the practical function, the conventional approximations, of everyday use without becoming frozen into the equally approximate conventions of a 'poetic diction'. If the writer, especially the poet, is concerned with verbal ways of giving relatively old ideas new implications, he is primarily a *craftsman*.

This is the point at which the most significant division of all comes into play. Some writers, particularly Cendrars and the

Gide of *Les Nourritures terrestres*, in seeking to break the hold of rationality, seek to eject with it all use of intellect. Others, like Valéry, formulate a new relationship between intellect and emotion. Any sign of pattern or irony is a re-assertion of this kind. Even the rhythmic variations of Cendrars' 'Pâques à New York' are evidence of such a control. As Eliot pointed out, no *vers* is *libre* for the man who wants to do a good job. The loose indulgence, or at least the incoherence, of some of Apollinaire's poetry is due to this lack of control, which in turn allows the poem to fall short of the objective status at which it aims. It says too much, too lavishly, and remains a subjective fragment. The same phenomenon in reverse can be seen in pieces like William Carlos Williams' 'The Red Wheelbarrow' and 'This Is To Say', where excessive understatement leads to a simple-mindedness which is equally subjective.

The line taken by Valéry and eventually Cocteau in asserting physical control over form is akin to that of Eliot and Pound. As the latter acidly observed in 'Hugh Selwyn Mauberley' (1920):

> The 'age demanded' chiefly a mould in plaster,
> Made with no loss of time,
> A prose kinema, not, not assuredly, alabaster
> Or the 'sculpture' of rhyme.

'Mauberley' is precisely Pound's attempt to offer a counter-current to the 'general floppiness [that] had gone too far' and for which he had prescribed as a remedy *Emaux et camées* or the *Bay State Hymn Book*. Cocteau's championing of simplicity and cubist analysis leads, in *Vocabulaire*, to something like the same emphasis. It is also noticeable that Valéry and Cocteau (who have, I hasten to say, precious little else obviously in common) are one with Pound and Eliot in the refusal to ignore anything but the obtrusively modern. They are not, to borrow another verse from 'Mauberley', writers for whom

> The tea-rose tea-gown etc.
> Supplants the mousseline of Cos,
> The pianola 'replaces'
> Sappho's barbitos.

Nor, whatever *Les Nourritures* might appear to suggest, is Gide, who was at all times interested in, for example, classical myth and Christian tradition as frameworks for his own ideas. Apollinaire, however, with his naïve enthusiasm for all things up-to-date, could be made to seem on the edge of rejecting all tradition, and was so to be made by the surrealists. In this way a great swathe of French writers were to turn drastically, and in some cases disastrously, from the direction taken by the mainstream of English and American literature.

I have concentrated in this chapter on poetry and to a lesser extent what might be called non-textual theatre — a genre where the experiments of the non-verbal arts could and did have substantial influence — and lyrical prose, where the hold of logic as an ordering force is of less importance than that of rhythm. This is because these are the genres where distinctively twentieth-century trends established themselves most swiftly, perhaps as a result of their obvious susceptibility to formal experiment. To borrow this time from Wallace Stevens:

> They said, 'You have a blue guitar,
> You do not play things as they are.'
>
> The man replied, 'Things as they are
> are changed upon the blue guitar.'

There is no intrinsic reason why the novel should not have responded to the influence of, say, cubism or the *Ballets russes*. Outside France, it did. Firbank's *Valmouth* and Carl Van Vechten's *The Tattooed Countess* show a Coctelian sense of novelty for which there are simply no French parallels. But the real impact on narrative prose was made by the new notions of reality, time, identity, and it was an impact which was felt much more slowly. French novelists were content to restring the guitars they already had. Nonetheless, here too things were soon 'becoming'.

CHAPTER 2
Literature and the Self

> I never *am*; I *become*.
> (André Gide)

I said to Hammett there is something that is puzzling. In the nineteenth century the men when they were writing did invent all kinds and a great number of men. The women on the other hand never could invent women they always made the women be themselves spendidly or sadly or heroically or beautifully or despairingly or gently, and they never could make any other kind of woman . . . Now in the twentieth century it is the men who do it. The men all write about themselves as strong or weak or mysterious or passionate or drunk or controlled but always themselves as the women used to do in the nineteenth century.

Gertrude Stein's observation to Dashiel Hammett in *Everybody's Autobiography* draws attention to a central feature of twentieth-century literature, though I doubt whether there is any real distinction by sex to be made between writers as far as this phenomenon goes. In the novel and poetry, above all in the rise of autobiography itself, concentration upon oneself, identity and self-exploration has become an important feature of literary creation. Stein makes Hammett identify the cause of this self-fascination as a lack of confidence in one's own character, but the reasons lie deeper, in the lack of confidence in any concept of reality outside the shifting perceptions of one's own experience.

An obvious symbol for self-fascination is the figure of Narcissus. It was indeed with the symbolists that the myth first became really popular. André Gide's *Traité de Narcisse* (1891) uses the motif of reflection in the water as an image through which to discuss problems of perception and aesthetics; Jean Royère's cycle of six poems, *Soeur de Narcisse nue*, and Paul Valéry's 'Narcisse parle' and the three 'Fragments du Narcisse' in *Charmes* all expand upon the mystical notions of identity which variant traditions of the myth suggest. The Narcissus legend points to the danger of self-fascination, a self-fascination which outstrips the mere fact that any author in some degree endows his characters with elements of his personality, even if he has no conscious interest in his own psychology. Narcissus stands for the figure of the writer as one whose task is *by definition* autobiographical, since his perception of existence passes through, and is transformed by, his individual consciousness. In that sense all writing is autobiographical.

The Narcissistic extreme leads, of course, to self-destruction, but the use to which the figure of Narcissus has been put by writers since Rousseau suggests that self-fascination has other and richer rewards: the artist must look into the mirror of his 'self' in order to reproduce not merely his own reality but a meaningful vision of the world around him. He may create an identity for himself, or he may explore the image which he sees reproduced there. The former leads us off into romanced autobiography and the novel, whereas the latter is more often thought of as the province of autobiography in the traditional (if not very accurately defined) sense. These mental probings elicit questions — where does identity lie? — and raise obstacles — Gide's 'What a distance there is between me and myself', Stendhal's 'the eye cannot see itself'. Conflict arises between the necessity for us to discover what we are and the difficulty of assembling and recording that knowledge into the 'historical' form of the autobiography; identity lies not in a single moment of one's past but in a succession of moments which lead into the present and carry on into the future. This highly personal literature is concerned then with the *process of recording* of the self, and thus with the act of writing, as much as with the mere description of a single complete image.

The significant personal element is not the bric-à-brac of a private life, but the whole unique sensibility of a creative mind. It is possible, admittedly, to read the novels of Colette (1873-1954), particularly the 'Claudine' series, as an amalgam of references to the author's own past. It is more revealing to read the novels in the context of the overtly self-descriptive works, *Vrilles de la vigne, Sido, La Naissance du jour*, and see how the themes of disillusion with love, the dignity of old age and the value of a heightened awareness of nature, help to reconstruct the unified psychology that created them. However, the reader is justified in asking whether his or her enjoyment of Colette's best novels, like *Chéri* with its effective period portrait of the relations between a handsome young man and his much older mistress, is in any way enhanced by an understanding of the autobiographical elements in it. The answer is clearly no. Yet it is not a big step from the introspection which gives rise to Colette's work to the deliberate self-examination of the novels of Gide.

Gide

In *Les Nourritures terrestres* Gide had proclaimed the need to open the self to every facet of experience. But in so doing he had raised the problem of continuity in identity and of the danger of the disintegration of the self, a problem which forms the subject of his play *Saül*. His two short novels (the French term is *récits*), *L'Immoraliste* and *La Porte étroite*, examine the effects of adopting what one might call respectively a life-orientated and a death-orientated approach to self-consistency. As his autobiography, *Si le grain ne meurt*, makes clear, he found these two approaches co-existent within himself, and projected each of them into a fictional work, with the intention of examining the effects of each tendency if taken to its logical extreme. Ideally he felt that both subjects should be treated within a single work, just as in his own case they existed within a single person. Unable to achieve this he had to content himself with remaining totally aware of the opposite of what he was writing in each case:

> ... the two subjects have developed concurrently in my mind, the excessiveness of each finding its justification in the excessiveness of the other, the two holding each other in balance. *(Journal)*

L'Immoraliste expresses, through its central theme of the rejection of normal sexual and social ties, the need to avoid all preconceptions about the nature and limits of human experience. The hero, Michel, finds in his arranged marriage to Marceline, his academic career and his inherited estate constraints upon his potential development. He comes to associate life, whose significance is brought home to him by a serious illness, with health and beauty, and in turn to associate these with a conscious subversion of normal moral values. At a key point in the story Michel meets the adventurer Ménalque, almost a philosophical abstraction, who embodies complete liberty by his absence of emotional commitments and physical possessions. By an irony of which he is completely unaware, Michel proceeds to model himself upon Ménalque, ignoring his intimations that each man's circumstances are unique and therefore cannot provide a pattern to his fellows. The cardinal rule of *Les Nourritures terrestres* has been broken. From here on the search for liberty itself becomes a form of constraint, as is reflected in the way in which Michel seeks to repeat the experience of his first African journey. He succeeds only in exasperating his wife's ill health to the point of killing her, and ends up as a listless failure, committed to all the superficial manifestations of moral rebellion, yet not able to develop in an unfettered way the potential of his own character. This is not to say that the character of Michel reveals no positive change. His illness and convalescence at the start of the book lead to an appreciation of the physical delights that bodily sensitivity can offer when the body is robust. The desire to reassess the whole pattern of thought which has been arbitrarily thrust upon him is clearly constructive in essence, as is shown by the period of positive work on his estate farm and of his preparation of the course that he will give at the Collège de France. This reassessment leads to a genuine appreciation of the non-rational potential that life offers. But once he defines in Ménalque a Nietzschean hero, and rather inadequately apes what he takes to be his morality, he can only decline into egoistic destruction both of his gentle and unresisting wife and ultimately of himself.

La Porte étroite is a less ambiguous work. Its portrait of the constrictions placed on its main characters by their upbringing and religious beliefs constitutes a straightforward rejection of Protestant ethics in particular and the submission of the self to any scheme of metaphysical values in general. The plot is slight. Jérôme records his love for his cousin Alissa, her equivocal attitude to his proposal of marriage and her eventual death. A section of Alissa's diary then exposes both Jérôme's short-sightedness and selfishness and Alissa's tragic confusion. The source of the problem is a simple clash of the demands of body and soul. Jérôme's Calvinist upbringing, coupled with an almost morbid passivity of temperament, leads him into an entirely false attitude towards Alissa, one in which her bedroom door and the 'narrow doorway' to Heaven form an overlapping image without his perceiving any incompatability or incongruity in the two images. He is content to pursue emotionally a relationship whose value he perceives as spiritual. Alissa is more complex. She has been scarred by her mother's adultery. Her devotion to God, her constant running away from Jérôme, her ascetic withdrawal from all that has given her pleasure in life are all eventually revealed as manifestations of the same inability to come to terms with her own potential sexuality. Although she is only fleetingly aware of this weakness in her religious vocation, the insights grow greater as she nears her end. It is in the tragic realisation of pointless self-sacrifice that she dies.

The theme of the destructiveness of value systems imposed from outside the individual is much clearer here. The symbolism of the novel, particularly the walled garden of the house at Fongeusemare, constantly suggests constraint. The focus of the story barely leaves the family unit. The doctrine of the body's sinfulness dominates every moment of physical proximity between the protagonists. It is difficult to see in what way either Jérôme, who remains supremely self-deceptive throughout the book, or Alissa, who struggles to deny the truth of her own perceptions, derives any even transitional benefit from their attitude to life. The way to God, one is firmly convinced, cannot be associated with any constraint of individual potential.

It is interesting to compare these two récits with the overtly autobiographical presentation of much of the same material in *Si le grain ne meurt*. Gide's attitude to autobiography awakens in his readers the same sense of the creation of an independent psychology whose development is being assessed that we feel in the case of the heroes of the *récits*. The narrator of *Si le grain* is a projected character, who represents a specific, if fundamental, aspect of the author, in the same way that Michel and Jérôme do. In all three works an older man is looking backward to a formative period of his life and ordering his recollections into an explanation of key events and tendencies. Protestations of attempting to establish the truth about the past, or apologies for gaps and inconsistencies, are as appropriate in the mouths of the fictional characters as in the 'non-fictional' narrator's. The point can be exaggerated of course. Autobiography as a genre has its own conventions, and Gide's is no more fictional, in some respects less so, than other such works. But if we examine the material of the three works, the way in which they represent three different projections of the same areas of experience becomes clearer. The atmosphere of *La Porte étroite* evokes the excessive puritanism of Gide's childhood, which occurs again in the reference to the Huguenot education given to Michel by his mother. The close links between Michel's new awareness of life's sensual possibilities, experienced in Africa, and Gide's own initiation into the delights of pederasty on his trip there in 1893 (the climax of his autobiography) are paralleled by the relationship between Gide's own professed spiritual love for his cousin Madeleine and its transposed fictional counterparts, Jérôme's love for Alissa and Michel's marriage with Marceline. Both the *récits* can then be read as interpretations of the problems posed by the attempt to reconcile Gide's own sensual and spiritual aspirations in the period 1880-1900; *Si le grain* is the synthesis of the two streams of experience, stopping short at the moment when the young Gide fully realises his own nature. In fact Gide himself draws attention to the unifiedly autobiographical nature of all his writing when he observes, in a note at the end of the first part of *Si le grain*:

> Memoirs are never more than half sincere however careful one is about their truthfulness. Everything is always more complex than one makes it sound. Perhaps one gets closer to the truth in a novel.

It is worth pursuing the point about the literary form of autobiography, since readers are not in the habit of considering how their responses are manipulated by what they tend to accept as factual writing, and since in France at least the genre has developed in the present century into the most characteristic form of first-person self-expression. As C.A. Tolton has pointed out, the relation of writer to reader in *Si le grain* is more or less the same as that in Proust's *A la recherche*:

> A man named André Gide lived a life which in his role as an author by the name of André Gide he has recreated in a book where a narrator (also named André Gide) tells the life of his younger self, the hero, who

of course was also called André Gide. This reminds one of nothing so much as a certain man called Marcel Proust who was also an author whose narrator . . . tells the story of himself (called Marcel) living and maturing with events and people surprisingly similar to those in the first Marcel Proust's life.

But whereas Proust writes in order to explore and record his attitudes to major problems of perception and identity, Gide writes for the specific purpose of dramatic self-revelation: 'I am writing these memoirs to provoke hostility towards myself.' Gide was writing to describe his awareness of homosexuality, while at the same time conveying to the reader his belief that this condition is not the result of any pernicious upbringing or unnatural elements in his character. At the same time he is careful to construct, in the opening chapters of part one, a sense of the determinist effects of the different influences brought into his childhood by his father and mother. In what constitutes the first 'Act' of the story, chapters 1-4, he creates the sense of an unformed being, a psychological embryo with concealed hints about both an unusual, precocious sexuality, and a passionate sensibility. The second Act of the Gidean drama (chapters 5-9) takes us out of the shadows of early childhood into an awareness of his difference. The narrative lurches forward as we follow Gide establishing himself amongst other people but constantly warning us that 'this isn't the really significant part of my narrative', as it were. Life is a search for new apartments, a round of grandparents and cousins, a blur of art, sensuality and religion. Moral temptation offers itself in the form of the amused prostitute from whom our hero flees (chapter 7). Yet he does not seem to flee for purely moral reasons, so much as from a natural indifference to the opposite sex. The progress of the self-portrait appears to be towards enlightenment of a religious sort, a seraphic state in which aesthetic and divine promptings illumine the soul. The artistic vocation presents itself and offers both a purpose and a liberation. Yet the young Gide is entering the world of André Walter, his cerebral passions more and more encroached upon by the call of the flesh.

Suddenly at the end of chapter 9 and thoughout chapter 10 Gide breaks off from his introspection, with all the hints of unrevealed complexities to which his analysis has constantly returned. The attention switches abruptly to people around him, particularly to the salon life into which the budding author was plunged. The individual is deliberately submerged in society. Just as Proust's Marcel, effaced observer in *Du côté des Guermantes* and *Sodome et Gomorrhe*, will become all the more dramatically the prime actor of the Albertine volumes, so the young Gide, constricted by the demands of his environment after the manner of Michel in Paris (*L'Immoraliste*), will suddenly be released to explore and develop his essential self in the North African journey of part two.

In this brief second part to the autobiography the chapters follow the familiar pattern of working to a thematic climax, with the author's skill evident in his prolonging of certain moments and his delaying tactics. There is more background to be filled in even though we know we are working towards 'the state of joy'. Algeria is to provide a resolution of the tormenting dualism that constantly reasserts itself and is expressed in appropriately biblical images of demon and devil. The element of travelogue performs the continued function of prolonging our anticipation until the young Ali achieves his seduction of the fascinated hero. The joy of sexual release brings a personal fulfilment echoed in the arrival of spring to the oasis. Nature and hero are transformed together.

Life cannot stand still. Nor therefore can Gide's liberation remain unchallenged from within or without. Michel must still, as it were, be faced by Alissa if the two tendencies are really to be united within the one book — the impossibility of presenting other than linearly forces at work within him simultaneously was a limitation which encouraged Gide to reject both *récit* and autobiography in favour of the more complex possibilities of the novel proper (see below pp260-3). Gide withdraws to Switzerland, symbol of the Calvinist gloom from which he had escaped. Though he returns to Algeria, for his second period of ecstasy (with a young musician), the death of his mother intervenes to arouse the other Gide. The African paradise is put aside. The childhood attachment to his cousin Emmanuèle (Madeleine) is revived, and their engagement announced. The retrospective narrator quotes ominously from Pascal, 'It is never people we love but only qualities in them,' and wonders whether it was not the quality of virtue as such that he loved in his wife-to-be. The marriage would appear to be flawed from its inception; hence the feeling of suspense with which the autobiography closes. After two Acts of anticipation, Gide has made a brief and profound investigation into his self in the climax to the third Act, only to withdraw again at the end, poised on the edge of a new uncertainty. One thinks of the criticism he voiced in the *Nouvelles nourritures terrestres* of the Delphic maxim 'know thyself'. It is not the search for oneself that he condemns but the arrogance of claiming to have pinned oneself down. Indeed, success at knowing oneself brings a limiting and impoverishment of the self. The structure of *Si le grain* suggests identification, but not resolution, of the complex elements in the narrator-hero's character.

In all this, the narrator's direct self-analysis is scattered, much of the account, like for example school life and piano lessons, consisting of narration in the past with interspersed critical comments in the present which often draw attention away from their self-justificatory function by adopting a critical tone or by phrasing the intervention in the form of a philosophical maxim which suggests the universality of the author's experience. Descriptions of both people and places, of Anna Shackleton, of the beautiful boy at the fancy-dress ball, Rubinstein, the Normandy countryside, the North African oases, La Fontaine d'Eure, the lake at Neuchâtel, are in the past or present tense according to the part of the time scale which Gide wishes to reinforce. There are also scenes of dialogue which help create the vivid presence, in particular, of Gide's companions in his African adventures, notably Oscar Wilde. There are even internal monologues to dramatise his own inner states. Like the style itself, with its modulations between controlled clarity, lyricism and occasional irony, the selection and balance of manner of presentation strengthens the sense of the work as a literary creation, designed to counterfeit a reality of the self just as much as any first-person fiction.

Proust
The Gidean works discussed above deal with the problem 'what am I becoming?'; Proust's novel asks 'what am I?'. Although Gide acknowledges the problem of imperfect self-recall, it does not seem to be one that concerns him. Whereas for Marcel, the spatial and temporal implications of the vagaries of memory are part of the broader problem of how to relate perception to reality, and thus have enormous import for the way in which the novel is constructed. It starts with a typical example of the loss of identity which derives from physical disorientation. This long description of how a bedroom can become unstable and anonymous because of the peculiar freedom which the newly awakened mind retains from sleep has three distinct functions. Firstly it begins the process by which childhood in Combray is re-established via the lighting up, as it were, of various rooms within a house, which then takes on a whole geographical identity within the little town. Secondly it introduces, in the character of each of the bedrooms remembered, specific moments of the past that will be enlarged upon later in the book. But most importantly, it establishes the autobiographical crux of the work (I use the term *autobiographical* here to mean relating to the reconstruction of the *narrator's* life by the narrator), Marcel's sense of his own fragmented contingency and the search for ways to create

a unified self which has a stable relationship to the world outside it.

In childhood Marcel possessed a confidence in the reality of the external world which he was gradually to lose. Truth is embodied for him in his mother and grandmother, in the books he reads, in the hawthorns along the way, in the bell-towers at Martinville. It lies hidden in people barely known to him, such as the Duchesse de Guermantes and Gilberte Swann. Life is to be a journey of discovery, in which he will apprehend reality through everything that is different from himself, in nature, society and art. Yet his awareness of his own difference is already an insurmountable obstacle to his complete identity with this alien truth. As he observes while reading in the garden at Combray:

> When I saw an external object, my awareness of the act of seeing it would remain between me and it, enclosing it in a slender mental outline which prevented me from ever coming directly in contact with its material state.

The desire to deny this total separation is strongly felt in his dependence on his mother's kiss, or the way in which he clings to his grandmother as a shield against the fear aroused in him by the unfamiliarity of his Balbec hotel room. But the desire for unity with the outside world is made more complex by the fact that no experience is really approached completely open-mindedly. Images of a complex and particular sort precede our visions of people and places. The Duchesse de Guermantes derives, from the associations of her family with the Combray church, a medieval patina which Marcel translates into tapestry and stained glass. It is not impossible for the interest of a person to survive closer acquaintance. Looking back near the end of *Le temps retrouvé* Marcel can even feel that life is made more poetic by the relationship between the Guermantes of his imagination, 'the mysterious race with the piercing eyes and beak-like noses, the unapproachable rose and gold race', and their flesh and blood representatives. Nonetheless, the difference between our vision of things and their reality is a constant source of disillusion. In so far as things survive this loss of prestige it is because we have precisely internalised them:

> ... as regards the Duchesse de Guermantes, I only perceived her charm, as was the case with certain pages of Bergotte, at a distance; when I was close to her, it faded away, for it had its being in my imagination and in my memory.

Marcel seems to want to find in the world around him both something completely new, the 'secret of half-intuited truth and beauty', and something which is the concrete embodiment of his own mental projections.

This ambiguity of the external world becomes a source of danger. When Marcel first visits Balbec he resents its failure to conform to his vision of a sea-girt Gothic church housing an 'ideal' statue of the Virgin. It is encased by the ordinary, and therefore familiar. Yet at the same time it contains no memories for him and is thus alien. Intellectual disappointment gives way to fear in the hotel bedroom, as the objects around him seem to crowd him out:

> It is our noticing them that puts things in a room, our growing used to them that takes them away again and makes room for us. Space for me there was none in my Balbec bedroom (mine in name alone); it was full of things which did not know me.

Caught off balance, as in the moments of awakening described at the start of the novel, the narrator succumbs to what Sartre sees as the 'thinginess' of things and suffers a consequent reduction in his own identity.

What Marcel lacks is any sense of continuity. For him loss of a relationship is the death of a self; the self who faces life after the end of his relationship with Albertine, or after the death of his grandmother, is represented as totally disconnected from the self which underwent the relevant experiences. If he goes on to modify this claim, it is only slightly:

> Doubtless this self maintained some continuity with the previous one . . . But I tended to become an entirely different character. It is not because other people are dead that our affection for them weakens, it is because we ourselves 'die'. Albertine had no cause to reproach her friend. The usurper of his name had merely inherited it . . . You only remember what you have known. My new self, whilst it had grown up in the shadow of my former self, had often heard Albertine spoken of; through that former self, through the stories collected about her, it felt it knew her, it found her congenial, it liked her; but it was only a second-hand emotion.

This feeling of a constant process of death and rebirth, without any accumulation of identity, necessitates the elaborate solution of creating an identity via a work of art with which *Le temps retrouvé* closes. But before examining this more closely, let us look at Marcel's attempts to find other solutions, in love, society and art, since it is this pursuit, and the growing disillusionment with the consequent experiences, which make up the bulk of the novel.

Marcel's most immediate attempts to relate to other people are through love, be it filial (with his mother and grandmother), amical (as with Saint Loup) or sexual (Gilberte Swann, Albertine). That Proust is claiming through his narrator to say something valid for more than just one individual is clear from the way in which Marcel's pattern of experience is echoed in Swann's relationship with Odette, Saint-Loup's with Rachel, Charlus' with Charlie Morel. The relationships all reflect the two-fold division which I have outlined above: the desire to penetrate to some entirely new truth and the desire completely to asssimilate the other person to one's own reality. With his mother, the emphasis of the relationship lies in assimilation. The secrets of the personality which she may reveal outside his company are less significant than the reiterated desire to demonstrate his emotional power over her. What is an understandable (if, in a teenage boy, slightly odd) form of jealousy in a domestic relationship comes to seem pathological in normal sexual relationships. 'The possession of what one loves is a joy still greater than love itself. Very often those who hide this possession from everybody do so merely because of their fear that the beloved object will be taken away from them. And this prudent silence causes the reduction of their happiness,' observes the narrator *à propos* of Charlus' pleasure in displaying his possession of Charlie Morel. The love relationships of the novel are in fact all images of the illusion of possession, particularly in the case of Albertine whom Marcel almost literally imprisons in his flat. Yet in every case the personality of the beloved remains elusive. It is not at whim that Proust devotes several pages to the description of Albertine asleep, for only at rest can the narrator have any significant illusion of controlling her. The recurrent symbol of his elusiveness is that of sexual desires in which the other partner cannot share. In the case of Albertine this is Lesbianism. With other characters, more subtle deviations are concocted — the Lesbian Lea's relationship with the bisexual Morel, or Rachel's proposition to a feminine young male dancer *en travesti* that he should form a threesome with her and another girl. In each case the underlying idea is that, respectively, the narrator, Charlus or Saint-Loup is unable to create in himself the nature of the desire felt by his beloved, and is thus kept at bay by the sense of a secret of experience from which he is by definition excluded.

This jealousy is not merely a yearning for the unattainably 'other': it is also part of the attempt to identify the self:

> I had since realised more clearly that when we are in love with a woman, we just project onto her our own state of mind, that consequently the important thing is not the intrinsic value of the woman but the intensity of the state.

Hence the enormous time and energy which Marcel expends interpreting the fluctuations of his relationships, only to come to the realisation that love is egocentric and that the beloved is the excuse for, rather than the object of, desire. What he deduces, then, is the history of his own mental states — affection, hostility, jealousy — as reflected in the particular strategies of possession that he adopted at given moments. This is not to say that the women who receive Marcel's attentions are reduced to interchangeable ciphers. On the contrary, our sharp awareness of the personal and social differences between Gilberte, the Duchesse and Albertine points up the degree to which the similarity in Marcel's response to them derives from something intrinsic to him. But all this is less important than what he does not and, in Proustian terms, *cannot* know.

Proust's views on love the average reader is likely to find both disagreeable and unacceptable. They also seem unreasonably biased towards the abnormal; by the end of the novel a rather extraordinary number of people turn out to have homosexual tendencies of one sort or another. It is therefore tempting to dismiss such a view of love as deriving from the instability of the author's own emotional life. It is not however sufficient to make the equation Albertine = Proust's chauffeur, Alberto, into an explanation of the novel's account of human relationships. Firstly the theory of love portrayed is quite similar to that proposed in *L'Etre et le Néant* by that violent anti-Proustian, Sartre (a man not known for his sympathy to homosexuality either), and exemplified in all his major creative works. Secondly, the concepts underlying the portrait of love are identical with those underlying that of social relationships in general. Proust's interest in society, or more to the point, Society, does not merely derive from snobbery (though to judge from his own correspondence he was no stranger to that particular vice). The fascination with the Guermantes that Marcel conceives in childhood derives from the coherence, tradition and therefore *essence* which their family history creates for them. They seem to demonstrate the incarnation of an identity, an illusion which it takes more than casual contact to deprive them of, as we can see from Marcel's comments as he watches the Guermantes group at the theatre. But, as he is inexorably to find out, the Guermantes are not deities out of a Meilhac and Halévy farce, ironically playing at *belle époque* drawing-room manners. There is a distressing similarity in kind, if not in detail, between a party at Mme de Saint-Euverte's and one at the Duchesse's or the Princesse de Guermantes'. There is even a distinct resemblance to the ghastly bourgeois salon of Mme Verdurin. This parallelism can be extended to include psychological identities between individuals which gradually break down Marcel's cherished notion that certain people embody secret qualities denied to the rest of us and to which he can with good fortune penetrate. The social laws that Marcel gradually extracts from his experience ruthlessly demolish the significance of anything but labels, the names and tags to which men are accustomed to attribute special meaning.

Marcel nonetheless continues to frequent society when he has long grown disillusioned with what it stands for. His lack of social ambitions gives him a clarity of perspective which makes for acute and humorous commentary on the ways of his fellows. Whereas love is never treated with detachment in the novel, society frequently is. We see the set rituals into which each social group falls and which prevent comprehension of the rules which govern other social groups — Marcel's parents refuse to accept that their friend Swann can also frequent aristocratic circles, Mme Verdurin is ignorant of the order of precedence which places Charlus above the Cambremers. The motivating force in society is ambition. The ambition can be for power over those within one's group, as in the tyrannical control which Mme Verdurin exercises over the personal relationships of her clan, or the refusal of Oriane de Guermantes to grace the salons of those of her relatives whom she judges to have slipped too far down the social ladder. Or it can be ambition to penetrate into groups whose secrets are as yet unknown, as we see with Bloch's unsteady but eventually successful attack on the Faubourg St Germain, Odettes' salon, marriage to Fourcheville and seduction of the ageing Duc de Guermantes, or Mme Verdurin's dizzying promotion to the status of Princesse de Guermantes. Each social group fights to maintain its exclusivity, and at the same time to extend its drawing power upwards. Mobility is achieved not by will-power but chance. Mme Verdurin backs Dreyfus (for all she is anti-Dreyfus by instinct), modern music and the *Ballets russes*. The first is a short-term loser; Odette Swann is much more successful by lionising the ageing author Bergotte and by using her husband's Jewish blood as a reason for supporting the anti-Dreyfusards. But Mme Verdurin knows a reliable long-term investment when she sees one:

> Mme Verdurin, in the Dreyfusiste cause, had attracted to her group writers of high quality who for the moment were of no social advantage to her because they were pro-Dreyfus. But political passions are like all others, they don't last . . . at each political crisis, at each new development in art, Mme Verdurin had little by little, the way a bird builds its nest, pulled out and collected the successive snippets, for the time being unusable, of what would one day be her salon. The Dreyfus Affair passed; Anatole France stayed.

The roulette wheel of political accident determines the changes in the face of society.

Proust's own and more apt image for this change is that of a kaleidoscope (an image also used by Gide in *Si le grain*). The bourgeoisie and the aristocracy are equal counters in the kaleidoscope, the subdivisions of the one group being superficially different from those of the other, but not different in kind. Hence the pointedly all-embracing observation by Marcel's grandmother that the snobbery of the woman who runs an exclusive public lavatory is 'typical of the Guermantes or the Verdurins and their little circle'. If one injects an arbitrary force for displacement, the counters change place and new patterns form. The sources of displacement here are provided firstly by the Dreyfus Affair, secondly by the Great War. Proust's attitude to the Affair is interesting. He was a Dreyfusard himself, and the sketches of moments and personalities embodied in the draft of his unfinished novel, *Jean Santeuil*, show that he closely concerned himself with the realities of the case (even if his interest as a novelist could loosely be called atmospheric rather than factual). Yet the presentation of the Affair in *A la recherche* is almost self-consciously counter-factual. Nobody seems to know or care about the rights or wrongs of what happened. Society thrives on gossip, or on a kind of perverse team-spirit. Proust most tellingly satirises this in the scene in *Du côté des Guermantes* where Marcel's butler, who is pro-Dreyfus, is exchanging words with the Guermantes' butler, who is anti. Marcel's butler purports to believe that Dreyfus is really guilty. He is uncertain whether there will be a re-trial and wants to deprive the Duc's butler of the pleasure of seeing the righteous cause done down. The Duc's butler thinks that if a re-trial is refused, Marcel's butler will be more indignant at the detention of an innocent man on Devil's island. He therefore purports to believe Dreyfus not guilty.

The effect of this jousting when transferred into the upper echelons of society, is to give to certain acquirable characteristics, notably nationalism and anti-Semitism, the power to open the doors of salons previously only accessible to those possessing certain inherited characteristics. Indeed, it is this that both Oriane and Charlus most bitterly hold against the Affair — they are expected to mix with social nobodies whose only virture is to be hostile to Dreyfus. The possession of the right label, or the failure to possess it, has a host of side effects. The Duc loses the presidency of the Jockey Club because Oriane is insufficiently anti-Dreyfusard; he blames his loss on his friendship with Swann. Saint-Loup champions the Dreyfusist cause despite his aristocratic and military background; he has a Jewish mistress. The effects of the Great War are more arbitrary still, but complete the kaleidoscopic process. A new set of faces are in possession of an old set of titles, such that the forgetful world confuses old and new. The key to society is not the individual, or even a set of values, but merely empty names.

What the narrator fails to find in individuals or groups around him, he also seeks in art itself, in the works of the novelist Bergotte, the painter Elstir, the composer Vinteuil, and ultimately in his own writing. Proust is careful to direct us away from both the collector's mentality, for example, the Guermantes and their insistence that their Elstirs are by definition the only ones of any value, and the critic's, as reflected in the aesthetic sterility wrought in Swann by his fascination with Vermeer. Marcel does isolate in works of art that individual essence of personality which he finds so inaccessible elsewhere. Right from his childhood reading of Bergotte's novels he has learnt to recognise what is typical of, and unique to, his author:

> ... recognising that same predilection for rare locutions, that same musical outpouring, that same idealist philosophy which had already on the previous occasions been the source of my pleasure, I no longer had the feeling of being in the presence of a particular passage of a particular book by Bergotte ... but rather of an 'ideal passage' of Bergotte, common to all his books.

The problem for the reader is that he is never fully convinced of Bergotte's identity as a writer. The evidence which one is offered, suggesting an uneasy and very dated blend of Anatole France and Maurice Barrès, does nothing to support the aesthetic importance which Marcel wants to attribute to him. The same kind of problem exists with Elstir, whose paintings are clearly impressionist in school. Marcel describes quite closely Elstir's technique of personal vision, his trick of transferring everything into a visual metaphor of something else — the sea seen in terms of a land mass, the land in terms of the sea. Yet the word-pictures the narrator creates remain tantalisingly abstract. Perhaps it is in the case of Vinteuil that we can most easily absorb Marcel's point of view, because we are used to having to make verbal approximates to describe the sensations which music, as an abstract art, creates in us. It is not that Marcel's description of the sonata as opening 'on a lily-white pastoral dawn' or the septet as beginning 'on a stormy morning . . . amid a bitter silence, in an infinite void' recreate a specific musical phrase or structure for us. But they do counterfeit the expression of a musical experience to which we are accustomed. What Marcel finds in Vinteuil's music is the distillation of his suffering, just as in Bergotte he finds a moral superiority which is the paradoxical product of the author's unsatisfactory life. As in Elstir's case, it is the translation of a special vision.

This makes Proust's view of art sound rather limited. In fact, as expressed in a passage in *La prisonnière*, this notion of distillation of essence —

> Wagner's harmony, Elstir's colour admit us to a knowledge of the qualitative essence of another person's sensations in a way that love for someone else does not

— is extended by the notion that the work at the same time contains an independent and complex world of its own, a comparison that Proust examines at some length and with particular reference to Wagner. All this is of great importance for our understanding of Marcel's final vocation as an artist himself, writing the book which is to be the one which we have just read. For Marcel's book also expresses the essence of his individual perception through its constantly metaphorical presentation of reality. It too creates an independent complex exterior world which is both an amalgam of its author's past experience and a system insisting on its own extension beyond that author's limits of perception. Here lies Marcel's solution to his original problem, how to cope simultaneously with the essential 'otherness' of the world around him and with his instinctive preference for his imagined and idealised view of objects and people, as opposed to their banal reality. For Marcel, the artist, the world is remembered in its own separate identity (via the curious process of affective memory, where familiar smells, sounds, tastes unleash an intense recall of areas of experience lost to our conscious mind), but because it is *remembered*, what was external has become a product of Marcel's own mind. Furthermore the self and the world created are not simply a resurrection of the past. As with an autobiographer's act of writing — and this is why I referred earlier to the narrator's autobiographical act in *A la recherche* — the tense of present consciousness embodied in a remembering 'I' absorbs all the other tense sequences. Past and present are contemporaneous in the literary character of the self constructed on the page.

The Gidean and Proustian autobiographical acts, though they have much in common, are considerably different in intent, as is perhaps reflected in their differing use of the kaleidoscope image. Gide models his work as self-exploration towards a future point, examining the logical possibilities of his own characteristics, or launches a rather complex self-revelation which seems to dramatise for the reader a process of knowledge previously attained by the writer. In both cases the nature of self-awareness is hardly in question. Proust determines his own nature by the act of writing a novel in which the hero determines his own nature by the act of writing the novel which the reader has just read. Common to the two approaches is the idea of a new self which grows out of the act of writing about the past self. This is, of course, by no means a traditional approach to self-portraiture. Even in works like Wordsworth's *The Prelude* where a process of change is forecast, it is a change wrought by self-comprehension rather than by self-creation. And the more standard strategies of autobiography, the confessional and didactic, normally depend by definition on the writer's awareness of his precise essence. Maurice Sach's *Le Sabbat* (first published 1946), a fascinating mixture of self-denunciation and self-exculpation in which sex, snobbery and religion are the main ingredients, though it pursues the idea of a unifying and ennobling characteristic which the author is certain exists within his character and has held it together throughout its long process of dissolution, assumes that this characteristic is to be revealed, and not created. However, there have been writers, particularly in the post-1930 period, who have expanded upon this concept of self-creation through first-person narrative with success. As an example of fiction proper we can take the works of Louis-Ferdinand Céline, for autobiography those of Michel Leiris.

Céline
The novels of Céline are a disconcerting blend of the traditional projection of the author's experience into a separate character, Bardamu, and the more ambiguous adoption, *à la* Proust, of one of the author's own first names, Ferdinand. Added to which the relationship between narrator and reader is itself not constant — sometimes a voice is present which asserts itself as the writer of the fiction rather than the actor of it. Céline's first and most famous novel, *Voyage au bout de la nuit* (1933), is in this respect the least interesting. Although its scenes of life at the Front and in war-time Paris, hospitals and lunatic asylums, colonial life in Africa and industrial society in America, relate to experiences in the author's life, the projection of his pessimism into the two characters, Bardamu and his friend Robinson, is no more than the extension and distortion of an author's life which is a commonplace of literary creation. *Mort à credit* (1936) complicates this process

by making its narrator, Ferdinand, also the novelist himself of the story that is being read. At the same time the 'biographical' element in the first part of the book is prominent. The description of Ferdinand's childhood is based on the author's experience of life as the son of a small shopkeeper and his wife, in the Passage Choiseul. It reflects the anxieties and prejudices of the lower middle class, patriotic and anti-Semitic, afraid of capitalism and looking down upon the proletariat. The pattern of jobs taken and lost, like the one as errand boy to a jeweller's, and the episode in which the boy is sent off to a school in England, are typical examples of material drawn from life. But the treatment of the material is a calculated deformation. The father is unbalanced and tyrannical, the mother makes a feature of both despair and resignation; the boy is shaped by a kind of class fate, poor but prevented by a code of morality from compensating for the restrictions imposed by that poverty. His life becomes a process of revolt and flight in which the nightmare qualities of exploitation, betrayal, the impossibility of winning against the odds of life all take precedence over normal psychological portraiture. This theme of defeat and disintegration transfers, in the second half of the book, onto a completely un-autobiographical level in Ferdinand's relationship with the larger-than-life figure of Courtial des Pereires, a crazy scientist who eventually commits suicide. There is, however, also a more complex relationship between novel and writer, because the history of the child Ferdinand forms the substance of a novel written by the adult Ferdinand. The work is also *about* the use of autobiographical material in a fictional context. The novelist Ferdinand quarrels with his mother because her version of his childhood is that of an exemplary lower-middle-class family working to uphold its standards and beliefs under the direction of a devoted father. This 'invention' Ferdinand rejects, and in so doing undermines the whole vision of existence on which his mother has depended. Thus Céline writes a novel in which he uses a distorted version of his childhood, and uses as his subject a man writing a novel in which he attacks a distorted version of his childhood which is in fact apparently similar in kind to Céline's real childhood. Ferdinand's quest for truth equals Céline's quest for self-mythicisation. To complicate matters further the idea of myth, in the form of the Krogold legend, is itself a subject of the novel too; the legend, a story recounted by Ferdinand, offers a parallel against which the events of the novel are to be viewed. All these elements, of necessity, inter-relate. Fiction implies autobiography; life implies fiction; self-recording necessitates self-creation.

The later novels extend and confirm these equations, particularly in the case of *Féerie pour une autre fois* (1952) and the trilogy *D'un château l'autre*, *Nord* and the posthumously published *Rigodon*. In *Féerie* the presence of an historical Céline is accentuated by the total reference of the work to the writer's situation, in prison in Denmark, and to the assimilation of the writer's past — his World War I experiences, his travels in Africa — to a time scale which is that of the narrator's mind. Ferdinand is plunged into the legal struggles of his creator to avoid extradition to France, and possessed by the obsessions of his creator over dreams of revenge on the world for its guilt and of recognition of his own innocence. *Mort à credit* has substantial impressionistic realism; *Féerie*, with its fragments of experience juxtaposed with fragments of fantasy within the context of a long and frenzied monologue of hatred, is only realism in the sense that it portrays a psychology. The trilogy takes up Céline's adventures in the closing stages of the war, as he wandered north through Germany on his way to Denmark. The episodes are not chronologically presented, because narrative is not the main feature of the books. *D'un château l'autre* again reduces all time to that of the narrator's psychology as he reconstructs his creator's experiences at Meudon and later in the company of the collaborationist and Vichy leaders in Sigmaringen. As in the previous novels the cosmic implications of those experiences are expressed through the mythical and fantastic status given to events and people; at one point, for example, the narrative shifts into a vision of Charon rowing his boat on the Seine, while in the castle of Sigmaringen itself Hell is symbolised by the mysterious room 36. *Nord*, which centres on the Simplon Hotel at Baden-Baden and then shifts to the destruction of Berlin, uses even more overtly Céline's experiences, to give a metaphysical analogue of the violence and pointlessness of human existence. *Rigodon*, in which the recurrent themes are pointless travel and the gradual disappearance of the characters, approaches the same theme of dissolution from a different angle. In all these works, both *Féerie* and the trilogy, the biographical elements are secondarily re-connected with the author, as in *Mort à credit*, by the theme of the artist, whose ability to reshape events into an artistic meaning of his own gradually declines as the annihilation of death approaches both narrator and author. As with the earlier work the significance of the self is asserted via the circular process of relating life to fiction, and fiction back to life.

Experimental autobiography
This process has been attempted in a very different way by Michel Leiris in his works as a whole, but more particularly in the autobiographies, *L'Age d'homme* (1939) and the tetralogy *La Règle du jeu (Biffures, Fourbis, Fibrilles* and *Frêle bruit*, 1948-76). From the poetry of his surrealist period in the late twenties it can already be seen how Leiris delights in the notion of words as a system of symbols or metaphors whose formal relationships disguise an inner secret. In the autobiographical works this notion is extended to the belief that by exploring the associations raised by inter-connections of language, the writer can assemble or create the essential elements of his own consciousness. *L'Age d'homme* is a step towards this approach. It owes its existence to a course of psycho-analysis

which Leiris underwent in 1929-30. This psycho-analysis, with its insistence on the importance of sexuality within his personality, allows Leiris to construct his autobiography around themes and images which draw on his memories, dreams and contemporary experiences. Autobiography here becomes self-therapy, although as he was to admit in 'De la littérature considérée comme une tauromachie', an essay added to a later edition of *L'Age d'homme*, 'at the bottom of all introspection is a taste for self-contemplation and . . . at the bottom of all confession is a desire for absolution'. Self-explanation is attempted primarily in terms of sexual obsessions, but the image which is present at the beginning and at the end of the book, and which Leiris is unable to banish, is that of death. It emerges that what Leiris is trying to extract from his past is an *ego*; sexuality increases his awareness of death, and death consumes the ego, effacing the Narcissistic image. *L'Age d'homme* suggests the close association between personal salvation and language which the volumes of *La Règle du jeu* will follow up. The first-person voice becomes little more than a linguistic function, and preservation is seen to lie in writing, a closed domain which points to the eternal:

> a means of attaining the eternal by simultaneously escaping growing old and finding an enclosed domain.

In *Biffures* (1948), leaving behind the limiting subject of sexuality, but attempting to exclude even further the subject of other people, Leiris uses as the principle of connexion the memory of how language itself and its relation to reality imposed themselves on his childhood consciousness; chronology and event are fragmented and the various aspects of the past subordinated to the complicated process of writing itself. The act of composing the autobiography assumes priority over all previous states of the writer's consciousness. The artist's reflection becomes totally dependent upon what he writes about himself; nothing appears to be known until the word gives it existence. In describing his method as 'a process of meditation zigzagging along the line of the writing itself' Leiris places importance on the act of writing in the process of the construction of an image of the self. Nevertheless, as John Sturrock has pointed out, *La Règle du jeu* though possibly a literary *tour de force* is also a personal fiasco, for with the expulsion of chronology from the autobiography, Leiris confronts the fact that it is not chronology which kills us but *time*, measured for the writer by the movement of his pen as remorselessly as by any watch.

Leiris' approach to autobiography seems closer to that of the novelists Céline and Proust — indeed the end of *Fibrilles* suggests a self-conscious inversion of *A la recherche*, a failure to achieve a Proustian consolidation of the past. Other autobiographers remain closer to traditional aims of recapturing or identifying the writer's identity, but, equally, attempt to transcend the positivist concept of experience on which the methods of traditional autobiography are based. A good example is André Gorz, whose *Le Traitre* (1958) received the commendation of Sartre. Gorz is writing from an existentialist position. For him, as for Leiris, the meaninglessness of life can be transcended in some degree by the act of writing itself. But writing is not only escape, it is also an *act* which affirms to the writer his own existence, using the past to expand his grasp of reality and thus give substance to the present. The first part of the book, 'Nous', outlines the problem of identity and the decision to attempt a written autobiographical solution. Gorz uses reminiscence of childhood both to create distance and, paradoxically, to reduce distance, between himself and his past. The child Gorz is presented as both particular — an alienated, bewildered Jewish boy — and as an example of a general condition, a classic case of Marxist alienation:

> he would curl up in obscure nooks and imagined he was a little animal, very small, in captivity, alone in the world, fallen out of a pocket or a hand, and which nobody wanted.

The world of childhood fantasy is replaced by a Marxist consciousness, and then by psycho-analysis. All this is designed to construct a picture of a child deprived of choices, who plays roles he does not understand — 'The child is a being almost totally invented.' From the identity of the self in 'Nous' he passes to the relationship of the self to the world in 'Eux'. We instantly recognise an aspect of the Proustian dilemma: '. . . he had always wanted to embody the complete opposite of what he was'. This is extended by a further desire, experienced since childhood, to be an invisible presence, 'not to be there'. The third major idea of the 'Eux' section is again Proustian. 'To be other than oneself while remaining oneself.' It is through the act of writing that Gorz perceives a solution to these problems: 'the act of writing . . . abolishes reality in favour of an absent Reality which is merely embodied in signs'. As with Leiris, writing takes on qualities of therapy: it is both escape (enabling the writer to become pure mind) and an involvement with reality by the very fact of its being an act. Writing is 'a purifying form of asceticism', the implication being that the emphasis is placed on the process rather than the product, that the act of writing is more highly valued than the completed book. For as Gorz declares; 'the writer who has written this book is a dead writer'. The Narcissus image has taken on a new aspect, in which the artist constructs a self-portrait by writing himself into existence on the page and thus abolishing himself as a significant historical entity. Gorz begins by referring to himself in the third person, setting himself up as an object of study. Horror of the self is translated into a horror of self-expression, the indirect 'he is repelled by the concept of myself' being preferred to 'I reject myself'. It is only at the conclusion of the book that the first person emerges and that the third-person reference designed to liquidate the past self can be abandoned in order to *define* the newly emerged present self.

Perhaps the new Narcissus was foreshadowed by Rousseau

when he called for a new language to cope with the demands of self-expression. There is no doubt that self-contemplation has become, in its more serious forms, less passive and indulgent than in the Greek myth, though just as ultimately destructive in some cases. Rousseau's contradictory personality, Stendhal's and Julien Green's dualities which create antagonistic forces in their autobiographies, all point towards the problems identified by Leiris and Gorz. Roland Barthes' ambiguously titled 'autobiography' (*roland barthes par roland barthes*) mocks Narcissus at the same time as appearing to pay court to him, the carefully chosen photographs of his youth indicating a stylised, fixed conception of self. From these we pass on to the text, where it becomes clear that the photographic image is a sort of pre-history, and that his real autobiography lies in the written word, in the texts that he has left behind. At this point the fictional and 'autobiographical' texts of self-exploration and self-creation come together; the distinction of genre is one of reader expectation rather than one inherent in the literary strategies. Which brings us back to Gertrude Stein's remarks to Dashiel Hammett . . .

CHAPTER 3
The Cult of Youth

> And when we bid adieu to youth,
>   Slaves to the spacious world's control,
> We sigh a long farewell to truth;
>   That world corrupts the noblest soul.
>   (Lord Byron)

In one of his *Carnets* Henry de Montherlant (1896-1972) wrote:

> I am in sympathy with children because our preoccupations are the same. It is a matter of enjoying oneself and living in the present moment, without prejudices and without any sense of obligation, particularly of gratitude.

In Montherlant's notebooks childhood and adolescence are portrayed as a Bergsonian paradise, open to the immediacy of sense impressions, unclouded by the conventions of reason, rebellious against the falsity of restraints which the child demolishes with a lucidity peculiar to its age-group. As such, the world of youth is the very emblem of *l'esprit nouveau*. This view represents a clear break with earlier tradition, and one which can partially be accounted for by changes within society itself. The idea that childhood and adolescence were states interesting in themselves and which should therefore receive some attention in literature had come later to France than to England. True, Jean-Jacques Rousseau, in his *Emile* (1762), had offered a philosophical encomium of the state of youth, portraying it as a time of purity which should be left as untainted by society as possible, the child only being forced to face the problems of rationality and adult emotion at fifteen years or more. In practice, however, the Catholic view of children as closest to the taint of original sin, and the consequent repressive régime imposed upon them, continued in the nineteenth century to lend weight to the socially convenient view that the offspring of the poor should be obliged to face the world as premature little adults, and those of the higher classes should be kept from disturbing the full social lives of their parents. Children, like servants, were best behind baize doors. Accordingly, the young appeared in literature merely as prefiguring adult states, as in Eugène Fromentin's *Dominique*, in sentimentalised portraits of pastoral charm (the rural novels of George Sand) or as paragons of brutalised innocence (Hugo's *Les Misérables*).

As the century wore on, the insistence on the necessity of authoritarianism in the upbringing of children declined very little. The natural inferiority of child to adult appeared, if anything, confirmed by the positivist school of psychology, according to which children possessed the cunning innate in animals. At best a benevolent altruism toward them was proposed, as in Bishop Dupanloup's popular work, *L'Enfant* (1869), and this attitude had modified very little even as late as Alfred Binet's relatively progressive *Les Idées modernes sur les enfants* (1910). In practice, however, a pattern of family life in which much closer relations existed between mother and child, while the father remained a distant, often tyrannical figure, emerged from the 1860s onwards.

Adolescence, as distinct from childhood proper, became a subject of concern only from around 1890, to judge first from the large number of novels on the topic (one hundred or more between 1890 and 1930) and secondly from the appearance of such psychological and educational studies as P. Mendousse's *L'Ame de l'adolescent* (1909), and of newspaper features on the problems of teenagers, of which the most famous by 'Agathon'

(H. Massis and H. Tardieu) was separately printed in 1913 as 'Les Jeunes Gens d'aujourd'hui'. The impetus for this sudden growth of concern was largely social, partly inspired by the effects on the young of the confused double-standards of sexual morality during both the Second Empire and the Third Republic (and one might add, ever since), and partly by the alarming increase in juvenile crime at the turn of the century. But in literature, the interest in both childhood and adolescence was greatly stimulated by the obvious symbolic connections between youth and all things *new*, between rebellion against the conventions of society and against the family as microcosm of that society. I do not mean that the novels written between 1890 and 1930 necessarily concerned themselves with revolt as such. Youth established itself as a focus of interest, an area with problems of definition and comprehension, in the same way that 'black consciousness' or the awareness of women's individual identity can be said to have preceded black or feminist revolt.

As early as 1879, Jules Vallès, the socialist agitator, had, in his autobiographical novel *L'Enfant*, scandalised the public by his attack on the thoughtless inhumanity of parents to children. It says much for the shift in public opinion that another denunciation of the myth of the united family, Jules Renard's *Poil de carotte* (1894 — later dramatised and filmed) received much more critical sympathy. It was beginning to be accepted that mothers were no longer sacrosanct figures. This did not prevent a new romanticisation of the mother-child relationship. Its theoretical expression is best found in the writings of the moralist Alain (1868-1951), notably *Les Sentiments familiaux* (1927), where the child is portrayed not only as the corporeal unification of the characteristics of its parents, but above all as forming with its mother the one perfect emotional unit. A similar if qualified notion, we shall see, lies behind some of the novels and plays of Cocteau. The contrary position is put forward by Montherlant in a note to his essay *La Relève du matin* (1920), where he observes that almost all French misapprehensions about children are precisely the result of this habit of thinking of ' "women-and-children" all in one, with hyphens'. Though Montherlant's misogyny informs even his views of children — it is only in boys that he shows an interest — his is not an isolated view, echoing as it does the ideas presented by Gide in *Les Nourritures* and *Le Retour de l'enfant prodigue* (1907). The relationship between mother and child, the struggle to reject or deny the significance of the relationship, forms one of the main strands in the 'youth' novels of the period up to World War II.

Another important theme is that of the separateness of children as a group. On this point at least both Alain and Montherlant agree, as can be seen from the charming chapter 'Le peuple enfant' in the former's *Les Idées et les ages* (1927) and from the latter's *La Relève du matin*, the whole of which is a lyrical hymn to the special qualities of adolescence. For Montherlant, a boy in his early 'teens is not only part of a special group (fostered by certain aspects of the educational system) but also endowed with qualities lost to the adult:

> . . . it is about thirteen that most males reach their point of greatest spiritual richness . . . how much we could learn from those who, adorned with the charm of youth, reveal to us a seriousness, a hatred of irony, a violence and extravagance in their attitude to life itself, an impetuous grasping of material reality, a way of blending themselves into the very heart of reality, whilst we 'grown-ups', set apart, are content with straying along its banks.

The major writers who exploit the theme of youth do so because, without necessarily going as far as Montherlant, they too identify their own aspirations with qualities which they find particular to childhood and adolescence.

Childhood as a lost paradise
What might be called the last of the great nineteenth-century novels, but one in which children hold the centre of the stage,

is Alain-Fournier's *Le Grand Meaulnes* (1913), whose most successful epigone is undoubtedly the magical *Eroica* (1938) of the Greek novelist Kosmas Politis. I say 'nineteenth-century novels' because of the suggestion that childhood is a 'paradise lost', another land yearned after as by a Baudelaire or a Rimbaud, and because one of the important characters, Franz, is the type of 'the young Romantic hero', as the narrator François Seurel himself calls him. Yet it is a moot point how far one can really speak of a complete destruction of the values of childhood. At the centre of the book is a sense of otherworldliness at times tipping dangerously close to the fey sentimentality of James Barrie. Meaulnes cannot attain the status of Peter Pan, but he belongs in the world of *The Little White Bird* (1902). As Alain-Fournier wrote in a letter to Jacques Rivière in 1906:

> My credo in art and literature is: childhood. To succeed in rendering it ... in all its profundity, touching on sacred mysteries. My book will perhaps constitute a perpetual, imperceptible to-and-fro between dream and reality; dream being understood as the vast, imprecise life of childhood hovering above the other world and continually ringing with echoes of it.

Le Grand Meaulnes is, indeed, dominated by children: by children who never quite, with one tragic exception, grow up. The first part of the novel, with its background of rural school-life, is focused on the restless, wild character of Augustin Meaulnes himself, and on the excitement and mystery of the strange festivities into which he accidentally strays at the 'lost domain'. Although the narrator, Seurel, is recalling the past with hindsight, he recreates, as from a non-omniscient standpoint, the suspense built up by Meaulnes' disappearance. The other-worldly magic of the party organised for Franz de Galais and his fiancée is seen step by step as it occurs, through the eyes of Meaulnes. The fête is a kaleidoscope of colour, sound, movement, in which the dominant note is given by the fancy dress of the revellers and by the fact that the organisation of events is in the hands of the children. When the magic is broken, it is by the intrusion of the adult world. Franz arrives alone, abandoned by his intended bride Valentine; suddenly, drunken grown-ups eclipse the delicacy and innocence of what has gone before. Yet the intrusion is of an unreal adult world. What matters is the apparently hopeless love which Meaulnes has conceived for a girl whose very name he does not know, and the melodrama of Franz's attempted suicide, presented as another kaleidoscope, as nightmarish as the preceding part of the episode had been idyllic.

Part two of the novel offers variations on the theme of pursuit frustrated, a succession of attempts to rediscover the path to the 'lost domain'. But as with childhood itself, banished by Meaulnes' fleeting proximity to love and death, there can be no true return to the château or to the girl, whose identity both, for the moment, elude Meaulnes. When, in part three, Seurel discovers for him that his beloved is Yvonne de Galais, sister of Franz, the second meeting of the ill-starred lovers, at a rather vulgar village outing, is a realistic 'parody' of the elements which had made a mood-poem of the original *fête*. Yvonne has, in a sense, retained her special qualities, at least those of beauty and purity, despite the decline in her family fortunes which have led to the destruction of the château and the sale of all the trappings which Meaulnes associates with it. It is, however, he himself who has changed irrevocably, corrupted by his incursion into the adult world of sexuality by a liaison with the woman who is, though he had not known it, Franz's former fiancée. Meaulnes can only attempt to redeem himself by re-integration into the world of childhood values. Thus, despite his marriage to Yvonne, he abandons her almost at once in order to honour a pledge to help Franz. It is Seurel who has again been the unwitting catalyst of disaster. Franz wants Meaulnes' help in tracing Valentine, and, thanks to Seurel, Meaulnes realises who she is and what responsibilities he owes to her. By the time Meaulnes returns to Yvonne, she has died in childbirth, leaving a baby daughter to Seurel's care.

This is not really a triumph for reality. At the end of the novel Franz and Valentine, united, are on the point of fashioning an idyllic life together in the cottage which his indulgent father had given Franz when he was still a boy. And Meaulnes holds in his arms the infant, symbol of his passion. The only loser is François Seurel, the quiet realist, the sole unhappy mortal condemned to grow up. He has never fully been able to enter the dream-world of Meaulnes, despite his immense admiration for him. Furthermore, it is precisely his tentative intrusions into this dream-world, his attempts to assimilate it to the laws of vulgar reality, which lead to the destruction of Yvonne, whom he clearly loves far more, in any meaningful sense, than does the barnstorming hero. It is the annihilation of this lone 'adult' that forms the last and most tragic note of the novel, when the baby, the only object left to give his life meaning, is taken from him:

> I had stepped back a little way to see them better. A little downcast and yet with a sense of wonderment I began to understand that the little girl had finally found the companion for whom, in some obscure fashion, she had been waiting. I felt keenly that Meaulnes had come back to deprive me of the only source of joy that he could have left me. Already I could picture him, by night, wrapping his daughter in a cloak and setting off with her on new adventures.

Reality, here, is the lame world of François Seurel, prevented from taking part to the full in the world of children by his early ill-health, condemned to the conventional petit-bourgeois path from pupil to school-teacher, shut out from the magic terrain of adventure and passion. Though childhood, as symbolised in the enchanted moment of the *fête étrange*, can never be brought back to life, it is those dreamers who retain within them something of its 'otherness', Meaulnes and Franz, who contrive to transcend the meaninglessness of adult reality.

Valery Larbaud's prose fiction, the *Journal de A.O. Barnabooth* which accompanies the poems, the novella *Fermina Márquez* (1911) and the short stories collected as *Enfantines* (1918), conveys the same sense of the special qualities of childhood but a more melancholy view of its power to withstand the encroachments of the adult world. Barnabooth is, of course, the adolescent who escapes; his diary is a mixture of comic Odyssey, sentimental education, analysis of the pursuit of pleasure, handbook of spiritual revolt. Yet even he, who is by definition only free of the restraints of conventional life because he is made larger than it by his unbounded wealth, is left with a sense of inadequacy and bitterness. In the fourth and last notebook of his diary, he expresses disgust for his past, distress for the future, and a sense of emptiness in the present. His very dreams of returning to South America and becoming part of everyday reality are false:

> Then I shall make my way to my up-country estates. I had tried to picture life there too: riding, the ranch, friendship with rough fellows, daily contact with the grandeur of plebeian souls . . . Ah well! it was just a bit of Walt Whitmanesque poetry; something very beautiful; but life is rarely as it is portrayed in the great classics.

The best that Barnabooth can manage is a Gidean renunciation of literature for action. By publishing his book he sheds the personality it records: 'It finishes. I begin'.

Barnabooth might be seen as symbolising something beyond his own personality, the 'unquiet soul' of modern man, caught between flesh and spirit, determined to achieve the utmost within the limits of human possibilities. The central figures of *Fermina Márquez* speak simply to us of adolescence, without idealisation and yet in a way which makes the rest of life into a decline. The novella is no less pessimistic in its conclusions than the *Journal*, but the experience it records are, somehow, more serious and more positive. The setting, delicately sketched in with all its curious blend of routine and excitement, is of life in a boarding-school of the cosmopolitan type which crops up in the memoirs and autobiographies of many writers of the 'thirties, from Maurice Sachs to Julien Green. There scarcely is a plot, merely a series of scenes designed to portray the last flowering of idealism, the first confusions of sexuality and emotion, the essence of the 'awkward age'. As the detached tones of the narrator put it:

> We were a band of sixteen-to-nineteen-year olds quite without shame or scruple, who made it a point of honour to stick at nothing in the way of rule-breaking and insolence.

The Fermina of the title is the sister of a Colombian new-boy. Her visits to the school with her indulgent aunt and her younger sister, Pilar, intended to help her brother settle into his new environment, serve as a pretext for Larbaud to present three studies in different types of young male who are captivated by her: Santos Iturria, charming, rich, madcap, notorious among his fellows for his nocturnal escapades in Montmartre; Joanny Léniot, whose prestige derives entirely from his outstanding intellectual prowess; and, more briefly delineated, Camille Moutier, only thirteen, dreamy, sensitive, shy. There is a deliberate haziness of time scale in the descriptions, and the action is confined to Joanny's winning Fermina's interest briefly away from Santos, then losing it to him again. What remains with the reader is a sense of the intensity of the mental world of adolescence. Fermina stands out for her confusion of religious conviction with moral scruple, as she struggles to suppress her own rising sexuality within the guide lines of a parroted life of St Rose of Lima (a very Firbankian saint). But it is Joanny who is the real centre of the book. He lives so intensely in his inner world, torn between despair at imagined inadequacies and exultation at prospective glories, he dreams so vividly of a future in which events as implausible as the restoration of the Holy Roman

Empire take place, that he hovers on the verge of what, in an adult, would seem mental illness. Yet Larbaud skilfully contrives to show his condition as a norm, and a positive state at that. He excels at nuancing the kind of shifts in thought and emotion which culminate in Joanny's renunciation of Fermina. He makes us believe in him as both deeply, almost pedantically, academic and yet able to cry out

> I despise the critical cast of mind, I hate knowledge, and I respect nothing but man's passions, because they are the only thing that counts in the midst of all the modern idiocies.

The narrative is not allowed to reach any kind of climax of action. It seems about to take off — will Santos become engaged to Fermina? will Joanny make something positive of the mood of self-satisfied humility which follows his crisis of honour (he throws away a gold watch given to him by Fermina's aunt because he sees it as 'payment' for his kindness to her nephew)? But, abruptly, Larbaud cuts the ground away from this neat and tidy world. An unspecified slab of time has elapsed. The narrator has returned to the college, now closed, and talked with the old concierge. The world of the school is put into a doubly different perspective: first, that of the concierge himself, who talks of the inhumanity of the boarding system, especially for the foreign boys; then of adult reality, as the adolescent charm and promise of the boys is wiped away by the historical truth of what has happened to them. Wealth has been its own destruction; some were ruined by women, others by gambling, others by the Stock Exchange. It is a tale of death, death by disease, by suicide, by dissipation. Santos? He married a German girl. And Joanny Léniot, the future restorer of Western civilisation?

> . . . he died in the barracks, during an epidemic, four months after he was called up. Garrison duty on the Eastern front is tough on the new recruits, especially in the block-houses. Anyway, he's dead. A lad who'd started so well, too. Seems he'd got two degrees and a prize from the Law Faculty in Paris, all before he was twenty-one.

Beyond adolescence there is only death, physical or metaphorical. Time seems the confederate of the murderous hand of adulthood, the obliterator of dreams.

This impression is greatly strengthened if one turns to the collection *Enfantines*. Mostly written over the period 1907-14, these stories reflect something of the repressive upbringing and poor physical health which sharpened in Larbaud the awareness of childhood as a process of living in one's own universe, while having to acknowledge the existence of what adults insist is reality. What the stories all convey is the *otherness* of children, which, despite the frequent presence of an adult voice remembering or observing, is presented without adverse comment. The narrative is composed of transverse slices of time; the characters, their thoughts, their milieu emerge from interior monologue, direct transmission of thoughts and memories in which adult and infant voices collude. Adult time, even if it is mentioned, is of little significance.

One could read the majority of these slight pieces as illustrations of what Alain says in 'Le peuple enfant', of children as a separate tribe with rites incomprehensible to the adult. Their games in particular, Alain says, should be sacrosanct, because they are the key to their universe. Games, in *Enfantines* constitute the creation of an alternative world. This can be a half-conscious creation, as in the constant plans of the dying Dolly in the story of that name, or the erotic fantasies of the sexually awakening heroine of 'Portrait d'Eliane à quatorze ans'. More often it is a transformation of reality, as in 'La grande époque', where Marcel, Françoise and Arthur translate the grounds of the house into a new world, into which they absorb fragments of history and geography as learnt at school. Time for them is the duration of their own creations. The metamorphosis of their territory into a huge railway system the year before is a century away as far as the children are concerned, just as when they play with Marcel's toy soldiers, it is quite natural for battles to be fought between Joan of Arc, Murat and the Black Prince. These new worlds are not inventions to the children. They are reality. In 'L'heure avec la figure', the face which the child sees in the veining of the marble mantelpiece, a face which 'the grown-ups are incapable of seeing, fortunately', transports the boy out of the room in which he is unenthusiastically waiting for his music-master and away into a vividly alive countryside, on a journey 'into the continents of the setting sun: the sky above the garden . . . like the blue and gold map of another world'.

The enemy are the adults, who ignore their children, like Dolly's mother, or misunderstand their dreaming, like Milou's in 'Le couperet'. Worse still, their rigid code of conduct intrudes upon the world of the children. Its caste system divides friends. Arthur and Françoise, children of the estate manager, have to address Marcel as *vous* now that he is going away to school. The narrator of 'Devoirs de vacances' is forbidden to play with Solange because her mother is 'not quite the thing'. Milou is separated from the servant girl, Justine, whom he secretly adores. Milou may have his moment of vengeance on the deadening world of materialist opportunism when he proclaims in front of his parents and their friends that he wants to be a servant when he grows up, rather than a Minister of the Republic. But adults, the reader knows, always win in the end.

The otherness of adolescence
In Larbaud's stories, youth possesses positive qualities, dream, emotion, the ability to experience the world with great intensity, rejection of the unnecessary categorisation imposed on existence by adults. This independent world is threatened or even destroyed by contact with the society of grown-ups. An extension of this view of youth, in which a different moral system, giving supreme value to emotional intensity, is lived out in defiance of the norm, is to be found in the novels of

Raymond Radiguet and Jean Cocteau, the Rimbaud and Verlaine of the 1920s (the description is too kind to Radiguet and a trifle hard on Cocteau). Radiguet (1903-23) lived a life more frenetic than anything invented by Aldous Huxley or Scott Fitzgerald, but his two novels, *Le Diable au corps* (1923) and *Le Bal du comte d'Orgel* (posthumously published in 1924), which should be seen in the context of Cocteau's *Le Grand Ecart* and *Thomas l'Imposteur* (both of 1923), are attempts to convey the otherness of adolescent emotion, its power to create a beauty absent from adult life, and the ultimate impossibility of its survival in a world of adult convention. *Le Bal* and *Thomas* are the more fantastical of the four. In the latter, the eponymous hero is a sixteen-year-old dreamer, who passes himself off as a general's nephew, and involves himself in life at the Front. The war itself is a backdrop to the exaltation created by his actions in the young Guillaume Thomas. When he dies, the bullet which kills him carries the force of that reality which will always shatter the glorious fictions of adolescence. In *Le Bal* François de Séryeuse, the incarnation of *insouciance*, makes the acquaintance of the Comte d'Orgel and his wife Mahaut, is drawn into their life of perpetual *divertissement* and becomes their close friend. François and Mahaut gradually fall in love, without admitting their feelings to one another. The latter loses her head, tells all to François' mother, learns she is loved in return, and tries to put things right by confessing to her husband. In accordance with the essence of his nature, which prevents him from taking seriously anything that can be kept private, the Count resolves that there shall be no break between François and the d'Orgels. Radiguet has created a fantasy world in which the adults conspire to play the game of life according to the rules of adolescence.

Le Diable au corps and *Le Grand Ecart* take the problem more seriously. In its opening paragraph *Le Diable au corps* brilliantly (and in 1923 shockingly) sets apart the mentality of its young protagonists from that of the older generation, by bluntly stating that for the very young — the narrator is twelve just before war breaks out — the war was simply a four-year 'summer hols'. The boy gradually finds himself unconsciously drawn, though still a child, into an emotional situation which a grown man would have found hard to handle. He falls in love with the young daughter of family friends, and his feelings are reciprocated, first platonically, later sexually. But Marthe is engaged to Jacques, who is at the Front. She marries him while he is on leave, although she no longer loves him. Her life is bound up in the sensual and emotional ecstasy of her relationship with the narrator. The core of the book is given over to recording the jealousy and the delight in power of the narrator himself, which combines with the pressures of the outside world, parental persuasion, scandal among the neighbours, letters and visits from Jacques, to destroy Marthe. She dies, and the child she has born to her boy-lover is accepted by her returning husband. Unlike Meaulnes, the narrator of *Le Diable* has lost everything. Order has re-established itself; the adult world has successfully excluded the non-conformist.

Le Grand Ecart portrays the sentimental education of Jacques Forestier. It is a much more sophisticated novel than *Le Diable au corps* in both style and content. It betrays more clearly an underlying philosophy of existence, and establishes a more elaborate triangular relationship between author, character and reader. This it achieves through the complex network of shifts from narrator-time to action-time, from interior monologue to detached comment, and by the use of maxims which delight in their own elegance while still defining an essential element of character or situation. Our fragmentary glimpses of Jacques' early adolescence show us three things about him that are very important: first, that he can be 'wounded' by beauty; second, that he learns from 'a disciple of Bergson and Taine' (strange and dangerous mixture) that he should make free use of his senses; third, that his nature is incapable of anything but excess. A stay in Venice reveals to him a significant paradox, that 'it is a fact that a masked ball unmasks men', ie, that anonymity removes the restraints imposed by convention. The anonymity of life in a Parisian *pension*, where he is living while he prepares for his *baccalauréat*, exposes him to the effects of such an unmasking. He is plunged into an intense emotional adventure with Germaine, the mistress of an older and richer man. The relationship is complicated by its entanglements with Germaine's protector, with her friend Louise, and with the other adolescent inhabitants of the *pension*, notably an English boy, Peter Stopwell, who 'would have been beautiful in the Greek style if long-jumping had not elongated him like a badly taken photograph' and whose sexual tastes are in some doubt. The key phrase of the novel is 'the undefined longing for beauty kills us'. Only certain people possess this longing, and Jacques is one of them. Hence his incompatability with Germaine. For she, like Stopwell, is of the 'race of diamonds', heartless and heart-breaking; Jacques, like Petitcopain, the youngster who adores Stopwell, is of the 'race of glass', his soul destined to be fatally marked. Jacques finally attempts suicide, a 'death' which Cocteau describes at length, like a foreshortened version of Golding's *Pincher Martin*, a comparison strengthened by the recurrent image of drowning. The suicide fails because of the intervention of chance — there are throughout the novel several references to destiny, and the names of Egyptian gods, Osiris, Anubis, Apis also crop up, prefiguring a favourite theme and manner of Cocteau's later plays and films. Yet there is no way in which Jacques can be integrated into the everyday world of deception and compromise. In an image from the book, he is an angel forced to live out a role in an alien world. The task is impossible:

> Jacques felt his mood darkening. He understood that life on earth obliges one to follow the fashion, and that hearts were not being worn this season.

In so far as the heroes of these four novels treat life as something to be enjoyed, live in the present moment without prejudices and lack any sense of obligation to a system of values outside themselves, they come very close to the definition of childhood given by Montherlant in his *Carnet*, even if the ages of the characters concerned range from twelve to twenty. Families, in so far as they appear at all, play an ambiguous role, over-protecting, meddling, and above all, as Mme Forestier with Jacques, failing to understand. Only *Le Grand Ecart* goes some way to elevating the problems of adolescence to an exemplification of wider ethical issues. Although Cocteau is not often thought of as a moralist — perhaps because, as he himself put it in *De la Responsabilité*, people confuse the notion of moralist with that of moraliser — three of his major collections of essays (perhaps 'thoughts' would be a better description), *Opium* (1930), *La Difficulté d'être* (1947) and *Journal d'un inconnu* (1952), all show a profound interest in the kind of practical ethics which are associated with the French seventeenth-century tradition of *moralistes*. There are, not surprisingly, comments in these works which throw light on Cocteau's view of youth, such as the well-known remark in 'De la jeunesse' (*La Difficulté d'être*):

> Childhood knows what it wants; it wants to get out of childhood. The feeling of malaise starts when it does get out of it. For youth knows what it doesn't want before it knows what it does. Now, what it *doesn't* want is whatever we do.

But for the very reason that Cocteau's moral essays are reductions of his own experience into aphorisms, and the reconstitution of real life into fictionalised moral principles, it is in two of his fully fictional works, the novel *Les Enfants terribles* and the play (far and away his best) *Les Parents terribles* (1938), that he projects most effectively a portrait of the meaning which he perceives in adolescence.

Adolescence is, for Cocteau, the time of the angels, both in the active and passive aspects of their Coctelian manifestation. *Les Enfants terribles* is a cocktail of their typical qualities, destructiveness and the will to be destroyed, corruption and purity, above all that disorder which is itself a higher form of order. The plot of the novel, self-consciously fictional though it is, barely matters. It starts with a snowball fight — snow, symbol of purity, recurs throughout — in which Paul is badly, and deliberately, injured by Dargelos, a slightly older gang-leader whom he adores. The victim is taken home by a schoolfriend, Gérard, and obliged to convalesce. Thereafter the book becomes a series of scenes showing his curious relationship with his sister Elisabeth, a relationship barely touched by the devoted friendship of Gérard, or even by Elisabeth's marriage to Michaël, a pawn introduced into the permanent game of chess between brother and sister and frivolously killed off in the manner of Isadora Duncan to show the character's unreality (Anouilh uses the same motif in *Léocadia*). However, a fourth character, Agathe, the female double of Dargelos, offers a real threat to the Paul–Elisabeth ménage, which can only triumph through a double suicide; perhaps it would be more accurate to say that Elisabeth brings about her brother's suicide, then times her own to coincide with it.

If the plot is unimportant, the characters themselves are not. Dargelos is the first *angel*, his beauty and treachery fatally wounding Paul. When the episode is used again, in Cocteau's film *Le Sang d'un poète* (1932), it shows how the image of one adolescent's power over another — the wound of homosexual attraction and its 'fatal' consequences — can coalesce with the image of the mysterious creative force which traumatises the poet from youth; for, the two images are expressed through the single symbol of the *angel*. But in *Les Enfants terribles* itself, Dargelos is hardly more than an aspect of fate. Attention is focused on the symbiotic relationship of the brother and sister, the first the passive representative of angelism, the second the active. They are two halves of an androgyne whose resolution can only be achieved in death. Yet this philosophical symbolism in no way detracts from the importance of adolescence in the novel. On the contrary, it enhances it. The action is played out in one of childhood's secret places: not a metamorphosed external terrain of the type favoured by Larbaud in *Enfantines*, but the more mundane, if potentially more claustrophobic, four walls of the children's shared bedroom. Even moving to the mansion Elisabeth inherits from her dead husband only leads to the reconstruction of the old room within the new setting, for it is a projection of two minds as much as a real entity. Life is, as for Alain's *'peuple enfant'*, a ritualised game from which adults are excluded: the children's ailing mother swiftly dies; Gérard and Agathe are orphans; Gérard's providentially rich uncle is simply deceived, as on the seaside holiday, or permanently absent abroad, and finally 'got rid of' by the author. All that matters is the formal competition between brother and sister to outwit one another, for the total disorder of their lives according to the code sanctified by bourgeois tradition constitutes the very perfection of the order whose rules govern their love-hate relationship. Dargelos' beauty, transposed into the figure of Agathe, is the sole force which can take Paul away from Elisabeth and into the adult world, symbolised by a normal love relationship.

In *Les Parents terribles* the symbiosis is the more sinister one of mother and son, Yvonne and Michel, whose disordered lives are again reflected in the disorder of their physical surroundings. The image of a gypsy caravan is applied to their flat (as it is to Paul and Elisabeth's bedroom), stressing the social unacceptability of the life-style. The intrusion into the emotionally incestuous unit of the girl, Madeleine, is made more complex by the revelation that she is Michel's father's mistress, and by the interference of Aunt Léo, Yvonne's sister, who has always secretly loved Michel's father. Yet here too the relationships take their meaning from the series of oppositions child/adult, pure/impure, disorder/order. As Cocteau puts it in his preface, the play centres on the balance between Michel, whose disorder is pure, and Aunt Léo, accomplice to the revolt of adolescence but whose order is impure. The dénouement allows an apparent resolution in favour of the creative anarchy of the adolescents, as opposed to the destructive disorder of Yvonne and her husband. This resolution is, however, only apparent, a factitiously theatrical ending of the type later favoured by Anouilh in his *Pièces roses*. Life, the dramatist suggests, is not like his play. It crushes the purity of youth with the false constraints of 'society'. Michel will marry Madeleine; they will in turn become 'parents terribles'. The only real way to preserve the purity of love is in the apotheosis of death.

Some critics have regarded novels such as *Le Grand Meaulnes*, *Fermina Márquez* and *Les Enfants terribles* as romanticisations of youth. They are plainly nothing of the sort. For overt romanticisation of youth one has only to turn to the right-wing literature of the late 'thirties to see the difference in tone. The reasons for this are obvious; as Michel Tournier observes in *Le Vent Paraclet*: 'In fact it is one of the characteristics of fascism to overvalue youth, to make out of it a value and an end in itself . . . A young movement, by and for the young, that was the most often repeated slogan in Italy.' In Robert Brasillach's *Les Sept Couleurs* (1939) the portrait of the emotional and political development of Cathérine, Patrice, and to a lesser extent François, centres upon the ideas expressed in the 'Reflexions' of the fourth section of the novel: 'There is nothing in life but youth and one passes the rest of one's days regretting its loss'; 'Those who die shortly after they are thirty are not consolidators but founders. They bring the world the sparkling example of their vitality, their mysteries, their conquests.' Such assumptions lend the essential poignant colouring to the Cornelian myth of love and duty which the characters play out — a political duty tied to the rise of fascism and finding its resolution in the Spanish Civil War. Alain Fournier, Larbaud and Cocteau do not mythologise youth in this way. They see in childhood and adolescence a moment during which some or all men are untainted by the compromise, narrowness of vision and hypocrisy of the adult world. It is arguable that the novel of 'manliness' with which I shall deal later, the glorification, that is, of virile action in the works of a Malraux or a Hemingway, is just a deceitful way of borrowing the savagery and disorder of youth and labelling them as the virtues of maturity. What happens as we move from Alain-Fournier to Cocteau is that the interplay of dream-world and conventional reality becomes closer and more violent. Cocteau goes beyond the other novelists considered hitherto in systematising the savagery, emotionalism and ritual of youth into an existential virtue in itself, a way of giving meaning to life. He has complicated the picture more than a little, however, by the suggestion of a 'fate' which negates even adolescent freedom, and by the exploitation of a suspiciously counter-Freudian *chic*, both of which elements come still more to the fore in a work such as his updated Oedipus play, *La Machine infernale* (1934).

It is interesting, then, to compare the Coctelian adolescent with his more ruthlessly egoistic counterpart in the novels and plays of Montherlant, from which such extraneous philosophical and psychological subterfuges are absent. Montherlant's use of the particularity of youth as a major theme for fiction, setting aside his glorification of it in his essays 'La Relève du matin' (1920) and 'Les Olympiques' (1924), appears most strongly in his earliest novels, *Le Songe* (1922) and *Les Bestiaires* (1926), and in his last, *Les Garçons* (1969), which forms a trilogy with the earlier two, and also re-expresses more cogently the autobiographical episodes portrayed in the play *La Ville dont le prince est un enfant* (1951). Both Montherlant and Cocteau could subscribe to the view expressed by Stephen Spender in his autobiography *World Within World* (1951):

> Most lives are like dishonest works of art in which the values are faked, certain passages blurred and confused, difficulties evaded, and refuge taken by those bad artists who are human beings in conventions which shirk unique experiences.

Neither Montherlant nor Cocteau would, doubtless, have been surprised that it is to his childhood self, and to the child permanently within himself, that Spender attributes his most significant perceptions. But Montherlant's heroes, unlike Cocteau's, could also be said to fulfil the ideal that 'Spender the child' vainly sought after, 'to know someone who saw himself continually in relation to the immensity of time and the universe: who admitted to himself the isolation of his spiritual search and the wholeness of his physical nature'. They are the embodiments of a philosophy in which the 'black' qualities of youth, its savagery and violence, are combined with its delight in the rules of 'playing' and the order implicit in peer-group structures. Whether facing a bull in the arena, as in *Les Bestiaires*, or the enemy at the Front, as in the World War I novel, *Le Songe*, Alban de Bricoule is seeking constantly to affirm his power as a male, his belief in the value of physical experience. Montherlant's personal ethic is one close to that of Gide in *Les Nourritures terrestres*; in a conventional sense an apologia of indulgence, it also demands an equal measure of *purity*, if one can use that term to suggest a mental self-restraint which is not imposed by conventional morality. Alban, like Montherlant's later, older heroes, is alone. His peer-group fail him (*Les Garçons*); war separates him from his friends first psychologically, then physically (the quarrel with Prinet and his death, in *Le Songe*); his interest in Rome and in bullfighting sets him apart in *Les Bestiaires*. Above all, he is independent of family: Mme de Bricoule absurdly misinterprets him in *Les Garçons*. He cannot trust those in authority over him: the Abbé de Pradts betrays him in both the versions of the incident at the Collège Sainte-Croix de Neuilly (also portrayed in Roger Peyrefitte's rather more salacious version, *Les Amitiés particulières* 1944). And he has no use for women, who are at best toys, like Douce in *Le Songe*, at worst distractions, like Dominique in the same novel.

The fullest portrait of what Montherlant is trying to express through his adolescents comes in *Les Bestiaires*. Despite its realistic descriptions of Spanish life — particularly of bullfighting and everything connected with it, from the hangers-on to the methods of rearing, selection and training of bulls — the novel is by no means naturalistic. Nor is it simply a sentimental education, though the plot centres on the way in which Alban, a schoolboy on holiday, is befriended by the Duke de la Cuesta, begins to learn the art of bullfighting on the Duke's estate, flirts with his daughter Soledad, and fights a dangerous bull, *Le Mauvais-Ange*, to win her favours. Alban's triumph over the bull makes him realise that Soledad is a distraction, although in a sensual sense a necessary one. But this is only part of the real meaning of the novel, which is brought out in the epilogue, a mythologised scene in which a dialogue between a high-priest of Mithras and a neophyte brings to a focus a series of constant motifs in the narrative: Alban's fascination with Imperial Rome, the elaborate parallels between the bullfight and the ritual of Catholicism, the comparison between Christ and Mithras. Alban has been initiated into the religion of individual heroism, where sensuality and sacrifice go hand in hand. He has identified himself as a member of that élite capable of giving a personal meaning to an 'absurd' existence.

The story of adolescent homosexual passion which forms the basis of *La Ville dont le prince est un enfant* and the first half of *Les Garçons*, 'Au paradis des enfants', is designed to show in a less specific context the same view of Alban's candidature for a neo-Stendhalian 'happy few'. As the latter work says:

> The strangest thing about Alban's *sangre torrera*, his 'torreador blood', was that it was not specific to a given art, but general to his whole life. It

was much less a question of watching *corridas*, or even of taking part in them, than of a certain way of facing up to life, which combined a taste for provocation with a taste for danger — the basis, together with technique, of bull-fighting, — the taste for domination, the taste for ignoring public opinion, and something one would have to call the taste for being afraid.

Montherlant's adolescents, like Cocteau's despise and refuse the world of compromise, although, as his later novels of the cycle *Les Jeunes Filles* (1934-9) show, in adulthood they cannot always hold out for long. Unlike Cocteau's heroes, they cannot blame fate for their lapse from what, we shall see later, is a form of self-elected secular grace. Nor can they retreat into the four walls of a private world. They can only long, in exile, for the communion of souls which they so briefly glimpsed at thirteen.

The works we have looked at, from *Le Grand Meaulnes* to *Les Garçons*, create a tradition in which the 'otherness' of childhood and adolescence is the feature in which the writer is principally interested. This otherness is seen as part of a process of *becoming* which will be perverted or suppressed by adulthood. It is difficult to find a parallel for such a tradition in Anglo-Saxon literature. In novels such as Virginia Woolf's *The Waves* and *To the Lighthouse* the portrayal of children, or childhood, though significant, is merely a small part of the search for a pattern or order in the disconnected perceptions of reality to which all human beings are subjected, and from which the texture of the novels is accordingly compounded. When the separateness of adolescent experience is touched upon by an English novelist, it is often in the incidental, if very perceptive, way that Iris Murdoch sketches in the affair between Patrick and Ralph in *An Accidental Man*, the advantage being that Patrick, whilst naïve, is also down-to-earth and lightly self-ironising in a way which Montherlant's rhetorical style or Cocteau's patina of frivolity rarely allow their characters to be. Where a book is wholly devoted to the young, it tends to study them as symbols of society as a whole, as William Golding's *Lord of the Flies*, or at least as representing the moral conflicts of certain typical relationships within society, as in L.P. Hartley's outstanding study of devourer and devoured in his trilogy *Eustace and Hilda*. The only major English novel of the period 1900–40 entirely concerned with youth is Joyce's *Portrait of the Artist as a Young Man*, in which the prominence given to the absorption of external reality into the mental world of the adolescent character, and to the particular theme of artistic consciousness in the making, severely restrict the extent to which the novel handles the theme of adolescence as such. Its central statements are about consciousness and art.

American literature, it is true, offers a tradition of the child or adolescent as 'noble savage', from Mark Twain to Salinger. But it is a tradition of romanticisation. The reader is not offered Huck Finn or Holden Caulfield (*Catcher in the Rye*) as representatives of the otherness of adolescence, but as romantic myths with whom he can self-indulgently identify, free-minded young chaps who embody a set of virtues in common, if differently expressed, with those of every good, all-American citizen. Equally, Kerouac, with his *On the Road* and *The Dharma Bums* is merely rehearsing a variant of the same set of American minority values, a new generation of Huck Finns, Whitmanised and free-wheeling. One has only to set such novels against the self-critical, lightly handled picaresque of Iris Murdoch's *Under the Net*, a work not inappropriately dedicated to Raymond Queneau, to see how far from any English tradition the American novels of adolescence are. Yet this brings them no closer to the French.

French literature too, of course, has other ways of treating youth. Romain Rolland's *Jean Christophe* (1904-12) in which, as Rolland himself says, 'The hero is Beethoven transferred into the world of today,' Roger Martin du Gard's *Les Thibault* (1922-40) and Jules Romains' *Les Hommes de bonne volonté* typify one approach. In each of these Trollopian suites of novels childhood is subordinated to some grander scheme; it merely provides a formative period, usually in a simple chronological sense, just as it does, in a very different social context, in some 'thirties' American fiction — James T. Farrell's *Studs Lonigan* trilogy, Edward Dahlberg's *Bottom Dogs*. Another class of French works uses youth symbolically. The young girls of certain of Jean Giraudoux's plays *Tessa* (1934, adapted from Margaret Kennedy's *The Constant Nymph*) or the eponymous sprite in *Ondine* (1939), embody types of perfection. Similarly the young people in his novels are disembodied figments of art. Giraudoux paints word-pictures of them as exquisite but imaginary creatures of purity, liberty and innocence, as with the heroine of *Suzanne et le Pacifique* (1921), a modern version of the Robinson Crusoe theme. This same sense of choosing a particular child or adolescent, rather than childhood or adolescence, as a vehicle for an aesthetic, philosophical or psychological statement attaches to works which I shall refer to elsewhere, such as Raymond Queneau's *Pierrot mon ami* and *Zazie dans le métro*, or the novels of Michel Tournier.

More closely related to the tradition which we have been examining, but still independent from it, are two major writers whose work is often associated with youth: Proust, whose *A l'Ombre des jeunes filles en fleurs* (the third part of *A la Recherche du temps perdu*) won the Prix Goncourt in 1919, and Gide, whose Lafcadio of *Les Caves du Vatican* and Bernard and Olivier of *Les Faux-Monnayeurs* are among the best-known adolescents in French literature. Neither of these authors is really interested in youth for its own sake, or even for what it can tell us about the shortcomings of the adult world. If, in *A la Recherche*, Proust seems to yearn a little for the 'paradise lost' of childhood days at Combray, it is in fact a minor fault in a structure whose argument precisely leads away from the misconceptions of Marcel the child towards the insights of the mature artist. As for Gide, what one meets with in the works from *L'Immoraliste* to *Les Faux-Monnayeurs* is an interest not in the qualities of adolescence, but in the possibilities of certain adolescents, under the guidance of the benign pederast. Lafcadio's independence from bourgeois conventions is symbolised in his illegitimacy and bisexuality. But, although Gide makes him a very attractive character, he uses him in the novel as one of the ways of expressing the falseness of those with whom he comes into touch, and at the same time undermines through him the whole notion of the *acte gratuit*, the completely unmotivated action. *Les Caves du Vatican* is a very funny satirical novel about bourgeois values, conventional concepts of psychology and the traditions of the French novel; it is only tangentially about youth. *Les Faux-Monnayeurs* makes more of its adolescent characters. They are indeed the only repositories of hope for a freer society, because they are capable of escaping from the counterfeiting which is an essential feature of adult society. Bernard, released from his duties to his family by the discovery of his illegitimacy, pursues a psychological odyssey that leads him through the sincere expression of what he thinks he is towards the authentic behaviour of one whose actions and essence are in harmony. Olivier, freeing himself from his fears and prejudices, accepts the tutelage of his loving uncle Edouard. But not all the adolescents achieve the same self-realisation. Armand, brother of Bernard's mistress, is corrupted by cynicism, while poor little Boris, a psychological wreck because of his neuroses about masturbation, is conned into shooting himself in a 'fixed' game of Russian roulette. This is a novel about social and psychological mechanisms; it is also a novel about novels (Edouard is writing one called *Les Faux-monnayeurs* . . .). Gide is indeed interested in the process of *becoming*, but in no individual work is it seen other than as part of the broader question of the problem of *being*.

Post-war French literature has seen in varied ways an

extension of earlier attitudes to the function of youth as a theme in fiction. This in part merely reflects changes in social *mores*. Roger Nimier's novels, of which the best are *Le Hussard bleu* (1950) and *Les Enfants tristes* (1951), begin a tradition in which the values of teenage society are assumed to be superior to that of their parents. The works of Françoise Sagan and Christiane Rochefort continue in the same vein, putting the emphasis on the female characters. More interesting than these facile glorifications of contemporary self-indulgence is a work like *Une Saison dans la vie d'Emmanuel* (1965) by the Canadian novelist, Marie-Claire Blaise, in which the children (very strange children) despite their fantastical reality seem to offer a metaphor of the paradoxical qualities which constitute mankind as a whole. In contrast, there are some effective attempts to analyse both the difference in the way that a child views the world, for example, Monique Wittig's *L'Opoponax*, and the complexity of re-establishing the role played by childhood in the development of an adult persona, as in Jacques Borel's rather heavily psycho-analytical *L'Adoration* and Camille Bourniquel's considerably more poetic *Le Lac*. However, a number of writers have also returned to portraying, in an elegiac way, childhood as a lost era, as in Hubert de Luze's *Cet enfant émerveillé*. Many of these works of the 1950s and 1960s seem implicitly to accept the principle enunciated by Maurice Sachs in *Le Sabbat* when he writes that man's whole life is an attempt to realise the dreams of his youth. Alain-Fournier, Larbaud, Cocteau, even Montherlant, might agree. The dangers of *becoming*, for Gide or Proust, lay precisely in the idea that childhood *can* exert just such a distorting influence on the central problem of what Cocteau has so aptly called 'the difficulty of being'.

CHAPTER 4
The Cult of Manliness

> Sometimes you hear, fifth-hand,
> As epitaph:
> *He chucked up everything*
> *And just cleared off,*
> And always the voice will sound
> Certain you approve
> This audacious, purifying,
> Elemental move.
>
> (Philip Larkin)

The cult of youth is, as modern society is proving to its cost, always an ultimately sterile and depressing approach to life, since the qualities held up for admiration are by definition destined to disappear fast. Already at the period when the theme of adolescence was having its greatest vogue, a parallel literary development sought to go beyond the temporal limitations of youth to an assertion of the values of manliness and comradeship. Here again we have an attempt to redefine the nature of man and to identify the possible meaning of human existence in a world from which the old moral and metaphysical certainties had been banished. Yet in some ways, as we shall see, the picture of man projected has more of the unattractive aspects of adolescence than does the cult of youth itself.

Manliness was by no means a new concept. The qualities seized upon are those which had an appeal to upholders of the old order. The meaning given to existence by the violent action of war and the relationship between adventure and spiritual health are proclaimed in the pre-War novels of Ernest Psichari, *Terres de soleil et de sommeil* (1908) and *L'Appel des armes* (1913). The comradeship of action is a theme taken up in the journalism of Charles Péguy and Maurice Barrès. Of course the best literature about World War I itself concentrates on exposing its horror and pointlessness, and rejects any notion of heroics. Henri Barbusse's *Le Feu* (1916) alternates between vignettes of the banal simplicity of the soldiers themselves and apocalyptic landscapes which encapsulate the horrors of trench warfare. Roland Dorgelès' *Les Croix de Bois* (1919) in a less moralising manner portrays the same themes through a series of self-contained episodes showing in particular the experiences of a new middle-class recruit. The same kind of indictment via description can be found in Georges Duhamel's *La Vie des martyrs* (1917) and, more explicitly and bitterly, *Civilisation* (1918). But, although the literature of war is dominated by this tradition, culminating in the powerful pacifist denunciation not only of war but of the modern society that produces it in Jean Giono's *Le Grand Troupeau* (1931), there is a secondary strain in which exaltation at self-assertion is the characteristic tone. Montherlant's *Le Songe* (1922) and *Chant funèbre pour les morts de Verdun* (1924) extol the opportunity offered by the chaos of war for individual heroics and brotherly love. Even the narrator of the six stories in Drieu la Rochelle's *La Comédie de Charleroi* (1934) finds a Nietzschean power to transcend the mediocrity of everyday life, although war in the modern world, as futile as all other aspects of life, ultimately exerts a negative force on individuality. By 1938 when Jules Romain's much-praised *Verdun* appeared (as part of his vast *roman fleuve, Les Hommes de bonne volonté*) it was possible to document with great precision conditions at the Front and at home, to analyse motivation and strategy, yet still to present the whole ghastly business as in some degree a liberating experience from the bonds of conventional existence.

It is this vision of man as engaged in a quest for male companionship in the face of danger wilfully pursued, often with all the attendant adolescent trappings of violence, coarseness, sexual indulgence and the repression of any significant emotion, which is a feature of the worlds portrayed by many inter-War novelists inside and outside France. These actions are the response to a spiritual malaise forcefully analysed by André Malraux in *La Tentation de l'Occident* (1926). In this work, according to 'A.D.' and his Chinese correspondent Ling W-Y, European man has lost not only his sense of God but his concept of Man. The awareness that nothing is permanent has left a demoralising sense of the essential meaninglessness of living. To this idea Malraux added in a brief essay of 1927, 'D'une jeunesse européenne', the picture of European man as so immured in his own subjectivity that he cannot establish meaningful relationships with others. There are no longer any common spiritual goals. All these notions underlie the writings not only of Malraux but of Antoine de Saint-Exupéry and, in a more ambiguous fashion, of Drieu and Céline.

Adventurers
Critics have reasonably attributed the tone of authenticity which Saint-Exupéry's novels possess to the close identification between the personality of the author and the subjects of his work. As a professional pilot, writing about the world of the aeroplane and the world as viewed from the aeroplane, he fashions an intimate unity between the experiences recorded and the moral meditations to which they give rise. As Sartre puts it in *Situations II*: 'Saint-Exupéry has shown that for the pilot the plane is an organ of perception.' Equally, though his thought centres on the nature of how man, aware of the precariousness of his position, can conquer his metaphysical

anguish and give a meaning to his life, he is not in revolt against the absurdity of existence, and the situations he paints are not revolutionary ones. In all other respects, however, his novels precisely represent the rejection of the everyday, the preference for the pursuit of danger and the praise of camaraderie which are the hallmarks of 'manly' literature of his period.

His literary output is relatively slight. It principally consists of four short novels, his allegory for children, *Le Petit Prince* (1942), and the bulky but very unfinished collection of maxims and parables, *Citadelle* (revised posthumous version 1959). *Courrier-Sud* (1929) introduces some of the essentials of its author's fictional world: the emptiness of materially based existence compared with the meaningfulness of the apparently empty life of the adventurer, and the notion of belonging to a special group, and of actions which are greater than the individuals who contribute to them. *Vol de nuit* (1931) expands upon similar themes, but in a much more concentrated way. There are only three main characters: Rivière the manager of the courrier line, the pilot Fabien who carries out a night flight between Buenos Aires and Patagonia, and his wife of six weeks' standing. The centre of the book is the portrait of Rivière, who ruthlessly moulds the lives of all those who work for him in the belief that by making men face danger in the pursuit of a common aim, he is raising them above their status as individuals. The plot is classical in its simplicity of time and action. Fabien is called out to fly south, but his plane meets a cyclone, he goes off track, runs out of petrol and disappears. His wife telephones to confirm his safe arrival and has to face the implications of 'no news'. Meanwhile Rivière runs his operations, reflecting on them, questioning and assessing his own actions, yet ultimately confident in the rightness of what he is doing. Saint-Exupéry's ideas are still very unformed. Rivière asserts to himself that the action which he extracts from his men, and which, he admits, runs counter to the conventional notions of happiness (embodied in Mme Fabien), preserves an important part of man which is more durable than the constituents of conventional happiness. Even concepts of defeat and victory are rejected as irrelevant (as they will be again in *Pilote de guerre* when Saint-Exupéry is analysing the collapse of France in 1940), since a material defeat can still lead to some sort of spiritual victory. But neither Rivière nor his creator is clear what the important and more durable part of man actually is. In the former's words '. . . if human life is priceless, we still act as if something surpassed it in value . . . but what?'

Saint-Exupéry's third book, *Terre des hommes*, which won him the Grand Prix du Roman (awarded by the Académie française) in 1939, is more developed in its ideas. It is in fact not a novel at all but a mixture of moral reflections and memories in which the unity is one of meaning, rather than of plot or character. The rejection of a materialist society and the extolling of a community in action are established from the outset:

> The greatness of a profession lies perhaps above all in the way in which it unites men; there is only one real luxury and that is the luxury of human relationships.
>
> When we work for material ends alone, we build ourselves our own prison. We place ourselves in solitary confinement with our money of ashes which will get us nothing which is worth living for.

The fragments of action presented move rapidly from topic to topic: for example, a record of the author's feelings when about to go on his first solo courrier trip; the experience of being lost over the desert at night; the adventures of his pioneering aviator friend Mermoz and his final disappearance. Like Drieu's hero at the end of *Gilles* the pilot is liberated by his very separation from possessions. When three planes of the line are grounded together in an area containing hostile natives, the sense of comradeship among the men in their encampment is heightened by its very sparseness:

> And yet we were infinitely poor. Wind, sand, stars. A lifestyle harsh enough for a Trappist. But on this ill-lit stretch six or seven men who owned nothing in the world but their memories shared invisible riches with one another.

This comradeship is further defined as the sense of working towards a unified aim, a theme already embodied in the image of the airmail lines of the first two novels and to be re-interpreted in that of the squadron in *Pilote de guerre*. The communal spirit thus formed affects the individual's view of himself. In the story of his friend Guillaumet who crashes in the Andes in winter and struggles on foot for five days to get back to base, as well as the idea that man's will allows him to exceed his mere animal instincts we find great stress on Guillaumet's spiritual links with his wife and friends, and above all on his equal responsibility for himself, the post he carries and the sorrows and joys of his comrades. Nor is this fellowship necessarily limited to particular groups. The exaltation which underlies all allegiances is the same: 'Under contradictory words it is the same impulses we are all expressing.' All ideologies are equally worthless except in so far as they help man realise a sense of his condition. The value of danger and of extreme situations is that they bring about this exaltation more immediately. It is not a question of despising death — Saint-Exupéry rejects a comparison with bullfighters and gamblers, and tells a contemptuous story of suicide — but of an intensity of living which he compares to that of the devoted gardener who finds meaning in the fruitful process of his work, since what gives a meaning to life also gives a meaning to death.

In *Pilote de guerre* (1942), Saint-Exupéry's autobiographical reverie on life during the collapse of France in the face of the German invasion, the exposition of the philosophy in a specific social context is more consequential, closely linked as it is with the crazy mission on which the pilot is sent and the view of France which it affords him. Initially the description of planes being sent out on fruitless reconnaissance flights is an illustration of the phrase in *Terre des hommes*: 'What makes a convict-prison is the giving of pick-axe blows which have no meaning.' In this context death itself becomes merely a sign and effect of disorder. The war is presented as a phoney adventure, since real adventure depends on the richness of the links it creates, the problems it poses and the transformations it provokes. Yet the drama of the flight itself, though it initially releases immense bitterness in the narrator, leads eventually to a reassessment. The intoxication of living through the flak creates a new spirit in the narrator. The attacks on the French administration and its inadaptability, crystallised around the way in which the plane's machinery is not built to function at the necessary altitude, and the disastrous evacuation orders imposed on every town and village by its petty functionaries, give way to an acceptance of the notion of universal responsibility for the defeat in which each must acknowledge his own part. The somewhat Vichyesque sentiment, 'Defeat can reveal the only path towards resurrection, despite its ugliness', for which one could find parallels in the political essays of Giraudoux and in his play, *Electre*, becomes a reassertion of the idea at the close of *Vol de nuit* that temporary notions of defeat and victory are irrelevant. The uncertain fumbling of Rivière for a more durable aspect of man is at last clarified (if uncertain clarity is an acceptable concept) by the enunciation of a metaphysics of Man, couched in religious terminology appropriate to the cultural inheritors of Christianity. Where man once perceived God in man, he now sees Man, a mystical notion which cannot be defined in the traditional language of humanism but which derives from the idea that the total potential of humanity is greater than the sum of the individuals which comprise it. Conventional concepts of collectivity, equality and liberty are all rejected as inadequate in themselves. Dignity in fraternity is the key to spiritual progress.

The morality formulated by Saint-Exupéry in *Pilote de guerre*, and which the unfinished and opaque *Citadelle* elaborates in a metaphysical dimension, is difficult to detach from the extreme situations which generated it. This is more glaringly true still of the ideas of Malraux. All his novels are set in violent situations, the first three in the Far East to boot. *Les Conquérants* (1928) starts from a broad canvas of revolution in South East Asia, narrows in on the fighting in Canton in which the hero, Garine, plays a leading part, and finally concentrates on the hero himself. Garine is anarchic. He compares himself to a gambler, whilst the narrator says of him that he draws his strength from his profound sense of the absurdity of existence. But action by itself eventually fails to satisfy him. As his health declines, undermined by malaria and dysentery, he parts company with his orthodox communist collaborators, Borodin and Nikolaieff, and becomes increasingly an individual at grips with his private metaphysical problem. *La Voie royale* (1930) also features a doomed adventurer, Perken, whose individualism is even more marked than Garine's. His sole aim has been 'to leave a scar on the map'. His attitude is of opposition to the world, as much in his eroticism — women are reduced to a system of sexual responses — as in his 'political' desire to impose his power on the jungle tribes in whose territory much of the action of the novel is played out. Ultimately his will to power is sapped by sheer and inevitable physical disintegration. The absurdity of death always triumphs.

These two novels have a great deal in common in addition to their philosophical basis. They assert the prime significance of action; they overflow with often gratuitous violence; they reduce relations between the sexes to a degrading eroticism; they both finish on an image of the fraternal, hinting at a meaningful communication between certain sorts of male which is little in evidence in the action of the stories. All four elements are repeated and developed in Malraux's best known novel, *La Condition humaine*. The action is the communist uprising in Shanghai. This forms the basis for a study in types, such as Tchen the professional killer, Katow and Kyo the revolutionaries, Ferral the banker and König the chief of police. But the characters are not studied for social or political significance. They embody attitudes to life. Tchen's will to murder is an attempt to conquer death by mastering it. He is a translation of Garine and Perken into a more abstract mode; ultimately, he shows us, the body betrays the will. His attempt to assassinate Chiang Kai-shek by throwing himself under his car while clutching a bomb not only fails politically (Chiang is not in the car), it also destroys the myth of his power over life and death. He remains conscious, in a horribly mangled state. Even his attempt to commit suicide fails in the sense that it is an involuntary spasm of his muscles, precipitated by pain, which causes his gun to fire. At the last his body has asserted its supremacy over his mind. Clappique, the mythomaniac, and Ferral, with his attempts to manipulate others through financial power or eroticism, finally turn tail on a world gone beyond their control. Gisors, Kyo's elderly father, though immensely perceptive, has abandoned action in favour of the oblivion of opium. All three have found ways of distracting themselves from the absurdity of existence, but the ways are very temporary. Kyo and Katow find their revolution betrayed and defeated, they are arrested and herded into a shed with other prisoners to await execution. Kyo takes his cyanide capsule; Katow gives his to two other prisoners whose nerve has failed, and accepts death in the form of being burned alive in the fire-box of a locomotive. The most nobly motivated forms of action seem destined to be as fruitless as the most selfish. Only death triumphs.

This, however, is not quite what Malraux appears to be saying. For Katow's death is worked up into an episode of more mystical significance. In passing his cyanide capsule to Souen and his companion, Katow is trying to protect 'human dignity'. In the dark the second prisoner, wounded in the hand, drops the two pieces of capsule. The three men feel anxiously around for the precious poison:

> Their hands brushed against his. Suddenly one of them took his, squeezed it and held it.
> 'Even if we can't find anything . . .', said one of the voices. Katow too squeezed the other hand, on the very edge of tears, gripped by this humble faceless expression of fraternity . . .

Human dignity, it appears, is sustained by this act of solidarity, symbolised in the moment of physical contact. It is the triumph of that 'virile fraternity' on which the two earlier novels close.

Yet one cannot help but wonder whether, in a novel where all hopes and actions are frustrated, corruption and misuse of power are everywhere in the ascendant, all relationships between the sexes lack any real meaning, families (as in the case of Hemmelrich) are merely an obstacle to self-fulfilment, and the so-called forces of liberty (in the shape of the Moscow communists) are indifferent to the plight of the revolution, it is enough to portray the justification of life as holding hands with a man to whom you have given your cyanide capsule, before being thrown alive into a furnace. Both Kyo and Katow face death with a resilient stoicism. Both deaths are ennobled by their tragic and heroic manner, by the manly affection which surrounds them, by the symbolic function which they assume:

> He was dying, as was each of the men lying there, because he had given life a meaning . . . It is easy to die if you do not die alone.

It is easy to see the contrast Malraux intends between this rising above the humiliation of death and Perken's dying cry that there is no death, only himself about to die. Yet the fraternity posited is a singularly ineffectual and meaningless one.

Malraux's next novel, *L'Espoir* (1937), posits a direction for human action, which places it aesthetically as 'committed' literature; it will therefore be considered separately in that context. Its successor, *Les Noyers d'Altembourg* (1943, first published as *La Lutte avec l'ange I*, but the work has never been continued), is a contemplation on the whole theory of human action, and as such throws light on Malraux's evaluation of his early view of life. The five parts of the work are not limited by any standard narrative connection. Their inter-relation is thematic. The first part, set in a prisoner-of-war camp in 1940, portrays man's capacity for adapting abnormal situations to familiar patterns. Life in the camp arouses in one of the soldiers, Berger, thoughts about the nature of man and his continuity, a subject on which his dead father, Vincent, a philosophy teacher, had left some reflections. The second part reveals the events which entitle Vincent Berger to have a more than theoretical view on such a subject. In a characterisation which owes a great deal to the figure of Lawrence of Arabia, Malraux portrays Vincent as a man of action and brilliant organiser working for the German propaganda service in pre-World War I Turkey. He becomes involved with the young Turks, is fired with a romantic vision of recreating an alliance of Central Asian peoples which proves totally illusory, and returns defeated to Europe. Part three portrays a conference of intellectuals at Altenburg at which Möllberg, a distinguished German anthropologist, rationally demolishes the notion that human destiny has any meaning by showing that civilisations do not communicate with one another horizontally and that there is therefore no process of continuous development. But Vincent Berger, gazing at the walnut trees on the crest of the hill, and watching how they 'framed Strasburg Cathedral . . . just as so many other tree trunks framed other cathedrals in the fields of the Western World', intuits a continuity of values which the intellectuals have not been able logically to identify. The fourth part allows Vincent to put his intuition to an empirical test. On the

Russian Front the Germany army is trying out poison gas. Appalled by the effects of the new weapon the German soldiers stumble back to their own lines carrying the bodies of the gassed Russians. Man's innate fraternity triumphs over other less attractive instincts. Symbolically, Vincent remembers the Altenburg walnut trees. In part five the younger Berger, caught in a tank trap with a radically varied group of men, experiences the same sense of common humanity. What Malraux seems to do here is to recap the achievements and inevitable disillusionment of the isolated adventurer, to set his dilemmas in the context of the philosophical posing of the issues, and to re-assert the existence of a continuity of brotherhood between men that can be intuitively perceived but not rationally proven.

In fact Malraux himself does believe that the continuity of cultures and values can be proven. The position which he attributes to his anthropologist character, Möllberg (akin to that of Spengler in *The Decline of the West*), is refuted in *La Psychologie de l'art* (1947-9) and rather more systematically in the reworking of that book in *Les Voix du silence* (1951). The four parts of the latter examine the meaning of art when displaced from its original context in time and space, how different styles inter-relate, what the individual artist derives from other art and how he achieves individuality, and finally what significance art has as an affirmation of human dignity and meaning in the face of the Absurd. Three key ideas appear: that each culture has its own style; that such a style is achieved by a forceful reshaping of another culture and its style, and that each artist develops his art by imitating his predecessors. Modern art with its access to a far wider range of other cultures is the great affirmation of man's ability to create a special human order in the face of the meaningless chaos of the universe. This replacement of action of an individual or political nature by artistic creation, already suggested in *Les Noyers* and more obliquely hinted at before in his work, for example, in the figures of Gisors and Kama in *La Condition humaine*, is summed up at the end of *Les Voix du silence* when Malraux explicitly rejects Saint-Exupéry's, 'I have done what no animal would have done' (*Terre des hommes*), and substitutes for it:

> We have refused the call of the animal in us and we want to rediscover man everywhere we have discovered what overwhelms him.'

The artist is privileged to undertake that task on behalf of his fellow men.

Malraux and Saint-Exupéry in their analyses of action make constant reference to the good of a wider community, be it group, tribe, nation or mankind. In contrast a completely solipsistic approach to the virtues of action, not doomed to the failure of Perken or Garine, is to be found in the works of Montherlant, particularly in his plays. The key to his view of man is to be found in the Nietzschean notion of the need to surpass oneself. As he puts it in his essay, *Service inutile* (1935):

> You think that man has something to do in this life. We think he has nothing to do but look for ways of rising higher.

From his first play, *L'Exil* (1914), in which the hero, Philippe, is torn between fighting in the war and staying with his mother, action is presented as self-fulfilment, an instrument for the perfecting of the self rather than a gesture of conformity with the outside world. All action which appears to serve others (and this applies to love too) is in fact self-directed:

> The secret of all service is that through it we serve our own ends without intending to; you think you are working for the community, out of duty or love, and in the end it's the individual that triumphs.
> *(Textes sous une Occupation* 1953)

Where a character in Montherlant asserts a nihilistic view of action, like Ferrante in *La Reine morte* (1942) for whom all action is equally pointless, the assertions prove to be only a disguise for a lack of faith in his own ability and power to achieve his aims.

Most of the plays portray the interior struggles of a character who retains a sense of the absolute within an overwhelming awareness of the pointlessness of almost everything, just such an awareness as Montherlant ascribes to himself from youth. Malatesta, hero of the play of that name (1946), is the only major character of Montherlant's theatre who wants to make his natural instincts and his attitudes towards them coincide. In this he is closest to 'total man' as portrayed in *L'Eventail de fer*, containing an alternation of opposites, for example, tenderness and cruelty, rationalism and emotion, and freely expressing this alternation:

> It's not just a question of living, but of living while being and seeming everything one is. (Act I sc8)

This fullness expresses itself in a virile philosophy which seeks meaning in the sheer intensity of existence:

> I have loved swords, manuscripts and women: this world of steel and blood, which I love more everyday, like one loves a sick child . . . My pleasure has always been extreme — and I have always found pleasure in myself. (Act IV sc2)

In seeking such a meaning Malatesta asserts sole responsibility for himself. As he himself puts it, it is he who is the instrument of his destiny and nobody else.

This self-sufficiency entails a rejection of conventional standards. Ferrante in *La Reine morte* suppresses normal paternal feelings for his son Pedro by having his wife put to death, and Alvaro in *Le Maître de Santiago* acts without reference to the interests of his daughter. Malatesta's contempt for ordinary morality comes out in his dismissive attitude towards the tribunal of Cardinals who had formerly condemned him to death (for a varied list of supposed crimes including rape, adultery, homosexual incest, necrophilia, parricide and heresy). Morality in Malatesta's eyes is a purely relative concept:

> ... anyone who accepts the task of passing judgment on his fellows condemns himself. For he well knows that he is always as guilty as the man he is judging. (Act II sc4)

This rejection is an inevitable concomitant of Montherlant's view that all action is inspired by self-interest (a view perfectly coherent with the ethical implications of Sartre's *L'Etre et le Néant*). This applies even to love. Love between the sexes is always an entirely negative force in Montherlant's work. Even the apparently balanced emotion of Isotta for Malatesta in fact creates a weakness in the latter which momentarily exposes him to Porcellio's revenge:

> [Malatesta to Isotta] Your love makes me lose in one respect what it gives me in another. Your trembling impairs my stability. Your constant admiration leads me into a false view of things.

But the cause of his downfall is not really the debilitating force of Isotta's love. His mistake is to put his faith in reputation, as represented by the 'Life' of him that Porcellio is writing. This lays him open to the revenge and destruction of the last scene, where as the hero lies immobilised by the poison that will kill him, Porcellio burns the only copy of the book before his eyes. The pursuit of reputation leads to a division between acting for what a man is and acting for what he will seem, for the creation of an image outside himself. It is only a character like Alvaro (*Le Maître de Santiago*) who can turn his back on the prospect of fame and fortune to be won in the Spanish conquest of South America, and retreat into isolation, to find self-knowledge in a monastery at the cost of sacrificing not only his own physical reality but Mariana's marriage prospects:

> Let us leave to find life. Let us leave to be dead, and living among the living. (Act 3 sc5)

Man in the works of Drieu, Saint-Exupéry, Malraux, and indeed in those of Montherlant or Robert Brasillach, analyses with peculiar lucidity his place in the universe, and attempts to create a meaning for himself by action, the assertion of power, an emotional identity with those he feels to be fighting the same battle (without exception fellow males). I think it is fair to make a comparison here with those writers, particularly Jean Giono in his pre-war works, who concentrated on a view of man in which, the intellectual lucidity gone, the struggle is an instinctive one between man and the forces of his environment. The distaste for Western materialist society which prompts Gilles Gambier or Patrice, Saint-Exupéry's pilots or Malraux's revolutionaries, and the mistrust of all these authors for intellectual solutions to their social and philosophical dilemmas, manifest themselves for other authors of the period in a re-examination of man's place in his natural context.

Man and nature
The poetry of Saint-John Perse is particularly germane to my argument. Almost all his early poems in *Eloges* (1910-11) evoke the flora and fauna of Guadeloupe, and the very titles of the series of long poems written in America during World War II reflect the dominant natural phenomena around which each is structured — rain, snow, wind, birds. But this is not pictorial poetry. It seeks to express the necessary harmony of man with nature, to explore the human condition, and in the later poems, *Amers* (1948) and *Chronique* (1959), to affirm human dignity and the poet's solidarity with his fellows. A particularly striking synthesis of these functions is to be found in *Anabase* (1922), the poem later translated by T.S. Eliot and which established Perse's international reputation. According to the poet's own interpretation as given in an interview in 1960 after he had been awarded the Nobel prize, he has in *Anabase* made the loneliness of the man of action his main theme. The poem evokes an expedition, vaguely located in Asia at a period

prior to the mechanisation of modern society. It is a world where the natural and animal aspects of human existence are accentuated. The ten cantos with their images of rise, fall and renewal, expressed in terms of organisation, building, disquiet, migration and the establishing of a new order, explore many themes which we have met in the novelists of the 'thirties: the need for action, the deliberate exposing of the self to a hostile environment, the acceptance of violence as a principle of existence. By a curious (to some infinitely irritating) technique of juxtaposition, a vast comparison of primitive and early Western cultures is drawn upon to suggest the kind of distillation of human potential which Malraux discusses in *Les Voix du silence*. Only the 'Leader', fulfilling an ambiguously defined role as military and civil ruler and as intellectual leader, suffers from anything approaching a metaphysical dilemma; it is his function to stop his fellow men from sinking into a sterile stasis which would prevent the fulfilment of their human potential. Like Saint-Exupéry, Saint-John Perse's later writings move closer to invoking an eternal principle as the focus of man's endeavour, if eternal principle is the right expression for what, in explicating *Amers*, he called 'great forces that create us, use us and control us'. The balance of imagery swings perhaps further in favour of nature, but the themes of the poetry remain the same.

Giono's world is also one in which man and nature have equal status, but here there is no question of nature having a symbolic role. In the three short novels *Colline* (1929), *Un de Baumugnes* (1929) and *Regain* (1930) Giono explores different aspects of man's relationship with the world about him. In the first the main body of the story is devoted to conveying the reality of the control which earth, water and fire have in the lives of a community, the hamlet Les Bastides Blanches, which is parasitic, exploiting nature rather than in partnership with her. Only man experiences the kind of solitude symbolised by the isolation of the hamlet, and in that isolation he is a prey to his imagination, which transforms the world around him into a magic universe of terror. The temptation either to dominate nature or to give in to it will both destroy the joy which derives from living in harmony with it. Protecting their farms from a forest fire welds the peasants into communal action. Yet the random killing of a wild boar at the end of the story poses the question of whether man can ever escape from his inner propensity to senseless violence and achieve a constructive relationship with his environment.

Un de Baumugnes is a fairy tale about redemption by love, in which the hero Albin is a mythological projection of the goodness that would typify a man truly born into a pastoral Utopia (Baumugnes). The human characters are forlorn, seedy, or locked in themselves, and can only be redeemed by the light and understanding which Albin may bring them. In *Regain* however the story does end with the triumph of those who live instinctively in partnership with nature. A key to the understanding of the book is perhaps the brief essay 'Magnétisme' in *Solitude de la pitié* (1932). The Apocalyptic theme of the destruction of civilisation is touched on earlier in that collection in 'Destruction de Paris', with its strange images of nature taking back her rights over the land of that city. In 'Magnétisme' the narrator posits the destruction of all human society except the village by whose café he is standing. He sees in the local peasants the true stock of the human race who, through their understanding of the natural cycle, would be able to withstand the Apocalypse because they have been bred by the silence, space and solitude to have courage and self-sufficiency. The peasant has both purity and the ability to maintain and develop his understanding of the world through his special crafts. In *Regain* a version of the Apocalypse has occurred. The book opens with the vision of a destroyed village sliding down its hillside, overtaken by natural growth. This force of destruction is embodied in the recurrent symbol of the wind, a natural and anarchic source of energy, yet potentially creative and itself a symbol of natural sexuality. What Giono goes on to portray is the regeneration of the community in the persons of Panturle and Arsule, who achieve instinctive communion with each other, conquer solitude, and by a conscious and hard-fought process learn to work within the natural cycle.

In *Le Chant du monde* (1934) the relationship between man and environment is taken for granted. Giono concentrates on exploring man's relations with man within that environment. The action centres on the opposition between Antonio, a man whose association with river and forest is established from the outset by the highly sensual description of his physical relationship with the river as he swims naked in it, and Maudru, the man of the mountains, whose dictatorship over *le Pays Rebeillard* is an obstacle to Antonio and his friend Matelot in their search for the latter's one surviving twin son. Only after being surpassed in strength and audacity by Antonio and the twin does Maudru yield up some of his semi-divine status by letting his daughter Gina go off with the invaders. In an adventure story full of motifs from the *Iliad*, devotion, fraternity and the desire to comfort the sufferings of others abound, whilst violence and hatred become natural cleansing qualities, devoid of viciousness, more akin to a hunter's kill. Death and life are merely two sides of the same coin, the former nourishing the latter, since, as Antonio says of the violent death of Maudru's nephew, it is the corpses that nourish the trees. The values of the book are not idealist in any Utopian sense. Giono tries to create a picture of a society of natural man in which happiness is the ultimate achievement, but doubt, emptiness, bitterness, weakness are all acknowledged as an inevitable part of man's condition. The over-riding liquid images, the physical harmony of Antonio with the river, the symbolic structuring of the story around the anarchic force of the river, pent-up in winter and consequently exploding into the climax of spring, all have a Lawrentian eroticism at their base. If man accommodates himself to the rhythms of nature and natural desire, the world will achieve a kind of primitive innocence, in which violence is not removed but made creative, or at least assimilated into a natural cycle of events. Man kills to eat, he kills to protect his mate, he kills to revenge the death of a relative. Otherwise he lives in harmony with his fellows and with himself.

Que ma joie demeure (1935) attempts to take the solutions and problems offered by the earlier works into the sphere of communal living on a broader scale (a whole plateau) and into a world more immediately faced with the problems of contemporary living. The question of how to give meaning to life in a society without spiritual values is tackled by the strange wandering 'artist' Bobi, who analyses the source of the peasants' malaise as excessive materialism, and tries to communicate his own passion for the useless. Hawthorns are planted to attract birds back to the plateau, but in order for them to be planted ground has to be used where crops would normally be sown. The ultimate act of this sort is the fetching of a live stag which, by its presence, encourages the various inhabitants of the area to travel in to see it and stay for celebrations afterwards. The impromptu feast, with its basic call to the primitive instincts of hunger, thirst and sexuality, provides the occasion which gives the community confidence in its ability to unite and share. The concept of private ownership is to be eliminated as selfish, and economic ties with the world outside the plateau, which place restraints on life within it, will be cut, all necessities being supplied from within the community. Beyond the arrival of the stag and the great feast there are two other group events which create the same sense of communal unity, the harvesting of the wheat and the installation and first working of the loom. The doctrine is not one of economic equality, for communism is firmly rejected, in the person of a doctrinaire farmer. It is a call for co-operation between man and man, and between man and nature, with the vision supplied by the artist:

> The true artist is always in the advance guard. He is perched in the crow's nest; he is the discoverer of new free lands, of all the sources of joy, nourishment and riches that await man . . .

Similar ideas gave rise to the slightly absurd practical experiment known as the Contadour venture (1935) with which Giono was closely identified. They are re-expressed in his essays of the period, particularly *Les Vraies Richesses* (1936) and *Triomphe de la vie* (1942). For example, in the first section of the latter he described life in an Alpine village, stressing the interdependence of the farmers and the various types of artesan in supplying the village's daily wants, and adding that what the community must have in order to achieve complete unity is someone to provide material for spiritual unity, to wit the creative artist. It is interesting therefore that Giono's faith in the viability of such a system should have wavered as early as *Que ma joie demeure*. For the novel ends with the failure of Bobi's schemes, his death and curious re-integration into the cycle of life. Bobi's death has in fact Apocalyptic status; it is caused by a heaven-sent thunderbolt planted between the shoulders as if in punishment for *hubris*. Where has he gone wrong? An aid to interpretation is a line in 'La ville des hirondelles', published in the collection of essays, *L'Eau vive* (1943): 'Let us simply say "Let my joy last" knowing we are the only ones responsible for it'. Bobi's teaching, though initially a creative stimulus, begins to impose on the community qualities which are essentially his own, deriving from his nomadic *jongleur* background (he is a travelling acrobat). The community itself explodes under the pressures of anarchic primitive emotions released by Bobi within it. The method and the nature of the perceptions offered to the plateau dwellers continue to be valid after his death, but the total community union he had envisaged is rejected.

Giono's description of the human condition is quite

different from that of his contemporaries in several obvious respects. His characters know no real *angst* (before *Que ma joie demeure*) because they are not plagued with the intellectual lucidity which characterises the adventurers. Yet they also belong to a world in which the major direction of society is false, corrupt and incompatible with any sort of happiness. They also are caught up in a consequent malaise which can only be dispelled by action, particularly if it includes the fraternity of communal co-operation. And although women play a greater role in Giono's novels, love being given significant status, it is still a world of male virtues and masculine dominance (as is the world of Saint-John Perse's *Anabase*). The world which appears from the novel is, in short, as curiously detached from everyday reality as the exotic action and settings of *Vol de nuit* or *Les Conquérants*, although at least Giono's heroes have the virtue of concerning themselves with how to live rather than how to die. Antonio, in *Le Chant du monde* is a dream-adventurer whose world never forces on him the compromise and defeat of Garine or Perken. Only in *Que ma joie demeure* are the limits of the philosophy adumbrated.

The writers I have been referring to in this chapter are not generally considered together. The conventional labels attached to them are quite different. Politically, for example, Drieu and Brasillach were pro-fascist, the pre-war Malraux pro-communist. Many ideas expressed by Saint-Exupéry and Giono could be identified with the Vichy government's views on corruption and regeneration, yet the former fought against Vichy, whilst Giono failed to establish any clear opposition to its policies. Such labels notwithstanding, the writers in question have much in common in their underlying assumptions about the human predicament. They all betray an instinctive anarchism, a deep suspicion over the limits of reason (though Malraux and Montherlant admit a lucidity in emotion which in some measure rehabilitates the intellect), a preference for what Malraux has described as the suppression of questions by a series of actions. In all of them some form of violence is accepted as a norm, whether it be the violence of nature or of man. Their political division in fact merely reflects a superficial disagreement, though one with enormous practical consequences in the climate of 'thirties' politics, as to the degree and type of fraternity which they find compatible with the full expression of individuality. Their weakness is that none of them is writing about reality at all: their characters live and act on a fictional plane not so very different from that of the *Boys Own Paper*. It is not surprising, then, that with the exception of Montherlant and Saint-John Perse, none of these writers was still expressing a philosophy of action in this form after the War. Drieu and Saint-Exupéry were dead; Malraux, as we have seen, moved on to a defence of cultural values; Giono shifted the focus of his study to the psychological mechanisms of the will to power. For some time action was to be respectable only in the context of social and political codes.

CHAPTER 5
Philosophical dilemmas

> The chief defect of the novel of ideas is that you must write about people who have ideas to express — which excludes all but about .01 per cent of the human race.
> (Aldous Huxley, *Point Counter Point*)

The introspection, youth-cult and impulse to constant revolt which characterise much of the literature of the first thirty years of this century were symptoms of a deep-seated dissatisfaction with the social and intellectual status quo. Between the wars writers began to take as their subject the representation and analysis of the source of this dissatisfaction — the new uncertainty as to what man is. The rise of fascism in Europe, the experiences of World War II, the advent of nuclear weapons added decade by decade to the disorientation and disillusionment of many intellectuals. The resulting metaphysical preoccupation is less surprising in France, a country where philosophy has long been considered an important part of the school curriculum, than it would have been in England or America. The new metaphysics was reflected in the novel and drama in diverse forms. Despite their apparent differences these can, however, be grouped around the two poles of contemporary thought: the belief that there are pre-existing and continuous concepts and values to which man can relate, and the belief that experience and choice create concepts and values that are contingent.

It is much simpler to outline the progress of these two types of thought among professional thinkers than to identify their precise reflection in literature proper. Continental philosophy has changed relatively little in its major preoccupations in the past four centuries; it continues to investigate ideas of morality and value judgment, the process of reason and the nature of concepts. All these problems have become progressively more affected in the present century by new attitudes to knowledge, identity and the contingency of time such as we have already met in characteristically French form in the work of Bergson.

There is some truth in the view that this kind of philosophy, especially as expounded by Ferdinand Alquié, Sartre and Merleau-Ponty, is an attempt to find a substitute for religious belief. Certainly, when translated into literature, metaphysics often undergoes the same kind of transformation that theology passes through in similar circumstances. The emphasis of the novel, play or poem will be ethical or psychological, while characterising the essential values or metaphysical revolt which the writer is upholding.

There is, nonetheless, a clear distinction between what one might call symptomatic and analytical representations of a philosophy in literature. Marguerite Yourcenar's *Alexis ou le traité du vain combat* (1929) is a study of homosexuality which makes interesting comparison with the *récits* of Gide; her novels, particularly *Mémoires d'Hadrien* (1951) and *L'Oeuvre au noir* (1968), contain substantial reflections on human nature. These analyses are based in a certain tradition of psychology and humanist values. A very different writer, Hervé Bazin, in novels ranging from *Vipère au poing* (1948) to *Les Bienheureux de la désolation* (1970) analyses different manifestations of social malaise in modern society. Both of these writers deal in symptoms, the surface of existence, though in Yourcenar's case these symptoms are reflected upon very acutely by the characters she creates. Such writing, profound in its own way, is quite different in kind from, let us say, that of the existentialists, or of Giraudoux, Queneau or Samuel Beckett, in that there the text is incomprehensible without reference to the metaphysical assumptions around which it is constructed.

Surrealism
The first substantial body of work of this kind was provided by the surrealists. The revolt against fixed values conducted by pre-1914 modernism had received a new impetus from World War I, whose horror and pointlessness emphasised the barrenness of the contemporary social values which had allowed or even encouraged it to take place. In 1916 the Dadaists, a group of intellectual 'bovver-boys' under the captaincy of Tristan Tzara, had introduced a new brand of adolescent nihilism into cultural manifestations. Gradually their simple rejection of everything but impulse as a basis for action gave way to surrealism, a systematic attempt to substitute for the conventional concept of reality a new kind of perception and expression.

The doctrines of the movement are set out in the manifestos issued by its leader, André Breton, in 1924 and 1929, whilst the nature of the surrealist way of life and thought is most compellingly reproduced in Breton's prose narrative *Nadja* (1928) and Louis Aragon's *Le Paysan de Paris* (1926) and *Traité du style* (1928). It is not surprising that the philosopher Alquié should have written a sympathetic account of a movement whose attitude to contingent experience has much in common with his own (*Philosophie du surréalisme*, 1955). The surrealists, however, did not only believe in complete freedom from all moral and aesthetic constraint and the irrelevance of the past to the present. Breton's definitions from the First Manifesto, formulated as mock-entries for dictionary and encyclopaedia, are explicit:

Surrealism, masc. noun: Pure mental automatism through which it is intended to express, be it orally, in writing or in any other fashion, the real processes of thought. Dictation by the mind freed from all rational restraint and without any aesthetic or moral preconceptions.

Encycl. Philos. Surrealism is based on a belief in the higher reality of certain forms of association previously neglected, in the supreme power of dreams, in the disinterested play of thought. It tends to the complete destruction of all other mental mechanisms and to substitute itself for them in the solving of the principal problems of life.

The surrealists in fact sought to fill the void of being with *le merveilleux*, a magic perception of reality in which all opposing tendencies are synthesized. To achieve this they drew heavily on dream and the unconscious (while denying the Freudian assessment of both).

The aesthetic implications of this experimentation are peculiar. In creating *le merveilleux* verbally they rejected the logic of language and the order of literary structure, adopting as their revelatory medium automatic writing, the deliberate juxtaposition of the rationally incompatible, sound-play and other word games. It is consequently not possible to make a literary judgment on surrealist writing in its purest forms. As Tzara put it, 'Criticism . . . only exists subjectively, for each individual.' By surrealist criteria all surrealist writing is perfect, by anyone else's it may be gibberish. Breton and Soupault's *Les Champs magnétiques*, Eluard and Péret's *152 proverbes mis au goût du jour*, the 'Rrose Sélavy' poems published by Robert Desnos in various periodicals are good examples of the genre at its most impenetrable or its most facetious. The more imaginatively accessible a surrealist text becomes in terms of its imagery, the less specifically surrealist it is, the more a natural extension of the manner of Cendrars or the so-called cubists. Eluard's poetry from *L'Amour la Poésie* (1929) onward, like the later love poetry of Aragon or the post-war collections of René Char, shows how the disruptive techniques exploited in surrealist poetry proper can be used to give force to a range of thought much more conventional than the one it was designed to create. There is, however, no substance to the critical commonplace that surrealism substantially altered the direction of modern French literature as far as poetry or prose is concerned. Dislocated images and verbal surprise are the stock-in-trade of Cendrars and some Apollinaire; humour is already important in Max Jacob; dream and the unconscious are explored in Cocteau's *Le Potomac* and its sequel as early as 1919. It would be possible to draw up an exhaustive list of the supposed legacy of the surrealists and demonstrate that all the major elements had been manifest in French literature prior to 1920.

Possibly it is in the theatre that we find the most interesting developments of surrealist literature (the term is a paradox, of course, since the surrealists repudiated the value judgment implicit in the very concept). The psychological and moral preoccupations of the ordinary dramatist, plus the notion of dramatic conventions and technical competence, were precisely the kind of 'content' and 'form' that the surrealists were committed to destroying. At the same time the circumstances of theatrical performance gave them an opportunity for an immediate public impact lacking in the printed word. Naïve attempts to shock the audience were not new on the Parisian stage: Jarry's *Ubu roi* (1896) and Apollinaire's *Les Mamelles de Tirésias* (1917) had both mixed fantasy with militant offensiveness. Yet they were less effective in creating uproar in the auditorium than Nijinsky's choreography for *Le sacre du printemps*. The surrealist theatre itself was a more constructive affair, exploring the potential of the stage as much as destroying the audience's preconceptions. Although there would be no reason now to revive such ephemera as Aragon's *L'Armoire à glace* or Breton and Soupault's *S'il vous plaît*, the movement produced at least one significant playwright, Roger Vitrac, and one project important in the development of French theatre, the Théâtre Alfred Jarry, founded by Vitrac,

Robert Aron and Antoine Artaud. It must however be noted that by founding this theatre Vitrac and Artaud cut themselves off from the surrealists. Artaud's concept of theatre as a means not an end, and his stress on the importance of the unconscious, dreams and chance as features of a dramatic text were all coherent with the principles of Breton's manifestos; Vitrac's best play, *Victor, ou les enfants au pouvoir*, with its bourgeois life-style turned upside down and its nightmare picture of childhood as the period closest to true values, was consonant with surrealist philosophy. But Breton and his clique could not tolerate the interest of Artaud and Vitrac in the development of theatre as such, and expelled them — to flourish outside the movement.

Essentialists in the theatre
The history of the French surrealist movement, its flirtation with the Communist Party, the endless expulsions, rows, reconciliations, its gradual reduction to a rump faction in the latter part of the 1930s, is a not particularly inspiring but fairly typical example of the in-fighting to which French artistic 'schools' of the last two hundred years have been subject. One can understand the hostility of Breton and his friends towards Cocteau, who also manipulated chance, the subconscious and the value of dreams, in plays like *Orphée* and *La Machine infernale*, who also created a poetry of objects on the stage, and who was much more successful at mobilising the avant-garde snobs than were his rivals. But Cocteau's concept of man, for all its surreal trappings, is essentialist. The themes of the purity of adolescence, the curse of impossible love (often incest as in *La Machine infernale* and *Les Parents terribles*), the fatal power of beauty, all of which appear in his novels, are here worked into a deterministic view of the universe with distinct overtones of Romantic doom. The elaborate game of theatrical illusion in which all this is cloaked, even more noticeable in the films, *Orphée* and *Le Testament d'Orphée*, reflects the

voluntary illusions of the hero, trapped in a cosmos that plots his destruction and pursuing perfection in a form incompatible with the taboos of society. Cocteau's metaphysics were as unacceptable to a surrealist as was his personality. However, the real antithesis to surrealism in its philosophical aspect, as far as the 1920s and 1930s are concerned, is the work of Jean Giraudoux, the most purely and abstractly essentialist of thinkers and at the same time the most self-consciously literary of stylists.

Giraudoux's plays belong to the same tradition of theatricality as Cocteau's. But in Cocteau the surface dazzle is usually designed to distract the spectator from the mysteries of the potential hidden meaning, to such an extent that certain critics, like Eric Bentley, have denied the existence of that meaning. In Giraudoux, theatricality is designed to persuade the spectator that not only is identification not meant to take place with the surface of the plot, but that the drama beneath the surface has a meaning accessible only to each spectator individually. Furthermore, the 'philosophy' embodied in each play is not the reason for its existence, the end-product (as it is in the case of Sartre or Gabriel Marcel); the reason for the existence of the philosophy is the creation of the theatrical experience.

This curious paradox underlies everything Giraudoux wrote on the theory of the theatre. Apart from the articles contained in his collection *Littérature*, probably the best source of information about his theory is embodied in his one-act play *L'Impromptu de Paris* (1937), which was first performed as a curtain-raiser to a revival of his best-known work *La Guerre de Troie n'aura pas lieu*. This conversation between actors and director suggests that they are in participation with the spectators to create an independent world which should not be experienced rationally

> People who want to understand at the theatre don't understand the theatre

but instinctively, through style in general and language in particular.

In so far as one can approximately talk about a function for this type of theatre, it is to give people back the instinctive perceptions about life which the process of compromise inherent in everyday existence has taken away from them. Man is reawakened to the creative force of his imagination, which has the power to resolve the kind of problems against which reason is of no avail. In the typical Giraudoux play a problem is taken and defined in what Jacques Guicharnaud has aptly called 'an aesthetic equilibrium between contrary definitions'. The metaphysical basis for this is set out in Giraudoux's definition of tragedy in his essay 'Bellac et la tragédie' (*Littérature*). There is a dichotomy between destiny, which represents a pure experience, and humanity, which represents compromise. The role of the protagonist is to be at the intersection of the two worlds, the absolute and the contingent, and to take part, either by choice or obligation, in both. In the early plays there tends to be a winner, in the sense of a resolution in favour of one force or the other — but the resolution can be ambiguous, as in *Siegfried* or *Intermezzo*. In the later plays, notably *Electre*, it becomes doubtful how far there is a resolution at all. In both cases the ultimate resolution can only be an emotional one effected within the individual spectator, since both the forces at play are rationally 'right'.

The central importance of the metaphysical conflict between destiny and humanity, which is by definition also a conflict between idealism and realism, means that the characters within the plays are not specific illustrations of general philosophic truths but incarnations of perfected essences. In the most literal sense Giraudoux's characters are what they say, such that, however highly individualised they are, they give the impression of being archetypes. The protagonists only gain the illusion of greater reality because they are more complex in definition, whereas secondary characters are deliberately imprisoned in a series of simple attitudes. This approach to characterisation causes certain problems in the novel, the form for which Giraudoux first became famous. The one-dimensionality of the very pure, very innocent, utterly free heroes and heroines of *Eglantine* or *Aventures de Jérôme Bardini* is accentuated by the two-dimensional presentation of the printed page. In the theatre the illusion of reality comes from the spectator's synthesis of all the concrete 'real' details which figure in the style. The world is reality reduced to a diagram in such a way that the continuity of certain lines, the existence of certain symmetries are detected. This diagram is then filled out with concrete 'real' content in the form of images. Giraudoux's characters are philosophical abstractions balanced against one another in a perfectly equipoised universe. They take their life from the complicity of the spectator's imagination as it is aroused by the language, structure and physical effects of the play in performance.

The two major fields in which Giraudoux explores the dichotomy destiny-versus-humanity are love and politics, though the two motifs are not entirely separable (the same is true of his novels, notably the Romeo-and-Juliet politics of *Bella*). There are four essentially political plays; the dialogue in *Siegfried* (1928), as in the parallel novel *Siegfried et le Limousin*, is between France and Germany, in *La Guerre de Troie n'aura pas lieu* (1935) between war and peace, in *Electre* between the two faces of justice, and in *La Folle de Chaillot* (written 1942, performed 1945) between repression and individualism. Sartre's criticism of Giraudoux in his article 'M. Giraudoux et la philosophie d'Aristote' (1940) takes the attitude that the positing of theoretical universes, which is what Sartre sees in Giraudoux, is a renunciation of the intellectual's duty to intervene in the world of reality. This view has tended to cast into the shade the evident relationship between the political plays and their historical context. It has also disguised the fact that Giraudoux pursued, over the period

1917-44, the writing of political essays from *Lectures pour une ombre* (1917) to *Sans pouvoirs* (posthumously published in 1946), which examined the nature and potential solution of the social problems of contemporary France. As a career civil servant attached to the Ministry of Foreign Affairs he was able to develop a documented perception of the reality of the European situation. This political experience and concern is naturally reflected in the dialectic of his plays, without necessarily being resolved in it, as we shall see.

Although in *Siegfried* the metaphysical dimensions of the problem are not fully developed within the play, the struggle between two sets of equal values, French and German, in the soul of Jacques/Siegfried, the amnesiac soldier who has risen to be 'chancellor' of Gotha before he is faced with his French origins, is expressed in the same exteriorised symbols as Giraudoux will later use for a more overtly philosophical purpose. In *Electre* Giraudoux has developed the potential inherent in his use of the political antitheses in *Siegfried*. He demonstrates that Siegfried's assertion about the assimilability of all contrary experiences is true in the sense that all meaningful experience contains the experience of its opposite, and false in respect to the rationally irreconcilable pulls of reality and idealism. He also develops a second, philosophically significant point — Geneviève's idea that Jacques has an essence which is the only thing meaningfully his and which his existence should develop — by opposing two such essences, discovered in the course of the action by their 'owners', Electre and Egisthe. The dialectical opposition in *Electre* is that of ideal justice and human justice. By encouraging Oreste to despatch Clytemnestre and Egisthe, Electre occasions the destruction of the innocent people of Argos at the hands of the invading Corinthians. For most of the play the characters build up the emotive oppositions of values in which truth is an impossible criterion. The audience may not select a cause on intellectual grounds because both poles of the opposition, even when symbolised by the opposition woman/young girl, are as repugnant as they are attractive. The action moves remorselessly to its inevitable climax. Purity of principle and human concern are irreconcilable. A world of compromise, adultery and manipulation has been destroyed: the question 'was that world worth saving?' is posed but not answered.

Giraudoux's own attitude to the destruction of France in his later essay 'L'Avenir de la France' suggests that he may have been sympathetic to the ruthlessness of Electre, seeing total destruction as a necessary preliminary to moral rebirth; the idea is born out by his use of the dawn image in the last scene of the play. I think however that this speech of Jouvet in *L'Impromptu de Paris*, written the same year as *Electre*, is more enlightening:

> It is the destiny of France to be the world's trouble-stirrer . . . She is justice, but only in so far as justice consists in preventing from being right those who have been right too long . . . In the application of integral justice she comes right after God and chronologically before him. It is not her role to make prudent choices between good and evil, the possible and the impossible. That way she's had it. Her originality is not in the equipoise which is justice, but in the weight she throws in to achieve equity, and which may be injustice.

If Giraudoux saw France as an Electre within the Argos of Western Europe, he must have got a very nasty shock in 1940.

The problem with using an elaborate argument of this kind to promote a political point is that people bring to these kinds of issue such clearly formulated prejudices of their own that they are likely to be relatively unsusceptible to the tissue of poetic images on which the play depends. Love, however, is a theme well-suited to such atmospheric persuasion. For this reason Giraudoux's two most effective plays, *Intermezzo* (1933) and *Ondine* (1939), are primarily about human relationships. In *Electre*, contact with the source of purity, Electre herself, frees Agathe from any sense of social responsibility and causes her to abandon her husband for love of everything and everybody around her. Release and authenticity are equally the facts behind the central predicament in *Intermezzo*. The schoolmistress, Isabelle, through her contact with a ghost, has activated the forces of purity in her little town. The system of social compromise has consequently broken down: the poorest man wins the lottery, women abandon their husbands for 'sober, smooth-skinned lovers', on their census forms husbands list not their real wives but the woman or even the female animal they regard as the perfect companion. The total disruption which in *Electre* is symbolised in black images is here posited in relatively comic terms. Against the ghost Giraudoux summons up both the most impossible of his bureaucrats, the Inspector, and the most human, the Deputy Inspector. The romantic, wayward and metaphysical is pitted not merely against the spirit of rationalisation, progress and belief in the unaided capacity of Man, but against the charm of the self-consciously contingent.

The weakness of *Intermezzo* has rightly been identified as the fact that the relationship between Isabelle and the ghost is not fully convincing as a love affair. Not until *Ondine* does the potential of a bond between a human and a metaphysical partner get full treatment. *Intermezzo*, like *Siegfried*, permitted a resolution, an end in human compromise: *Ondine*, like *Electre*, ends in the destruction of the two main characters, but with the ambiguous sense that something may outlive that destruction. The centre of the relationship between Hans and Ondine is the portrait of total sensuality. Love is no longer, as with the pale, ethereal ghost in *Intermezzo* — who is presented as a fin-de-siècle Hamlet — a source of potential knowledge. It is born of a physical experience. The dialectic of the play encompasses absolute love, the love of Ondine for Hans, and human love, the compromised social relationship of Hans and Bertha.

The plot of the play, derived from an old German folk-tale *Undine* by Friedrich de la Motte-Fouqué (1811), is simple enough. Hans, a medieval knight-errant, falls in love with Ondine, the adopted daughter of fisher-folk but in reality a sea-sprite. He abandons his fiancée and takes Ondine back to the court as his wife. But the very qualities which make Ondine's love for him so special are the source of her social failure. Hans tries to rid himself of her by accusing her of infidelity. At the absurd trial, however, he reveals that it is he who has betrayed her, with Bertha. Hans' life is forfeit to the king of the sea-sprites, and Ondine must return to her people. The schema of the forces in the play is closer to *Intermezzo* than *Electre*. The sea-sprites, particularly their king, and the court, particularly Bertha, provide the extremes of the value system, with Ondine as the force of destiny made manifest and Hans the point of contact between ideal and real. Yet the focus of the play is really quite different from *Intermezzo*. The sea-sprites play an active part in Acts 1 and 3, their king is the illusionist who manipulates the whole action of Act 2. At the same time reality is more embracingly portrayed and satirised, but with less close everyday reference. Above all, the focus of the play is not on the mortal contact, the wretched and rather absurd Hans, but on Ondine and her opposite number, Bertha.

Ondine combines two roles. As well as the embodiment of pure love she is the active representative of the natural world — 'Ondine's nature is Nature itself'. The sun, similarly used in *Intermezzo*, symbolises this: 'Blond. The sun and she go by together', is how Hans describes her. Bertha is the opposite of Ondine both physically and in character. It is her pride which motivates her maltreatment of Hans, her hostility to Ondine, her ugly reaction to the discovery that she is the real daughter of Ondine's adoptive parents. She is without capacity for genuine physical or emotional affection, but completely endowed with the ability to fulfil the social patterns laid down for her. Between these two women Hans evolves during the course of the play from being pure man — encased in a suit of armour which suggests the rigidity of artifice dividing man from nature — to an awareness of the superior attractions of the ideal, brought home to him by his contact with Ondine. In the reconciliation scene (Act 3 sc6) before his death, though he cries out against the injustice which condemns an ordinary man like himself to be the object of so ultimate an experience, his cry is not one of rejection, but of despair at being torn between the ideal he cannot achieve and the tawdriness of the compromise that is within his grasp. This climactic scene presents the rebirth of the love of Hans and Ondine through the pattern of the words: its opening echoes precisely that of Act I sc5 when they communicated alone for the first time. The significance and effect of the scene cannot be over-estimated. The attempt of Ondine to fulfil a human pattern, of Hans to love the ideal, leads not merely to the annihilation of Hans, but to the obliteration in Ondine's mind of the fact that Hans ever existed. As Ionesco wrote in a tribute to Giraudoux:

> Never have I been so overwhelmed by the theme of separation, love, absence, death — more than death, for there was something still more terrible there: the suppression, retrospectively as it were, of an essential event, rooted out of the universe, thrown out into the void of cosmic oblivion; life, struck out of life, not only no longer existed but, through being returned to the increate, never had been . . . What could there be more dreadful than the awareness of the total uselessness of our pain, of our existence, declared null and void, unrecorded by the memory of the universe, by any god?

The pointlessness of human existence, not just ended but obliterated, never to have been at all, lies at the end of the play. Yet ambiguity is not totally eradicated. For Ondine proclaims her preparation for this fated separation, the creation of a physical 'memory', a sequence of steps and motions which will unconsciously keep alive in her the days when those steps and motions were part of the routine of her earthly life with Hans. The human will maintain a place within the heart of the ideal:

... separated by oblivion, death, time, race, we shall be in accord, we shall be faithful to one another.

The spectator cannot but be committed, within the emotional framework of the play, to the losing side, while remaining aware that his own frail humanity condemns him to the experience of the Pyrrhic victor, reality.

The quotation from Ionesco above should give one pause for thought as to whether the Sartrean view of Giraudoux as a detached composer of intellectual games designed to lull the bourgeoisie into satisfied contemplation of the status quo is really applicable to his plays at all. It is perfectly true that, like the novels, the plays represent the extension to the ultimate of certain values and an intellectual, though by no means rational, exploration of the implications of such extremes. But the conclusions are not particularly comforting ones. The powerlessness of Hans shows man very close to the edge of the void: life is a set of meaningless rituals in which the intrusion of ideals is not only destructive but also perhaps a figment of man's imagination. *Ondine* was the most lavishly staged production of its epoque (and that is saying something), and nowhere does Giraudoux more effectively embody his desire — which is certainly part of his literary credo — to restore harmony to his fellows through the literary and theatrical experience of beauty, than in this play. However, it seems, in a typically Giralducian paradox, to be made illusory by the nihilism of the text itself. The essentialism of *Electre* gives way to a vision of something close to what later writers will call 'the absurd'.

The absurdity of life
The rejection of the compromise and corruption of French society in the 1920s and 1930s was, of course, common to writers of vastly differing vision. There is a spectrum of responses that ranges from those who merely chronicle it, like Roger Martin du Gard and Georges Duhamel, through those

who satirise aspects of it, as Paul Morand in *Bouddha vivant* and *France-la-Doulce*, to the delirious attacks of Céline and of Drieu la Rochelle (*L'Homme couvert de femmes, Le Feu-follet, Gilles*). All these writers deal principally or entirely with symptoms. Giraudoux and Sartre deal in causes. But while Giraudoux's metaphysical conceits offer both an analysis of the decay in terms of what is wrong with human nature and a highly stylised projection of theoretical alternatives, it was Sartre who first expressed in fictional form the philosophical crisis underlying the moral void. In his startling first novel, *La Nausée* (1938), the hero, Antoine Roquentin, lives in isolation in the provincial town of Bouville. He has no aim in life except, fitfully, to write the biography of an eighteenth-century aristocrat, the marquis de Rollebon. The text of the novel is cast in diary form, which is really a substitute for internal monologue. Roquentin reflects on the nature of immediate experience and finds it profoundly disagreeable. His problem, at least initially, is largely a question of his relationship to things; he feels disgust in the face of the sheer materiality of the universe, its self-contained alienness to the human condition. He measures his responses against those of a humanist, l'Autodidacte, against the bourgeoisie of Bouville, against Annie his former girlfriend, and uncovers the contingency of man, the falseness of all attempts to give human life shape or meaning. Only in the disembodied phrase of a jazz song, from a record in his local café, does he detect a solution (of sorts) to his dilemma.

The power of *La Nausée* derives less from its thought than from the brilliant interplay of form and idea. The monologue effect gives us a sense of the urgency, the *presentness* of the problems depicted and emphasises that the consciousness involved is avidly seeking a solution, and that it really is a reflective consciousness and not a passive receptor of experience (like Virginia Woolf's Clarissa Dalloway). The sense of nausea which certain detached trivial experiences arouse is communicated both through fragmented analyses and set-piece scenes. The 'events' the novel possesses are merely necessary stages in one's appreciation of the rejection of conventional solutions to the metaphysical dilemma. Where other characters are focused upon, it is so that Roquentin can analyse their place in the scheme of things, whether like Dr Rogé they are deliberately refusing to recognise their own (philosophical) absurdity or whether like Annie they have arrived at the same realisation as Roquentin by a different route. As each new stage of philosophical awareness is reached, it is exemplified in a set-piece, as at the intellectual climax of the novel, where the root of a chestnut tree really brings home to Roquentin the 'thinginess' of things. Although it is true that the drily intellectual nature of Roquentin's personality is rebarbative and the absence of any reflection upon him by other characters emphasises the disembodied, almost one-dimensional nature of the narrative voice, this only enhances the horror of the hero's predicament. Though one might read the novel as the case-history of a psychotic, it would be difficult not to share to some degree in the mental turmoil that is portrayed.

Sartre only expressed his philosophical position in its full form in *L'Etre et le Néant*, five years after writing *La Nausée*, but the earlier work embodies in fictional form the implications of his main ideas. Unlike the material world which is self-contained and static, man merely exists, a blank sheet, and is conscious of the anomaly of his own existence. It is up to the individual to create himself by his actions, and since he is entirely free to choose what he becomes, he is also entirely responsible for himself. *La Nausée* stops short at identifying the initial premisses. With *Les Mouches* (1943), *Huis clos* (1944) and *L'Age de raison* (1945, first volume of *Les Chemins de la liberté*) Sartre followed through his position to look at the problem of the individual in his social context. In the last-named, Daniel who 'wants *to be* homosexual the way an oak *is* an oak' and Mathieu whose freedom condemns him to life in a vacuum, are excellent embodiments of two obsessions with aspects of the philosophical impasse. However, in other respects, *L'Age de raison*, like *Les Mouches*, begins the uneasy and philosophically untenable transition from existentialism to political commitment, and is best looked at in that context. The assumption in both works that the best choice for the individual must also be beneficial to the majority of his fellows is based on a humanitarian leap of faith that has nothing to do with the bleak metaphysics of *L'Etre et le Néant*, as Mary Warnock in her critique of Sartre's ethics has conclusively shown.

Huis clos, on the other hand, is a purely philosophical play and perhaps for that reason the most effective thing he wrote apart from *La Nausée*. The gloomy lesson on man's relationship with man to be derived from *L'Etre et le Néant* is that all attempts at relationships are the fruit of self-interest or bad faith, and that there is no more merit in leading a nation than in getting drunk on your own. Each person wants to use his neighbour as a mirror of his own being, a way of 'fixing' his own image; even if the resulting conflict of interests between two people can be temporarily resolved, the presence of a third person judging the relationship upsets the balance of interest. In *Huis clos* Sartre takes his characters, Garcin, Estelle and Inès, at the point where they have no choices, no development left open to them: they are dead. The scene is Hell, transposed into the perfect symbol of bourgeois materialism, a Second Empire drawing room. Garcin and Estelle begin by attempting to project on to each other the image of their past lives as they would like to see them; Inès breaks down their pretences. Estelle, it transpires, drove her lover to suicide by killing their child. Inès, a Lesbian, seduced a married woman, persuaded her that their relationship had driven her husband to his death, and caused her to kill herself and Inès. Garcin, after a longer attempt at hiding the truth, proves to have been a coward in the face of war, who broke down at his execution. But the course of the play does not merely lay bare the bad faith of the ill-assorted trio. It proves their dependence on one another, symbolised by Estelle's need to mirror herself in Inès' eyes in order to arrange her hair. Her image is only confirmable in the reflection offered by a second person's attention. The three are locked together for eternity in a complicated interplay of hatred and necessity. It is easy to see why Sartre should have come to the conclusion, in *L'Etre et le Néant*, that 'man is a useless passion'. Though he effectively portrayed the mechanisms of bad faith in his reworking of Alexandre Dumas' play *Kean* and investigated the theme of the irrevocability of past acts very neatly in his film-scenario *Les Jeux sont faits*, none of his later plays integrate quite so perfectly philosophical principle, psychological development and dramatic impact as *Huis clos*.

It is interesting to contrast with Sartrean existentialism the philosophical views that Camus expounded in his essay *Le Mythe de Sisyphe* and exemplified in his novel *L'Etranger* (both 1942). The absurdity of life, the clash between the meaninglessness of the universe and the desire of man for meaning, is a concept at which Camus arrived by a quite different route from Sartre. Roquentin's crisis is an intellectual one, dependent on the sense of viscosity which afflicts his consciousness in certain circumstances. Meursault, the protagonist of *L'Etranger*, experiences this same alienation instinctively, finding his meaning only in the disconnected moments of physical sensation which constitute his existence. This is perfectly in tune with the views expressed in Camus' early works, *L'Envers et l'endroit* (1937) and *Noces* (1938). It conforms in particular with the affirmation in the latter that physical happiness, associated with the sensual beauty of Mediterranean scenery, is the only possible source of transcendent values. *Le Mythe de Sisyphe* transfers the argument on to an apparently more cerebral plane, but the 'truths' which it asserts are held together by the author's emotional convictions rather than logic. The metaphysical absurdity of which Malraux had spoken in *La Tentation de l'occident* is for Camus something which should not be denied by the kind of leap of faith he associates with both Christian existentialists and the metaphysicians in general, nor should it be taken as a reason for physical suicide. It should simply be kept in focus, as a reason for a defiant affirmation of the value of life itself. By revolting against the implications of our own absurdity, we sharpen our sense of being alive.

Meursault lacks the lucidity necessary to be an absurdist hero in the terms laid down by *Le Mythe*. He is equally untouched by any of the normal human tendencies to create patterns of meaning in one's own life and make them comply with accepted social standards. The novel falls into two unequal parts. The first, which is very fragmentary, traces certain events in the protagonist's life, from the news of his mother's death through to his killing of an Arab. Throughout he is a man for whom no time exists but the present, no values but the physical, no motivation but the instinctual. He moves alone in a world of intense light and heat. The first-person narrative plunges the reader into all this; the disjointed view of life is the only vision of it vouchsafed to us. For the same reason the vocabulary is concrete, the syntax limited in range, except at the complex and hallucinatory moment when Meursault, entirely in the power of the midday sun, shoots the Arab. The second half of the book, with Meursault awaiting trial and execution, is a reflection upon the first half. It embodies a condemnation of the society that judges a man upon false principles and an analysis of the growing lucidity of the hero as he realises the importance of the physical existence he is about to lose. The reader has been put in the place of a character almost certainly quite unlike himself and is implicitly required to judge his own prejudices as they are reflected in the society of the novel.

Camus approaches the same problems from a different angle in his play *Caligula* (written around 1939 but not performed until 1945). There he explores a man at the opposite pole of existence from Meursault, in that he is completely lucid and also in full control of society rather than in its power. Like a Giralducian hero, Caligula is the spirit of the absolute caught in a world of compromise — '. . . everything all around me is lies; I want people to live in truth'. The death of his sister, Drusilla, with whom he has been having an incestuous affair, has awakened him to man's powerlessness in the face of death, to the relativity of human happiness that this powerlessness implies. Acts 2 to 4 explore the moral and political consequences of Caligula's decision to revolt against the implications of the absurd by attacking the world. Caligula is in fact making himself the instrument of death in order to bring home to mankind the truth that he has perceived. He is not however alone in his perception. He is matched by Cherea, an intellectual with humanist impulses — 'I believe that there are some actions which are finer than others' — who has resisted the implications of the absurd. But the only force which can stop Caligula is himself. It is the realisation that his revolt is futile, his power no less relative, that leads him to submit to assassination. Camus, like Sartre but again for quite different reasons, is very loath to accept that any man can stand alone.

Camus went on to further dramatic exploration of the nature of the absurd in *Le Malentendu* (1944). But, for a progression in his moral position we should look to *La Chute* (1956). The monologue form of this novel creates an ambiguity of purpose by robbing the reader of firm criteria by which to judge the sincerity of the speaker, Jean-Baptiste Clamence. Clamence, once a successful lawyer who prided himself on a philanthropic career, let a woman die because of his cowardice. Since then he has undergone a constant decline until he is reduced to his present occupation, confessing his failure to total strangers whom he buttonholes in an Amsterdam bar. The egoistic verbosity of Clamence strikes a false chord. His truthfulness and his motivation are impossible to determine. His critique of society seems right, yet his attempts to incriminate his listener by association suggest a desire for self-exculpation. If his is a fall from grace, as the title seems to suggest, there is certainly no suggestion of redemption. The simplicity of Meursault and the lucidity of Caligula have been replaced by complexity and obscurity, by a remorse that seems to stultify. Perhaps, as at the end of his essay *L'Homme révolté*, Camus is proclaiming that the modern world has lost the power of loving life.

Despite the obvious differences between the four responses to man's condition represented by the surrealists, Giraudoux, Camus, and Sartre and his followers, they have several points in common. All rejected the primacy of reason in human life; all denigrate the compromise that constitutes social existence; all portray the pursuit of ideals as impossible or dishonest. To this Sartre and Camus add anguish at the incoherence between man and the universe, and an appreciation of the dangers of solitude and the stultifying effect of *ennui*. What is end-stopped in these expressions of metaphysical crisis is less the content than the form, particularly as regards the intellectual contrivance, the literary artifice which marked all but the surrealists. The most important developments in post-war representations of the absurd are the result of experiments designed to break down the superficial rationalism imposed by literary language and structure.

The 'Theatre of the Absurd' was the most radical of these experiments. It renounced argument about the human condition in favour of concrete stage images of absurdity. Language became devalued. Stage action often contradicted the actual words spoken. A new kind of dramatic suspense was created: the problem posed is no longer 'What is going to happen?' but 'What is happening?'. The plays give no solutions; they challenge the spectator to pose questions. In other words, writers have moved from the identification and analysis of the metaphysical crisis to an attempt to bring home the nature of that crisis by steeping the spectator in its atmosphere. Eugène Ionesco (1912-   ) established himself in the public mind as the leader of the new style. His definition of the absurd as '. . . that which is devoid of purpose . . . Cut off from his religious, metaphysical and transcendental roots man is lost: all his actions become senseless, absurd, useless' is much more the description of an intuition than the elaboration of a concept like Camus', let alone the deduction of a principle like Sartre's, but it is obvious that all three are referring to the same experience. In order to give full expression to the sense of unbearable futility which characterises man's attempts to invent meaning in life, the writer, in Ionesco's view, must create a form of drama in which every aspect is pushed to its fullest tension. Only the unendurable is profoundly tragic, comic, theatrical, because only the unendurable gives the sense of being insoluble and therefore leaves the audience with the right sense of desperation.

The way Ionesco chooses to achieve this maximum tension which results in a sense of the unendurable is by emphasising the conventions of theatre to the point of revealing their inner absurdity. Drama is created by the extreme exaggeration of feeling and action, by caricature, the grotesque and above all by violence, so as to dislocate flat everyday reality. In this context the distinction between comic and tragic is invalid: the comic is inexorable, and thus hopeless, whereas tragedy, by presupposing the reality of fate and destiny, reduces the futility of human helplessness to a kind of comedy. Hence the mixed classifications that Ionesco gives his plays: *Les Chaises* is a 'tragic farce' since, as the author observed in a programme note, 'Beings drowned in the absence of sense can only be grotesque, their suffering can only be ridiculously tragic.' It is this tension between opposing qualities, tragic/comic, realistic/fantastic, ordinary/strange and the crisis of communication which accompanies it that are Ionesco's major weapons.

His best works are his earliest — *La Cantatrice chauve* (1950), *La Leçon* (1951), *Les Chaises* (1952). Each expands on a single image. In *La Cantatrice chauve* the middle-class couples hang on grimly to their assumption that their reality is unassailable, only to find language itself disintegrating in their mouths. In *La Leçon* language is a deadly instrument which the teacher cannot control and which destroys his student. In *Les Chaises* objects proliferate; the crowds imagined by the two elderly caretakers are projected into reality as an ever-increasing swell of empty chairs which eventually drive out the two humans to their death. The same motifs, language and proliferation, occur in later plays — the millions of eggs in *L'Avenir est dans les oeufs* (1957), the men metamorphosed into rhinoceroses in *Rhinocéros* (1960) — but the balance of these plays is changed; the central characters are made more human, and what might be called themes, or at least recurrent obsessions (death, the dangers of totalitarianism, false dreams of paradise), are introduced. Although the dream-like quality of the action in *Le Piéton dans l'air* (1962), with its vision of Hell, and the symbolism of the plague in *Jeux de massacre* (1970) are clever vehicles for Ionesco's personal philosophical and political feelings, they provide a less taut and integrated dramatic structure than that of the early plays.

One striking quality about Ionesco's theatre as a whole is its total pessimism. Whereas Sartre and Camus move on to affirmations about how to improve the lot of mankind, Ionesco becomes more and more emphatic about the individual's isolation and the destructive power of all attempts to group man, however well intentioned the ideology on which they are based. In *Macbett* (sic, 1972) there is even a sense of regret for the humanist values which he, as much as any one, has helped to bury. However, the purest expression of metaphysical despair is not to be found in Ionesco or in any of those writers, such as Ferdinand Arrabal, who could be linked with him under the heading 'Theatre of proliferation', since their worlds become deliberately more and more overburdened with objects, words or images. It is contained in the increasingly spare plays of Samuel Beckett.

Beckett began his career as a novelist, writing in English. *Murphy*, orginally published in 1938, he recreated in French in 1947, but *Watt* had to wait until 1968 to appear in its new language. His first major works in French were *Molloy* and *Malone meurt* (both of the same year, 1951). The themes, characters and general development of his novels prefigure or parallel major aspects of his plays. His entire work could be defined as the paring down of an emotional response to the horror of existence, a horror stemming from the gap between a consciousness fated to meditate on its eventual destruction and the uselessness of the material world, particularly the human body, whose gradual corrosion is a symbol of the process of extinction. The earliest characters embodying this condition are already very detached from the usual patterns of life; Murphy does nothing and relates to nobody, though he briefly warms to the inmates of a mental hospital because he feels they have succeeded in completely shutting themselves off from the 'contingencies of the contingent world'; Watt arouses curiosity or anger in his fellows but is quite detached from them as he pursues his journey to nowhere via another mental institution. In *Murphy* the action is extravagant and parodic, the language exuberant; in *Watt* the contours of place and character are beginning to fade as the hero loses contact with external reality altogether. The long-unpublished *Mercier et Camier* places the focus more precisely on the 'journey to nowhere' motif; *Molloy* consecrates the tramp-outcast as the type-figure of the human condition; *Malone meurt* develops the image of human decay and the theme of the search for identity in the face of encroaching death; *L'Innommable* centres on a truncated barely sentient figure dazedly musing in a twilight zone. Gradually Beckett has peeled away the indifference and ugliness of the world, the absurdity of sex, the falsity of conventional communication. Knowledge becomes useless, feeling evaporates.

In the first of the plays, *En attendant Godot* (1952), the characters are outcasts and the themes of the early novels, non-communication, repetition, frustrated expectation, are all present. In the first half, two tramp-like figures, Estragon and Vladimir, are passing the time on a road somewhere, near a tree, waiting for someone called Godot, whom they expect to reward them in some way for turning up. The boredom of uncertain waiting — are they in the right place? is it the right day? — is relieved by the arrival of Pozzo and Lucky, loosely definable as master and servant, who temporarily divert and disturb. Eventually a boy arrives to inform them that Godot will not come today. The tramps contemplate suicide, decide to leave, but take no steps to do so. The second act is simply a variant on the first, the main changes being that Pozzo is now blind, Lucky dumb, and that the relationship between all the characters is more violent. A noticeable aspect of the play, given its unconventional content, is its concession to traditional theatrics. It demands a separation of audience and stage; it plays with the effects of words, whether in a Pinteresque way or as dislocated rhetoric. As we move on through Beckett's later plays, the colour, movement and verbal ingenuity are deliberately drained out. In *Fin de partie* Hamm in his wheelchair, Nell and Nagg in their dustbins, even Clov with his stiff, tottering walk are a step nearer physical destruction; the boredom is unbroken even by a Pozzo or a Lucky. *Oh, les beaux jours* (1963) buries one of its elderly characters, Winnie, up to her waist in sand, and confines the other, Willie, to limited physical activity, for example, lying on the ground behind Winnie for much of the second act. The elements of fragmented knowledge still stock the minds of the characters, but their verbal coherence gradually degenerates, such that Winnie's long speech (almost a third of the total text) near the close of the second act breaks down into scattered phrases at times. The three characters of *Comédie* (1966) are part of their funeral urns, no more human than the central figure of *L'Innommable*. *Pas moi* (1974) features a 'Voice' coming from about eight feet above the stage and addressing in syntactically disconnected phrases the silhouette of an entirely silent listener whose sole contribution is four brief gestures, each less perceptible than the previous. Both thought and presentation have been stylised down to a level of abstraction beyond which there can be no further development without retrogression — except perhaps in the neat self-parody *Souffle*, where the stage is littered with miscellaneous rubbish and the 'text' consists of two babies' cries and a bit of heavy breathing, punctuated by lighting effects, total running time thirty-five seconds.

Fortunately there are a lot of French authors who would accept the implications of the existentialist analysis of the human condition without restricting their expression of the world to the extremely narrow range of language and image Beckett has adopted. Jacques Prévert employs a neo-Dadaist impertinence against traditional values which expresses itself as pure derision in his poetry, for example *Paroles, Spectacles*. Jean Genet exhibits in his novels a *fin-de-siècle* idealisation of everything conventionally held evil, from transsexual prostitution in *Notre Dame des Fleurs* to murder in *Querelle de Brest*. The 'thinginess' of things is celebrated with immense detail in the work of Francis Ponge, particularly the descriptive 'definitions' of animals and objects in *Parti pris des choses* (1942). The isolation and alienation of the individual is the object of study in Jean Giono's later novels, of which *Un Roi sans divertissement* and *Les Ames fortes* are particularly satisfying in that their form obliges the reader to take an active part in the process of constructing the meaning. Equally effective are the novels and plays of Marguerite Duras, notably *Les Petits Chevaux de Tarquinia* (1953), *Moderato cantabile* (1958) and *La Musica* (1965), in which the meaninglessness of life is represented by undermining the conventional properties of time, memory and communication and by paring away the certainties of human identity. However, the clearest refurbishers of what one might call the old orthodoxies (essentialism and existentialism) are Jean Anouilh and Raymond Queneau, whilst specifically post-war developments are represented in the work of the new mythologisers Julien Gracq and Michel Tournier. An analysis of the work of these writers gives some idea how the remarkably unified metaphysical obsessions of the century have gradually become absorbed over the past forty years into less acutely intellectual forms.

Playing at meaning
Anouilh was the successor to Giraudoux as much in philosophy as in stage craft, since unresolved tension between idealism and pragmatism runs through his plays. But whereas Giraudoux saw self-conscious theatricality as a catalyst, Anouilh uses it nihilistically. He is just as much the successor to Armand Salacrou, whose *L'Inconnu d'Arras* (1936), portraying a man's life relived in his dying moment, suggests a world where even contingency is predetermined, and man lacks the very freedom to forge himself a meaning. For Anouilh's characters life is a choice between an everyday world inevitably corrupted by compromise and the pursuit of the ideal. Only the heroine or hero will choose the latter. The pursuit of the ideal is a self-deluding process doomed to failure. Antigone's stand against Créon gives her a moment of self-induced meaning; Julien's attempt to mould his wife to fit his vision of purity in *Colombe* is merely self-destructive. The difference lies merely in the context of the act and the manner of its presentation. Anouilh has rung all the changes on both: his contexts have been mythical, historical, fantastic, realistic; his manner sentimental (*Eurydice*), optimistic (*Léocadia*), pessimistic (*Ardèle*), flippant (*L'Invitation au château*). It is really to these variations, and not to modifications of substance, that the titles of his collections of plays refer: *Pièces*

roses, Pièces noires, Pièces brillantes, Pièces grinçantes, Pièces costumées, Pièces baroques.

It is, in consequence, in the exploration of his theatrical means of expression that the development of Anouilh's career lies. The elements he chooses are often the most hackneyed of conventions in themselves, piled together to seem as self-consciously artifical as possible. The centre of his meaning comes to be the theatrical metaphor itself. Characters literally adopt a role: Amanda is hired to impersonate the dead Léocadia in the play of that name, Isabelle is paid by Horace to pose as an heiress in *L'Invitation au château*, Lady Hurf thrusts the identity of the duc de Miraflor upon Peterbono, La Surette tries to force Julien into the role of cuckold in *Colombe*. Other characters admit that their whole life is an act — the vocabulary of the theatre is constantly in the mouth of Créon in *Antigone*, of Robert in the third act of *Le Rendez-vous de Senlis*. More integrally still, Eurydice belongs to a travelling theatre company, the guests in *La Répétition* are rehearsing a play by Marivaux. Finally we arrive at those plays of which the theatre is the subject, *Colombe, Cher Antoine, Le Directeur de l'Opéra, Ne réveillez pas madame* (the last three, perhaps significantly, all written towards the end of his career, between 1969 and 1972). The symbolism is not merely of the fragility of identity, though this plays a part. It suggests a fundamental falseness to life, the paradox of trying, on the stage, to represent one illusion by another. Hence the shock tactic of the bogus ending, as in *Le Voyageur sans bagage*, where the amnesiac Georges is saved from reassuming a personality he does not want by the last-minute arrival of an English orphan who provides him with another, quite false, identity. The ending is not an escape but a way of underlining by its very artificiality the ineluctability of real life.

To say that the theatre of Anouilh is escapist is a rather odd judgment, especially with regard to such later plays as the overtly Pirandellian *La Grotte*. Like Salacrou he constructs a world of inescapable contingency. The conventionality of the plays lies rather in their superficial concern with ethical questions reminiscent of the old-style problem play and in their acceptance of a traditional logic of character and plot. In these respects there is as great a gap between Anouilh and Raymond Queneau as between Giraudoux and Sartre. For Queneau's novels are philosophical games which make very little concession to the action and psychology of the conventional novel. Yet it could be said of both authors that their work has a serious core or starting point which is developed into something outwardly entertaining. Medicine is no less efficient for being sugar-coated.

Queneau, as a young man, joined the surrealists: his eventual break with them because of their woolly metaphysics and over-seriousness is evoked in an early novel, *Odile* (1937). The influence of the movement comes out more clearly in one of his first collections of poetry, *Les Ziaux* (1943); thereafter, in *Fendre la foule* (1966) and *Battre la campagne* (1968), his fondness for celebrating the everyday life of the little man and for deriding traditional moral and intellectual values brings his verse much closer to that of Jacques Prévert, on whom he wrote a sympathetic article now collected in *Bâtons, chiffres et lettres*. While accepting that man's contact with the world does give rise, philosophically, to the sense of the absurd, Queneau has no desire to transcend this condition in the sense that Sartre or Camus attempt to; his characters are comfortably installed inside it, finding for themselves a way of coping with the practicalities of life, growing to doubt the meaning of what is around them but losing faith in their doubt. If all appearances are untrustworthy there is as little to be gained from suspecting them as from accepting them. Any character who tries to disprove a philosophical point in a Queneau novel will end up by giving a virtuoso display of pointless sophistry, as with the *concierge*, Saturnin Belhôtel, in *Le Chiendent*, who demonstrates in a hilarious parody of rational argument that 'being isn't, whereas not-being is'. Otherwise he will, like Uncle Gabriel in *Zazie dans le métro*, come to the conclusion that the search for truth has nothing to do with life:

> — Truth! exclaims Gabriel (gesture), as if you knew what it is. As if anyone in the world knew what it is. All that (gesture), all that, it's a load of codswallop: the Pantheon, Les Invalides, the Reuilly barracks, all of it. Codswallop, that's what it is.

This is not to say that the anxiety caused by death, and particularly by man-made disasters like war, is not constantly referred to. But if you do not ask too much of life, certain positive experiences can be derived from it. Though *happiness* does not exist, moments of happiness do. Though life is irrational, there are reasons for living. The only momentary escape is in play, particularly the games of the mathematician and of the controlled artist playing with the formal possibilities of his art.

It is the perfect, gratuitous symmetries of structure and the unique form of language used that are half the 'meaning' of a Queneau novel. The aesthetic principles which led him to write ninety versions of the same incident in as many different styles (*Exercices de style*, 1947) and ten sonnets with interchangeable lines capable of arrangement into 10^{14} other sonnets — whence the title *Cent mille milliards de poèmes* — generate the seven chapters, each of thirteen sections, which Queneau claims to be the structure of *Le Chiendent*, the parallelism of *Loin de Rueil* in which Michou lives through exactly the same situations and dreams as his grandfather at the same age, the grouping together of all the characters in one place for the final scenes of *Pierrot mon ami* and *Zazie*, the use of circular motifs and repetitions *passim*. Queneau is emphatic that these structures, which in his article 'Technique du roman' (*Bâtons, chiffres et lettres*) he compares with the discipline imposed on medieval poets by such forms as the ballade and the rondo, are not random but represent the rhythm of what the novel is expressing. Certainly the structural curiosities do not obtrude themselves.

The stylistic ones, however, do. In several polemical articles Queneau attacks the concept of literary French, its orthography, the distance of its syntax from that of the spoken language, the limitations of its vocabulary. What he himself writes is, of course, not remotely like spoken French. The metamorphosis begins with the more obvious elisions of unpronounced syllables and, in the more extreme passages, the complete phonetic collapse of whole phrases, for example, *'Ltipstu'* for *'Le type se tut'* (approximately 'thbloakshtup' for 'the bloke shut up'); it goes on to the common syntactic rearrangements of oral register. To these he adds structures and words imitated or transcribed from other languages or from earlier stages of French, neologisms and slang. Between these very different sorts of language and traditional written forms he then moves without warning, such that conventional concepts of style, let alone register, do not apply. Puns, alliterations, hidden verse structures, accumulations and enumerations all help to break up the normal patterns of prose, creating a unique style which keeps the reader constantly alert and at the same time entertained. The final touch to this self-consciousness is given by the overt authorial manipulation not only of the characters but of events, descriptions or any element that takes his fancy. This, the intervening voice points out, is only fiction.

The funniest of Queneau's novels is *Zazie*, with its awful child-heroine and burlesque supporting cast of villains, bemused tourists and eccentrics. The cleverest of the novels is *Les Fleurs bleues* (1965) in which the time-sequence oscillates comically between 'now' and the middle ages, the language oscillating with it. The classic work, however, is probably still the first, *Le Chiendent* (1933). At one level the novel is a study in the relation of appearance to reality. It starts with an unnamed silhouette which by stages acquires full human status. Sartre's Roquentin declares that his existence depends on his thought, but by that he means that his existence takes its significance from his thought. In *Le Chiendent* Etienne literally takes on three dimensions only as he acquires the power to think. Finally he becomes 'visible' to other men — Mme Cloche recognises him as the man almost run over by a taxi outside the Gare du Nord; he has the right now to be given a name, Etienne Marcel. From this point on the absurdity of the world is completely revealed to him, neither he nor anything around him is stable or predictable. There is a further complication in the philosophical position posited by Queneau. For Etienne's transformation depends in part on its being observed, in this case by an anonymous observer who himself later takes on a role in the text. When eventually the mysterious Pierre, the observer, disappears, Etienne, now unobserved, begins the gradual process of deflation which returns him to one dimension at the end of the novel. Pierre also takes on the role of philosophical mentor, instructing Etienne in the detection of the deceptiveness of appearances. The comedy of the novel derives precisely from the imprudence of the other characters in failing to recognise this deceptiveness. Mme Cloche for example insists on forcing all experience into a pattern; hence her belief that Etienne, Pierre and Narceuse are gangsters and that the old rag'n'bone man, Grampa Taupe, is a millionaire. Taupe's blue door is in fact the main deceptive object in a large part of the novel. Taken out of its context, that is, no longer functioning as a door but merely hanging on a wall, it precipitates a series of absurd explanations all of which assume that its appearance masks a set of serious realities. When there is found to be no treasure behind the door, the whole process of deflating the fictional world can begin. In the final episode the characters, acknowledging that they are only a part of a book, undertake to suppress themselves, to obliterate everything and simply start again. It would be difficult to talk of the philosophical proposition of the novel as more than the occasion for showing that life and fiction are equally absurd, in both senses of the word.

New mythologies
Anouilh and Queneau, as I have said, acknowledge the absurdist view of the world without accepting either the philosophical or literary consequences of it drawn by their contemporaries. Two more recent writers have broken more radically with the absurdist tradition in creating their own mythologies of modern man. The older of the two, Julien Gracq, has philosophical affinities with the surrealists and earlier traditions of irrational poetry, affinities confirmed by his critical essays on André Breton, Poe, Lautréamont and Rimbaud. Surrealists have tended, particularly since World War II, to put emphasis on the need for a new mythology to express the gap between human desire and the means available to satisfy it and to embody a potential solution to the problems posed by this permanent conflict. Artaud in *Textes mexicains pour un nouveau mythe* (1953) and Benjamin Péret in *Anthologie des mythes, légendes et contes populaires d'Amérique* (1959) looked to Central and South America for possible sources, but others have seen the anti-rationalist qualities of Celtic myth as equally fruitful. It is not surprising then that Gracq's first two novels, *Au Château d'Argol* (1939) and *Un beau ténébreux* (1945) and the title story of *La Presqu'île* (1970) are all set in Brittany, the centre of France's Celtic tradition, or that his play *Le Roi pêcheur* (1948) is based on an episode from the Grail legend (to which thematic allusion is also made in *Au Château d'Argol*). This is not to say that Gracq uses pre-existing myths as a special kind of intellectual or emotional vehicle in the way that Giraudoux and Sartre do. He is not using a familiar framework to promote new responses to details. He is developing a new interpretation of existence which has its roots in a particular medieval tradition.

His introduction to *Le Roi pêcheur* is rich in indications of what he considers the function of myth to be. As one might expect from the man who wrote of Kleist's *Penthesilea*, which he translated in 1954, that like all truly symbolic works the play had no precise meaning, he is anxious to preserve the open-endedness of myth. Hence his distaste for the closed circle of fault and retribution inherent in both classical and Christian traditions. In the Arthurian cycle, with its 'elective community' and quests for the suprahuman, he finds a particular resonance:

> The companionship of the Round Table, the passionate quest for an ideal treasure which, however obstinately it withdraws, is always represented to us as within our grasp, these figure . . . quite easily as a background reference — an indefinite reverberation — for certain of the most typical aspects of contemporary phenomena, among them surrealism.

It is particularly the status given to desire, the temptation of absolute love which Tristan represents, the temptation of divinity embodied in Perceval, which Gracq finds significant. He is emphatic that the Christian overtones of Arthurian myth, especially the Grail stories, are an accretion. Their symbolism can express a wider concept of man's search for the meaning of existence than the traditional religious interpretation permits.

Gracq's first novel *Au Château d'Argol* is set in an atmosphere only one remove from the legendary events of *Le Roi pêcheur*. Its hero, Albert, like Perceval, has begun his quest for complete knowledge at the age of fifteen, and is particularly interested in the inner meaning of myths. In his Gothic retreat Albert is visited by Herminien, 'his double and his opposite', and by Heide, a hauntingly beautiful girl who incarnates the temptation of the feminine principle. These characters, according to Gracq's own 'Avis au lecteur', are involved in a demonic version of the Parsifal story, demonic because Herminien represents the evil side of Albert's own nature and because the moral values of the book are deliberately confused. The tension that builds up between Albert and Herminien leads to a vicious attack by the latter on Heide in the forest and thence to Albert's discovery of his own fascination with blood, in the form of Heide's wound. It is in the attempt to free himself from this attraction that he murders Herminien. So that what began as a quest for metaphysical revelation ends in violence. Throughout this narrative a sense of foreboding and fatality are maintained; for example, Albert carves Heide's name on a cross without yet knowing who she is. What is not clear is how far the action represents destruction and failure, how far purification and achievement. As with Perceval's decision not to see the Grail at the end of *Le Roi pêcheur*, the symbolism is deliberately ambiguous.

Un beau ténébreux transposes the same themes a stage closer to the surface of modern life. The remote location this time is a hotel, the isolated group among whom the drama is played out are youngish people on holiday; each of them has a type role, sometimes clear — Jacques the adolescent, Irene carnal womanhood — sometimes indefinite — Gérard, dreamer endowed with some kind of second sight, Christel elect spirit destined for sorrow. At the core of the novel is the figure of Allan, the *'beau ténébreux'* of the title, who awakens instant fascination or hostility in the other characters. He is a catalyst bringing destruction yet like Perceval a man in motion unlike the static world around him. As Christel puts it in her letter to Gérard:

> In the middle of so many people at rest, who are as comfortable and non-existent as furniture, he is moving, already going somewhere. He has the look of a traveller at the carriage window as the train slowly begins to start off.

The climax of the story is again highly ambiguous, for Allan's search for the meaning of existence (he himself compares it to the Grail quest) leads him to suicide, despite the efforts of Gérard and Christel to deflect him. His death is an act of pride, a desire to achieve god-like status in the eyes of the faithful. Yet at the same time it is an act into which he has been forced. In an interesting image, Gérard, in his forebodings, has prepared us for just this ambiguity. He observes that the part of the Christ story which most appeals to him is the period between the Resurrection and Ascension, when mysterious forces seem at work everywhere, and there is an immediate contrast between the feverish activity of the initiates, aware that their hero is about to go away, and the hostility of the settled part of humanity, 'that taste for merciless man-hunting which awakens in the heart of closed families'. The tension between the real world and a man who, far more than Hugo's Hernani, has the right to say of himself 'I am a force in motion', leads to revelation for the few and destruction for the hero himself, but the destruction remains a higher destiny than that of those who refuse life's possibilities by their acceptance of compromise and convention.

This theme of electing for death is developed further in Gracq's third novel, *Le Rivage des Syrtes* (selected for the Prix Goncourt in 1951, though the author indignantly rejected the award in protest against the whole French prize system). At times one feels uneasily that this novel has moved too far towards the paradox which Giraudoux expresses in *Electre*, for the hero Aldo arouses his fatherland, Orsenna, from the state of torpor in which it has lain for three hundred years by deliberately provoking a war with the neighbouring state of Farghestan which will completely annihilate Orsenna. Like Electre, who is in Giralducian terms also a creature of destiny, Aldo cures spiritual malaise at the price of complete physical destruction. This rather clumsily abstract novel does, however, emphasise a new aspect, anticipation, which is almost the entire subject of *Un Balcon en forêt* (1958). This could hardly be more different from its predecessors in superficial subject, since it is set in the Ardennes during the 'phoney war' period before the German offensive there in May 1940. In fact, however, familiar themes reassert themselves. Grange the central character grows to find spiritual fulfilment in his dream-like communion with the forest where he is stationed in an isolated outpost. A mediator in this fulfilment is Mona, another incarnation of the special power of love. But spiritual fulfilment leads to detachment from physical reality: Grange ignores the imminent reality of the war, and allows himself to be killed (if his final falling asleep *is* death) by the inevitable German attack.

In his last major work, *La Presqu'île*, a collection of three long stories, the tension between mind and body is presented in a much less violent form. 'La route' and 'Le roi Cophetua' are stories touched by war in the background, but the long central story which gives its name to the collection is another study in waiting, set in the Breton countryside. Simon is waiting at the station for Irmgard; the whole of the story is outlined in his passing thought: '. . . she won't come . . . Perhaps it's even better if she doesn't come now'. When she fails to come by the morning train, he decides to spend the rest of the day exploring the peninsula where he had spent his childhood holidays, before returning to the station in the evening. What follows is a long exploration of the form and mood of the Breton landscape intercut with Simon's anxieties. The mythical level is kept to odd images and references, for example, '. . . it was almost like the thickets of thorn bush and the more than usually drab stretches of moorland which lead travellers astray on the very edge of the Castle Perilous'. Gradually Simon realises that meaning and pleasure lie more in expectation than in fulfilment. Irmgard's arrival is an anticlimax:

> . . . he felt that the hollow opening up within him for joy was not filling; all that was left was a neutral rather abstract feeling of security which was doubtless happiness at finding Irmgard again.

The *doubtless* undercuts all. Simon's quest is over; he is condemned to stasis.

Gracq's attempts to extend ideas explored by the surrealists within a highly controlled literary form are aimed at establishing a mythical framework valid for man in general. Michel Tournier's myths are more egocentric in their origins. The key to an understanding of his work lies in the long autobiographical and critical essay *Le vent Paraclet* (1977). Tournier's masters appear to be a curious bunch, from Gaston Bachelard, whose critical method was based on Jungian archetypes, to Roger Nimier, the author of five novels of fashionably disenchanted youth-cult who killed himself at the wheel of his Aston Martin in 1962. He is particularly amusing about Sartre, whose *L'Etre et le Néant* had been the philosophical bombshell of his adolescence but whose subsequent development as the leader of a School and supporter of Good Causes occasioned him considerable disillusion:

> Sartre seems always to have suffered from excessive moral scruples. The throbbing fear of slipping into what he considers the camp of the 'dishonest' has undoubtedly diminished his strength and his creative power. You cannot live healthily and fully, I believe, without a minimum of indifference for the ills of others ... Perhaps one should go further. Perhaps this Marxist has never been able to give up the secret ambition to become a saint.

Equally enlightening is his analysis of the necessity he felt to discover a myth which would bridge the gap between his metaphysical perceptions and the form of the novel, a bridge which he sees myth as essentially designed to create, because its basis is pure story, while its upper tiers pass through theory of knowledge, ethics, metaphysics and ontology without ceasing to be the same tale. His attraction to myth is, however, not purely formalist. He thinks it to be an essential part of the formation of the human consciousness:

> Man only becomes man, acquires a human sex, heart and imagination thanks to the murmur of stories and the kaleidoscope of images which surround the baby in its cradle and accompany it right to the tomb.

At the same time myth should not become fixed or allegorical. It is the writer's job to extend and modify myths, keeping them living creative forces in his society.

Tournier's first novel, *Vendredi, ou les limbes du Pacifique* (1967), takes as its base the Robinson Crusoe story, which he considers a myth generative of its own modern versions, from the *Swiss Family Robinson* and Jules Verne's *L'Ile mystérieuse* to Giraudoux's *Suzanne et le Pacifique* and Saint-John Perse's *Images à Crusoé*. The Robinson myth exemplified certain fundamental aspects of man's condition in the twentieth century. In particular, it represents the overcoming of the dangers of solitude — solitude as danger because, 'As society progresses in well-being and freedom of time you can see falling by the wayside an increasing number of victims too weak to support the isolation which is the corollary of these two "achievements"'. Secondly, through the figure of Man Friday, whose mythological status has only become possible in the age of the ethnographer, the story offers a counter to the whole contemporary concept of civilisation. In *Vendredi* Tournier has attempted to show Robinson being stripped down to the basic psychological elements of man, under the pressure of the solitude he undergoes, and then with the pure help of Friday tentatively creating a new mode of being.

His second novel, *Le Roi des Aulnes* (1970), is more complex, less derivative. The narrative concerns Abel Tiffauges, a garage mechanic whose negative childhood and adolescence cut him off from his fellow men. Taken prisoner in 1940 he ends up in Eastern Prussia, where he gradually finds fulfilment denied him in his native France. His employment at the hunting reserve at Romintern, Göring's special haunt, leads to his transfer to a *napola*, special SS military schools for the young, at Kaltenborn. Here he becomes a one-man pressgang, collecting fresh flesh for cannon fodder, until the destruction of his charges at the hands of the advancing Russian troops causes him to leave, bearing off to an ambiguous death in the marshes Ephraim, a Jewish boy whom he had rescued.

This narrative is only significant as a vehicle for the symbols and meditations around which the intellectual core of the novel develops. There are two major areas of focus: Nazi Germany, and the theme of the prisoner who finds his 'homeland' in exile and his liberty in captivity. Linking them is the myth of the Ogre, represented both by Abel and by fascism in its generality. What Tournier calls 'the ogress vocation' of the Nazi régime is reflected in its youth-cult, for example, the incorporation of all ten-year-olds into youth organisations on 19 April each year, the eve of Hitler's birthday, which makes the Führer into a Minotaur figure 'for whose birthday an offering is made of an entire generation of little children'. Less metaphorically the preparation of the boys at Kaltenborn for the sacrifice of their flesh to the political mania of Hitler represents a similar offering to the ogre.

Tiffauges is an ogre in a more intangible sense. His magic powers certainly exist within his own conviction. When he is to be disciplined at school he wishes the school would burn down, and it does. War breaks out and saves him from trial for a rape he has not committed. He also has an appetite for anything fresh, which leads to an especial attraction to children. The malefic aspect of this fascination is implied both by the title of the novel, with its reference to the sprite in Goethe's poem who abducts and kills a child, and by Abel's role in forcibly recruiting boys for the *napola*. But the 'carrying off' motif is linked to a 'carrying' motif, for which he uses the term *phorie*, connected with St Christopher for example. The theme of *phorie* runs through the images of the entire book. In the moment when he lifts the wounded Jeannot in his arms at the garage Abel experiences a total ecstasy for which he then seeks symbols and analogues in the world around him and in myth (Atlas, Hermes, even Adam in the curious hermaphroditic image Abel creates of him). It is in

Kaltenborn, where he becomes both servant and master, that his cult of *phorie* reaches its climax. The ambiguity of this state of both serving and controlling what can be benevolent or destructive is never finally resolved.

We are not merely dealing with the psychological case of an individual, even one whose *amor fati* leads him to espouse and develop the direction he is apparently already destined to take. The speech of the Commandant of Kaltenborn to Abel reminds us that Tiffauges the ogre and Hitler the ogre are two faces of the same phenomenon:

> The signs are powerful, Tiffauges. They have brought you here. The signs are quick to anger. A flouted sign becomes diabolic. From a centre of light and harmony it makes itself into a power of darkness and destruction. Your vocation has revealed to you the existence of *phorie*, its malefic inversion, and saturation. You have still to learn the ultimate in the mechanism of these symbols, *the union of these three figures into a single one synonymous with apocalypse.*

The Commandant goes on to explain the malefic inversion of *phorie*, in which the thing carried usurps the function of the carrier: Abel has already glimpsed the way in which war itself has usurped the functions of the warrior by placing man *inside* his weapons, the tank, the aeroplane. The Nazis are thus the end of a metaphysical process, unleashing an Apocalypse in which, symbolically, the death scene of Abel's three charges, Haro, Haio and Lothar, speared on their swords, forms a coat-of-arms fit for an ogre — both Abel and Hitler. Here is the fulfilment of Abel's words at the beginning of the novel:

> Yes, I believe in my magical nature, I mean in that secret connivance which closely entwines my own adventure with the course of things.

In Tournier's third novel, *Les Météores*, the move away from a unilinear, literary myth, as in *Vendredi*, to a cluster of inter-related motifs creating a 'new' myth is complete. It is impossible to define the work in terms of plot, since it consists of a complex thematic structure which is overlaid on a sketchy chronological development involving a pair of identical twins, their parents Edouard and Maria-Barbara and their homosexual paternal uncle, Alexandre. The theme of isolation previously studied in Robinson and Abel now becomes the more complex phenomenon of isolation-in-companionship represented by the twins, Jean and Paul. At one level this is extended to an examination of the couple, represented by Edouard and Maria-Barbara and by various people encountered by the twins on their (separate) travels around the world. In counterpoint is the elaborate presentation of the theme of homosexuality through the adventures and aggressive commentaries of Alexandre. The relationship between the twins overlaps with both issues, through their incest on the one hand and Jean's attempt to break out into a separate relationship with Sophie on the other. Tournier's belief that the novelist should reveal his characters by allowing them to 'explain' themselves leads to the construction of a series of partial arguments about the relative achievements of each type of relationship. For example, Thomas Koussek, an old schoolfriend of Alexandre's, elaborates a contrast between hetero- and homosexuality based on the notion that contemporary heterosexuals, in attempting to negate the procreative function of their act, are aping homosexuality in the same way that M. Jourdain in Molière's *Le Bourgeois gentilhomme* apes the aristocracy. Much later in the novel Paul uses the same comparison to contrast twinship with homosexuality. This time it is the homosexual who is the would-be usurper:

> Homosexuals are like the *Bourgeois Gentilhomme*. Their common birth destines them for utilitarian tasks and family life, but they crazily lay claim to the life of disinterested play of a gentleman [ie, a twin].

These views are modified again when Paul meets Ralph, surviving partner of a heterosexual partnership which had tried to achieve twin-like status by geographical isolation. And all these various relationships have to be re-evaluated in the light of Paul's final discoveries about himself, after the 'disappearance' of Jean.

The novel does not confine itself to these limited areas of meaning. The twin relationship also raises questions of heredity and environment which become part of a mythology of personality. Paul wishes to conserve the perfection of the twinship:

> This game had only one aim: . . . to cleanse us of the contamination from the atmosphere of dialectic in which we had been steeped, despite ourselves, since our lapse into temporality, and to restore to us the eternal, unmoving, unchangeable identity with which we are by right endowed.

Jean reacts against this stasis, firstly in his failed relationship with Sophie, then in travel; he subjects himself entirely to environment just as his brother confines himself to heredity. The realisation to which Paul comes is that, for twins, there is always a third element. The 'space' separating identical twins is part of their unit:

> This inter-twin space — the soul unfurled — is capable of limitless extension or contraction. It can be reduced almost to nothing when identical twin brothers sleep intertwined so as to make an oval shape. But if one of them goes a long way away the 'space' stretches and becomes finer — without ever actually tearing — until its dimensions envelop earth and sky.

Paul's final adventure in his pursuit of Jean involves him in the amputation of his left arm and leg, as a result of being trapped in an underground tunnel while escaping from East Berlin. Setting aside the political implications of tying the twins' ultimate separation to the moment when the Berlin Wall is being built to divide the two Germanies irrevocably, we can see in the final vision of the bed-ridden Paul the same sort of achievement by *'amor fati'* that was Abel's destiny. In the development of his phantom limbs he feels the presence of his brother. By making their 'inter-twin space' infinite, they have mystically annulled it.

  These very difficult ideas are expressed through complex metaphors of time and weather which recur as leitmotivs, from the twins' childhood relationship with the mental defective, Frantz, who is governed by the calendar and the seasons, through to Paul's final aspirations to dominate the elements as a prerequisite for re-absorbing Jean into the twin unit. Paul is associated with precision, the calendar, the clock, Jean with natural phenomena; there are, in particular, references to Jules Vernes' *Around the World in Eight Days*, comparing Paul to Phileas Fogg with his determination to control time and weather, and Jean to Passepartout, the rover who relates intuitively to his environment. The association of twins with the elements, especially in view of the ambiguity *ciel* (both 'sky' and 'heaven') and the complex discussions of the various meanings of Hebrew *ruah* ('wind' and 'holy spirit'), has metaphysical overtones which raises twinship to full mythical status.

  Although Tournier's approach to myth as a vehicle for metaphysics in the novel is very different from Gracq's, they both stem from a surrealist tradition. Indeed certain aspects, like the status given to chance and the use of *amor fati*, are common to both. But whereas Gracq derives from the Gothic side of French literature, Tournier compares his techniques with those of the surrealist *painters*. Just as the latter took ultra-realism to the point where it destroyed itself, Tournier wants to take classical metaphysics and build out of it systems which fracture its rational framework. He seems to regret the death of the antique concept of wisdom as identifiable with the totality of human experience and to reject the division of mental and affective activity introduced during the eighteenth century. His concept of the absolute gives unique status to each person, each phenomenon, each experience, a status that can only be achieved by isolation, the isolation of Robinson's island, of the closed garden (there is a lot on gardens in *Les Météores*). It is a harsh philosophy — one can see why he was so attracted to *L'Etre et le Néant* — but a challenging one, expressed in a thought-provoking manner.

The range of philosophical literature in modern France has been expanding consistently in both form and content such that it is almost impossible to draw any conclusions about aesthetic principles. It is however noticeable that the 'intellectual' novel or play accounts for only a small proportion of the works we have been looking at. Though it is possible to hold that Cocteau, Giraudoux and Anouilh subordinate intellect to aesthetics in a rather frivolous way, it is more difficult to make the same charge stick against most post-war prose writers, even Queneau. Even the highly rational premisses of a Sartre or Camus are most effectively communicated through the filter of a temperament, Roquentin, Garcin, Meursault, Clamence. It is, however, the mythologisers in the broadest sense who seem to have created the most subtle expressions of contemporary dilemmas, in works as strikingly different as *Ondine, En attendant Godot, Un beau ténébreux, Les Météores.*

CHAPTER 6
Christian Convictions

> Operationally, God is beginning to resemble not a ruler but the last fading smile of a cosmic Cheshire cat. (Julian Huxley)

It is all too easy to suppose that philosophical speculation in twentieth-century France, and the reflection of such speculation in literature, is a phenomenon from which religious thought is excluded. This is untrue. Setting aside for the moment the question of non-Christian belief, there has been an active renewal of Catholic speculation on theological and moral issues which has influenced literary expression in all genres. The alliance between the Church and the Nationalists, as exemplified in the influence of the *Action française* movement (until the Papal condemnation of it in 1926), indicates the strength of ecclesiastical conservatism. This was more than counterbalanced by more radical forces. Even Jacques Maritain (1882-1973), who initially sympathised with the theological traditionalists and developed a neo-Thomist approach hostile to the prevailing Bergsonism, was to disassociate himself in *La Primauté du spirituel* (1927) from the political aims of the Right. Later, at the time of the Spanish Civil War, he strove, as did Mauriac and Bernanos, to prevent any compromise between Church and fascism. Maritain's theological conservatism was intended to defend the primacy of intellect, something that secular movements in philosophy were also attempting. At the same time he rejected philosophical, moral and social materialism.

At the opposite pole to Maritain, Maurice Blondel (1862-1949) borrows from Bergson's arguments against reason. In *L'Action* (1893, revised 1936-7) and *La Pensée* (1934) he argued for a greater role for intuition and action, attempting to revive a mystical attitude to the transcendental. Blondel's existentialist approach to Christian ethics can be accounted a force behind Marc Sangnier's Social Catholic movement *Le Sillon*, a forerunner of the worker-priest movement. The former is evoked in Mauriac's *L'Enfant chargé de chaînes* (1912); the latter is documented in Gilbert Cesbron's novel *Les Saints vont en enfer* (1953).

Finally, there is the most distinguished of the Catholic philosophers, Gabriel Marcel (1889-1973) whose *Journal métaphysique* (1927) and *Etre et avoir* (1935) propound what has come to be known as Christian existentialism. The form of his philosophical works is an indication of the way in which the thought they embody has been formulated. They are meditations upon the experience of spiritual life, without any attempt at systematic deduction from rational principles. Marcel's philosophy is exceptionally difficult, maintaining as it does an idealist element, a phenomenological element and a belief in knowledge by faith. It can be broadly defined as anti-Thomist and pro-Bergsonian. In his interpretation of human existence there are three central notions: the fact that the individual is inseparable from his physical incarnation, the fact that he resides in a particular situation definable not only spatially and temporally but also as a constantly developing phenomenon related to the existence of one's fellow creatures, and the fact that the self develops its individuality through action, in conscious confrontation with the basic situations of existence. The full meaning of this human condition only becomes clear in the context of the kind of devotion to the good of others which exalts us beyond our limits and sets us in motion towards transcendence. The approach to a transcendental reality, in other words religious experience, can be understood through an interpretation of certain human experiences such as hoping, promising, loyalty and trust, which cause such exaltation.

As with so many existentialist writers, Marcel achieves the most forceful communication of his ideas in his plays, which he saw as acting out in concrete terms what he elsewhere meditates upon in abstract form. A typical example is the problem of authenticity, so important for Gide and Sartre. Are we what we think we are? Marcel investigates this in the best of his early plays, *Un Homme de Dieu* (1925). Claude Lemoyne, a successful and devoted Protestant pastor, had forgiven his wife Edmée for deceiving him with another man in the early years of their marriage, and had accepted her illegitimate child, Osmonde, as his own. Now the other man, Michel, about to die, wishes to see his daughter. Suddenly the motives for past actions are called into question. Did Edmée admit what she had done because she was afraid of Michel and felt certain of getting Claude's pity? Did Claude deny his own human reactions and pardon Edmée as a professional gesture? These questions are not of merely historical interest, for they undermine the characters' confidence in their entire personalities:

> Claude: Did I love you then? And did you love me? We can't remember. Perhaps we never knew. On the strength of a glance, an inflexion, you committed your life. A glance promising . . . what? That mysterious promise hasn't been kept, and that's the whole story of our life together . . . And when I think of God, it's the same. I've sometimes thought I heard him speaking to me, but perhaps it was only my heightened state deceiving me. Who am I? When I try to come to grips with myself, I slip out of my own grasp.   (Act IV sc 11)

Claude has confused himself and his role as priest, with

disastrous results. The problem, for Marcel, is that people see self-knowledge as possession, a reduction of the self to the state of object, whereas the indivisible and continuous process of being cannot be 'known' in that way.

This philosophical problem, which forms the basis of the later essay 'Etre et avoir', is further developed in another of Marcel's major plays, *Le Monde cassé* (1933), whose concrete examples are generalised in the essay 'Positions et approches concrètes du mystère ontologique' which was published as a postface to the play. *Le Monde cassé* contains the first of Marcel's sustained satirical attacks on the contemporary world, painted in the same terms of decadence as one finds in novels of the period, from Drieu la Rochelle's *L'Homme couvert de femmes* to Sartre's *L'Age de raison* (and on into the works of Françoise Sagan). This satire is not an end in itself. The central character, Christiane Chesnaye, lives in a world of superficial amusement whose inner aimlessness and anguish finds its logical end in the suicide of her friend Denise. Her husband Laurent mistakes his own weakness and self-doubt for a liberated attitude to adult relationships. This world of marital indifference and feverish pursuit of pleasure turns out not to be 'reality' for Christiane, as she herself already dimly perceives in the first act:

> Don't you sometimes have the feeling that we live . . . if you can call it living . . . in a broken world. Yes, broken, like a broken watch.

Christiane had loved Jacques Decroy, who joined the Benedictine order. When she learns of his death, it seems as if the underlying and unacknowledged reason for her not giving herself entirely up to the nihilism of the world around her (or even to suicide) has disappeared. But just as the force of her unrealised love had partially saved her despite her separation from Jacques, so it can transcend his death, for his sister Geneviève reveals that he had eventually been wakened to his own love for Christiane, and had found a profound religious significance in it which he prayed that she might share. The play ends on a note of hope. Christiane will transfer into her previously meaningless relationship with Laurent the lesson of human communion which she has learned:

> We're not alone; no-one is alone . . . There is a communion of sinners . . . There is a communion of Saints . . . Laurent, I am your wife.
> (Act IV sc7)

Christiane's 'soul' had been separated from her life. The miracle of enlightenment which comes to her via Geneviève not only reincorporates her soul within herself but restores her contact with the mystical supra-reality from which modern life has become detached.

The rejection of reason
With the exception of Marcel, particular schools of theological thought are rarely individually reflected in the novels, plays and poetry of the period. One can however detect certain general attachments. The major Catholic writers tend to an anti-intellectual, or at least a mystical, position, extending as far as the near-pantheism of Alphonse de Chateaubriant in *Monsieur des Lourdines* (1911), *La Brière* (1923) and *La Réponse du Seigneur* (1933), in the first of which, for example, the eponymous hero communicates through the music of his violin the divine love which will prevent Anthime's suicide. The later plays of Claudel are extreme examples of the exclusion of reason, continuing to celebrate the doctrines embodied in *L'Annonce faite à Marie*. The trilogy *L'Otage, Le Pain dur* and *Le Père humilié* (1910-16) deal with what, in Claudelian terms, could be called the birth of the modern world: the collapse of the *Ancien régime* personified by Georges and Sygne de Coûfontaine in the first play, the triumph of materialism under the Restoration in the second, and the end to the temporal power of the Papacy (in the dying

year of the French Second Empire) in the third. But the underlying themes are still the need for total submission to God and redemption through sacrifice, together with the complex inter-relation of divine and human love which had received its fullest expression hitherto in the autobiographical *Partage de midi*.

The completest expression of the Claudelian universe is to be found in *Le Soulier de satin* (1924). Rodrigue, whose youthful career enables him to incarnate the full potential of the Nietzschean Will to Power, and Prouhèze, whose marriage to the elderly don Pélage has taught her peace without her ever experiencing the creative benefits of suffering, are destined to love one another, but to be for ever physically separated (generally at least a continent apart). What they love in one another, through the symbol of their mutual passion, is the divine love that motivates them both. Their complex sufferings, involving Prouhèze's remarriage to the satanic Camille, eventual renegade to Islam, and Rodrigue's final disgrace in the king's service, allow Claudel to bring into the play not merely another drama of thwarted love but a whole picture of the Renaissance world and of the triumphs that are achieved in God's name whatever the temporal loss to the individual.

Universality is sought in a different way in the poetry of Patrice de la Tour du Pin. For him, too, the relationship between human and divine love is a central issue. In his major work, the *Somme de poésie* (1946-59), he explores it through a series of mystical allegories of man's development, placed within the framework of an assertion of the mystery of the poet's self. In the second part of the work, a mixture of verse and prose, the presence of love which has been defined in the first part is now traced in the disarray of the modern world via the spiritual journey of a central character, André Vincentenaire.

La Tour du Pin's approach to his religion differs in one vital respect from Claudel's, in that he acknowledges man's anguish in the face of his condition. In this he is close to the two other major metaphysical poets of the century, Pierre-Jean Jouve (1887-1976) and Pierre Emmanuel. Emmanuel sums up the notion perfectly in one of his volumes of autobiography, *Qui est cet homme* (1947):

> ... the anguish of being embedded in rock, agonisingly forced into shape, is a feeling I have known since childhood, and today I see in it far more than an adolescent obsession. It is man's eternal condition.

In his poetry, particularly in his major collections *Sodome* (1944) and *Babel* (1951), and in *Jacob* (1970), this anguish is expressed through the idea of man as exiled from God and feeling his exile as a short-coming in himself. All action must be a striving towards total union with the divine principle. Like La Tour du Pin, but without his wishy-washy Lamartinean allegory, Emmanuel clothes his central ideas in mythical symbols. He defines the images in which he works as deriving from two sources, the agony of Christ in the tomb, neither human nor yet divine, from Good Friday to Easter Sunday, and the figure of Orpheus in Hades reaching out to take Eurydice and finding it is Christ he has seized upon. The Orpheus image represents the poet's descent into his own consciousness in order to come to terms with the significance of death and the problem of God's existence as posed by the Christ image. Clearly one is not dealing with orthodox dogma but with transcendental myths of highly personal significance yet rooted in the biblical tradition. What seems important to the poet is not the definition of the nature of faith but the continual expression of being possessed by the problem of faith.

Jouve's poetry has little overt Christian reference, and yet it is often strongly reminiscent of Christian doctrines, particularly those dear to Claudel. In *Le Paradis perdu* (1929) he presents what is clearly a personal spiritual quest. He takes a pessimistic, almost Manichean, view of the place of evil in the universe, identifying lust as the primary sin. *Les Noces* (1931) suggests the pursuit of mythical union with a divine presence whose nature is only dimly comprehended. The themes of voluntary suffering and renunciation as necessary preparation for such a union are central (one could make comparison with *Le Soulier de satin*). In his later work a greater awareness of contemporary events shows through, as in the Apocalyptic attitude to war in *La Vierge de Paris* (1946), though Jouve never comes close to the degree of commitment which Emmanuel sometimes shows. Both poets could be said to see in art man's quest for spiritual certainty. In Jouve's words:

> *Tout poème a Dieu pour témoin et coeur et vrai receptacle*
> *Tout chant est substance à Dieu et même si Dieu absent*

[Every poem has God as its witness, heart and true repository/ Every song is substance to God even if God be absent].

A world without God

A mystical approach to religion predominates in the novelists of the period too, but the surface of their work is quite different. 'Even if God be absent' could be taken as their epigraph. Nonetheless, they handle many of the same themes. An obsession with the relationship between human and divine love, for example, can be found in much of the work of François Mauriac (1885-1970). In his essay *Souffrances et bonheur du chrétien* he went so far as to suggest that the sensual and spiritual could never co-exist within a man, although they might alternate. Evil is symbolised by sexuality, as *Le Mal* (1924, but revised 1952) is devoted to showing us. Marriage is no solution; in his *Journal* it is referred to as a 'caricature of divine union'. Hence its portraiture as a state in which physical and spiritual dissatisfaction cause equal frustration. Two of Mauriac's major novels, *Le Baiser au lepreux* and *Génétrix*, are concerned entirely with this theme. But although the rejection of human love is an important motif in these novels, it is at best equal with Mauriac's other obsession, the destructiveness of the family unit.

Even when trying to portray a family unit as a positive force in life, as in *Le Mystère Frontenac* (1933), Mauriac's approach is, as John Flower has pointed out, equivocal. Although the marriage of Blanche and Michel seems to have been emotionally fulfilling, the other relationships described, particularly of Jean-Louis and Madeleine and of uncle Xavier and his mistress Josefa, are conditioned by the patterns of bourgeois relationships which Mauriac elsewhere condemns. Where his attitude to the family is consciously negative, as in *Le Noeud de vipères* (1932), it becomes the microcosm of the faults of humanity. Of all his novels it can be generalised that they portray a world in which material wealth is ruthlessly pursued, spiritual values are ignored or decried or are distorted hypocritical conformism, and affection is betrayed. In *Le Noeud de vipères* the intense hatred between husband and wife, the scheming of the family and the superficiality of traditional Catholicism are violently presented. Here, however, for the first time we also find a degree of redemption, in the genuine affection between old Louis and his granddaughter Janine, and in Louis' gradual awakening to the love of God, which the diary form of the book allows us to infer near the close of the story.

This raises an important question. In what sense are Mauriac's novels expressions of his religious beliefs? In *Le Noeud de vipères* Louis' conversion is meant to demonstrate the workings of Grace, something shown more clumsily in later works such as *La Fin de la nuit* (1936) and *La Pharisienne* (1941). The earlier works have no such overt reference. They are nonetheless the product of a Christian perception of life. Mauriac is obsessed with sin. The world which he evokes is divided between those who are too self-satisfied to be aware of the evil within them, as with the whole Desqueyroux clan in *Thérèse Desqueyroux* (1927) and those whose very desperation marks them out as redeemable. Thérèse herself is a prime example. Married to a man who is coarse and insensitive, condemned to a stifling *ennui* by the materialism, small-mindedness and hypocrisy of her environment, she tries to break out by gradually poisoning her husband. The greater sin, it is hinted, is not hers, for her rebellion is a sign of an inner yearning to transcend the limitations of a profoundly irreligious society. Accessibility to the Devil is paradoxically a mark of potential accessibility to God. How successful Mauriac is in making the reader aware of what he calls 'the wretchedness of man without God' is a problem I shall look at shortly.

Sexuality as evil
The same obsession with sin, especially in the form of sexuality, plays an important role in the works of Julien Green (1900-). His four volumes of autobiography, *Partir avant le jour, Mille chemins ouverts, Terre lointaine* and *Jeunesse*, portray very vividly both his spiritual odyssey and his discovery of his own sexuality (homo-erotic). As late as 1949 he writes in his *Journal*:

> The truth I have come to after so many years of struggling and reflexion is that I hate the sexual instinct . . .

the end of which phrase is echoed in the mouth of Joseph Day, the violently puritan hero of *Moïra* (1950). Green's vision of the relationship between human and divine love is not, in fact, simply the negative vision of Mauriac, for he retains his awareness that sexual instinct too comes from God. The problem of the double instinct within man of the spiritual and the carnal is therefore an issue of great importance. As he expresses it elsewhere in his *Journal*:

> You hear the body and soul spoken of as if the body were the container and the soul the contents . . . Between the two there is no perceptible dividing line, or none at least which is not crossed every minute as if it

were not there. The soul is to be reached via the body and the body via the soul; there lies the whole drama of the human condition, which makes such mysterious creatures of us.

Although one can see constant thematic obsessions in Green's work, particularly with death, sexuality and the notion that material reality may be less real than some transcendent alternative, there is also a considerable modulation of attitudes which coincides with his own intellectual crises. Born a Protestant, he was converted to Catholicism at the age of sixteen, only to lose his faith as a result of his inner conflict between faith and physical desire:

> Later I turned away from Christ because he was a barrier to the slaking of my carnal appetite, but I dared not deny him completely. I tried to ignore his existence; I could not contrive that he forget mine.
> (*Mille chemins ouverts*)

Over a long period he returned slowly to Catholicism via an interest in Buddhism (reflected particularly in *Varouna*, 1940). The only works of his which are strictly Christian are *Moïra*, *Chaque homme dans sa nuit* (1960), and the plays of the same period, particularly *L'Ennemi* (1954). It is accordingly dangerous to examine ideas from any of his works out of their chronological context, and even more dangerous to quote from his *Journal* without reference to the period of writing.

In the early novels such as *Adrienne Mesurat* (1927) and *Leviathan* (1929) the world is filled with a violence and despair that outstrips Mauriac's efforts to suggest the absence of God. The sinners are compelled to their actions by unidentified dark inner forces. In *Minuit* (1936), parts one and two portray the *ennui* and terror of the human condition, but part three suggests a metaphysical solution which will allow man both to escape from the limits of his condition and to transcend death (the only way out envisaged in the earlier novels). The precise nature of this transcendence is unclear, but the prerequisite for it is significant. In attempting to escape from the castle of

Fontfroide with Elisabeth, Serge, her lover, falls to his death. She in turn falls, but is 'saved' by the mystical figure of the dead M. Agnel, whose name and role suggest something akin to a Christ figure. Salvation, then, is at the cost of a renunciation of physical love.

It is in *Moïra* that this problem is first developed within a Christian context. The novel can be read in the light of the third volume of Green's autobiography, *Terre lointaine* (1966), in which the author's experiences at the University of Virginia (USA) are described. In the novel he proceeds in a rather Gidean way to take certain tendencies in himself and project them in an extreme form. The protagonist, Joseph Day, is a handsome, if startlingly red-headed, hillbilly from a fundamentalist sect. He has only come to university so that he can learn to study the New Testament in the original. His intolerance makes him a somewhat absurd figure — he tears up his copy of *Romeo and Juliet* because he finds the play corrupting. In the context of the adolescent lewdness and cynicism of his contemporaries his innocence is nonetheless a very positive quality. But it disguises a strange confusion. As Joseph says to his friend David, the milk-and-water theology student who fails completely to perceive the true nature of Joseph's problems:

> You love The Lord in peace. It's a frenzied desire for God that grips me. My love must always be violent, because I am a man of passion.

His religious fanaticism feeds on a passion which is taking other forms; for example, his wrestling with the mysterious Praileau masks a sexual attraction he does not identify. This repressed sensuality explodes into violence when some of his contemporaries maliciously arrange to shut him up with Moïra, an amiable girl of low morals. Though Joseph at first rejects her in silence, when she goes to leave he throws himself upon her and initiates himself sexually. The next morning he murders her and buries her body in the garden. Rejecting the chance of escape offered by Praileau (the temptation of homosexuality) he then gives himself up to the police, to meet the death which is the only way of resolving his interior conflict. He is a man who kills what attracts him. In murdering Moïra, he kills the carnal man within himself.

The meaning of Joseph's self-sacrifice is more cloudy than this bald summary might suggest. The forces that motivate Joseph are more than psychological; the violence stems not only from unacknowledged erotic attraction but also from an exasperation with what seems to stand between him and total purity. Hence the notes of approval for Joseph which we find in Green's *Journal*. The author regretted that he found too late for use as an epigraph to the novel Father de Caussade's Claudelian sentiment, 'The action of man is a veil covering the profound mysteries of divine action.' If we take this remark in the context of a passage from the *Journal*:

> There are times when I think that many men will be saved despite their moral lapses, because of their loyalty to Faith and Charity amidst the most violent of crises . . .

it would seem that Joseph's act may not represent a capitulation to Satan at all, but a rather macabre expression of divine will through which he is spiritually saved.

The problem is taken a stage further in *Chaque homme dans sa nuit*, the title of which, a half-line from Hugo, suggests that each man will find his way from the darkness of this world to his own spiritual illumination, for as Green notes in the *Journal*, 'Every human life is a road leading to God.' Wilfred Ingram, the central character, is obsessed by sensuality and constantly yields to temptations. He is also a devout Catholic, filled with remorse at his own sinfulness, and will accordingly be saved. There is no doubt where the balance of value lies. As his cousin Angus, one of the several men in the book who are unavailingly drawn to Wilfred, rightly observes: 'You are eaten up by passions, but in spite of everything you have kept your faith.' Wilfred's dilemmas are matched against a series of other studies in religious belief: his debauched uncle Hector dying in a state of fear at his own sinfulness, his sternly puritan cousin, James Knight, whose angelic wife, Phoebe, is adored by Wilfred, and above all Max, a mentally unstable male prostitute obsessed with a desire to commit sacrilege as a form of self-abasement. Max has seen Wilfred praying in the Polish church. He pursues an acquaintance with him, oscillating between rejection of God and a masochistic desire for suffering:

> I suffer when I believe in a certain way . . . Yet I need this suffering. I need Him, you see, and this suffering is the closest I can get to the happiness I have never known.

Is Max an agent of the Devil or of divine providence? As with Joseph it is hard to say. For when, in a fit of anger, he shoots Wilfred, he is the instrument of the latter's salvation. Wilfred pardons him and dies in a state of serenity unknown to any previous character in a Green novel.

The message, if that is an appropriate word, of the later works seems to be that the true gift of faith allows one to experience the workings of divine love despite one's submission to the material world. Hence the redemption of Wilfred. It is not a question of conscious acts. Elisabeth in *L'Ennemi* is deranged by the time that she feels the absence of barriers between her love for Pierre (by now dead) and her love of God. The prostitute Karin in *L'Autre* (1971) is accorded a divine revelation which suggests that despite her apparent unbelief she may yet be saved. Both women have seen beyond the veil of material reality to the metaphysical truth of God's love.

Good and evil: the novels of Bernanos
Although the hostility to the flesh, and the sense that certain sinners are especially privileged for redemption are reminiscent of the world of Mauriac, the metaphysical side to Green's

work, the presence of forces of dark and light, the unreality of the world around us, is all much closer in tone to the novels of Georges Bernanos. Bernanos had nothing but contempt for Mauriac's obsession with the carnal. His own vision is a much more Apocalyptic one, in the style of Léon Bloy. He belongs to the tradition of doctrinal and political intransigeants associated with the *Action française*. His polemical work retains the same violence whether it belongs to his right-wing phase or his radical period. Thus his attack on the decadence of middle-class Catholicism between the wars in *La grande peur des bien-pensants* (1931) is matched in vehemence by the account, in *Les grands cimetières sous la lune*, of the experiences in Majorca 1936-7 which caused him to denounce the conspiracy of Church and state. What Bernanos finds in the world around him is the broad canvas of a vast and unceasing battle between Good and Evil, whose expression demands more than the analysis of individual sins.

From his first short story, *Madame Dargent*, Bernanos portrays a world divided between predestined communities of saints and sinners. As in Green's last works, Satan is presented as a force whose most violent expression also makes a man most accessible to the redemption of God; in Bernanos' own words, 'Once the human soul has reached a certain degree of abasement and sacrilegious dissipation, the notion of redemption is forced upon the mind.' His novels are focused upon these extreme moments, which he nonetheless sees as typical of the human condition. In *Sous le soleil de Satan*, for example, Mouchette (nickname of Germaine Malorthy) represents the ultimate degree of abasement; the abbé Donissan, the man destined to take on himself the suffering necessary to buy out her sins, is as close to sainthood as the inherent sinfulness of man will allow.

The themes of vicarious suffering and sainthood are rather differently presented in Bernanos' best-known work, *Journal d'un curé de campagne* (1936). It is a novel written in a much lower key, and all the more effective for that. The curé d'Ambricourt, whose diary the title refers to, is right when he observes in his opening words: 'My parish is a parish like any other. All parishes are alike.' The curé carries out his ministry in a world stifled by *ennui* and hypocrisy. Gradually he gains a deeper understanding both of the villagers' spiritual problems and of how to approach them. His childlike simplicity is complemented by the robust practicality of his well-meaning but insensitive colleague, the curé de Torcy, the two men standing in contrast to the moral weaknesses of the established church in general — as represented by the numerous more transitory clergy who appear in the story. But it is the curé d'Ambricourt whose acceptance of poverty and capacity for pure love make him the unique instrument of grace. The cancer from which he suffers and which finally destroys him is symbolic of the evil around him, whose burden he assumes. The melodramatic saintliness of Donissan has been exchanged for a childlike acceptance of God's mission.

The blackest of Bernanos' works belong, roughly speaking, to the same period as the *Journal*, forming a counterpoint to its relative optimism. In *Nouvelle histoire de Mouchette* (1937) the fourteen-year-old heroine, unconnected with Germaine Malorthy though the choice of name is a deliberate echo, lives in a world unredeemed by any curé d'Ambricourt. The theme of social justice, strongly represented in the *Journal* by de Torcy and the count's nephew Olivier, became more important for Bernanos as the events in Spain impressed on him the incompatibility of his political allegiances with his ethical beliefs. At first sight there is little in common between the war-time fate of the Spanish poor and the story of the rape and suicide of a French peasant girl. But the author himself affirmed that he started writing the story on seeing lorry-loads of republican hostages destined to be shot the next day for reasons beyond their comprehension. It was not a case of transposing what he had seen, yet had he not seen such things, he would not have written as he did. This account has to be put in the context of an earlier note to his publisher, stating his intention of writing a story that would show the feeling of purity quickening in a child of wretched circumstances. These two themes, the relentless force of poverty and the awakening of an instinctive purity in the most impure of conditions, bring together the social and religious dimensions of the story. One evening Mouchette gets lost, and is befriended by the drunken poacher Arsène, who helps her shelter from the bad weather but involves her in an elaborate conspiracy to disguise the fact that he has shot the gamekeeper, Mathieu. Mouchette is both afraid of Arsène and emotionally drawn to him. But he doubly betrays her confidence, firstly because he rapes her, secondly because it later transpires that Mathieu is unharmed. When the girl reaches home in the early hours of the morning, her mother is dying; thus the last person who is capable of showing her tenderness is removed. In the village next day she receives only humiliation and rejection. Mathieu's wife tries to show greater understanding, but in so doing she proves a threat to Arsène, whom Mouchette instinctively protects. Her ultimate resort, suicide, is not presented as a defeat but as an escape, offered by God, from the corrupt world in which the child's innocence can find no place.

Monsieur Ouine, begun in 1931 but not published until 1943, is a blacker book still. The *Nouvelle histoire* is a study in abject misery in some degree relieved by the seeds of purity. *Monsieur Ouine* is an attempt to portray the essence of ultimate evil. To achieve this Bernanos abandons even the degree of realism to be found in *Sous le soleil de Satan*, and evokes a dreamlike world comparable with that of the middle-period Green novels. Why people are there or what they are, what the precise nature of events is, these are questions often best left unasked, for the meaning of the novel lies not in narrative but in atmosphere. The *ennui* of Ambricourt is transformed into a total and apparently irremediable lethargy. As the curé proclaims at the funeral of the murdered cow-hand, the parish is dead, so dead that the devil himself will leave it to the solitary hell of its own sin. It is a symbol for the whole rotten state of contemporary materialist society, condemned to be the basis for the rule of the Prince of Darkness. The world is one of madness, lust and destruction, yet essentially lifeless, like Monsieur Ouine himself, who seems able to generate the chaos by his presence and yet is merely a presence, watching, at most giving 'an imperceptible push', as he puts it in his deathbed speech to Steeny, the acolyte he has spiritually (and perhaps sexually) perverted. Ouine is the embodiment of evil, but not the fighting demon of *Sous le soleil*. As described by Mme de Néréis, the eccentric châtelaine of Wambescourt, he is simply a force for annihilation, absorbing and eradicating all warmth and love: 'The genius of M. Ouine, you see, is coldness.'

We have, then, in Bernanos' work a much more fundamental exposure of a world without God than Mauriac's, and an even more visionary presentation of the force of evil than in Green. The world is divided between those possessed by the devil and those few special beings who have the strength to redeem the sins of their fellows through vicarious suffering, the only exponents of love in the full Pauline sense of 'charity' as Bernanos views it. Nonetheless, despite the clearly very Catholic nature of this doctrine, it is interesting to what extent the world-view on which it depends corresponds with that of the atheist writers of Bernanos' day in certain key respects. Firstly, man is presented as in a state of anguish over the apparent pointlessness of his existence. Secondly, the bulk of men seek to avoid facing that anguish by 'bad faith'; they hide behind ready-made criteria of behaviour and put up false absolutes as aims in life. Thirdly, the essential feature lacking is a common human bond which would lead to the defence of mankind in general, rather than the promotion of particular groups. Fourthly, it is only through a special and self-sacrificing commitment on the part of individuals that such a common bond can ever be forged. The comparisons with Malraux, Sartre, & Camus, though not to be pushed too far, emphasise the community of spirit from which hostile creeds sprang, just as we see the same phenomenon in left and right-wing doctrines of action at the same period.

The aesthetic dilemma
So far I have confined myself to talking about the *matter* of Catholic literature. This is in some ways its less interesting facet. For the mere expression 'Catholic literature' raises the question of forms of communication and clashes of aesthetic and doctrinal interest. Jacques Maritain, in his influential *Art et scolastique* (1920), gives an instruction which is easier to applaud than to follow:

> Don't separate your art and your faith. But make a distinction between things that are distinct. Don't try to force together what life is good at blending naturally. If you made an article of faith out of your aesthetic, you would do harm to your faith. If you made a canon of art out of your piety, or turned your concern for edification into a tool of your art, you would do harm to your art.

Most of the writers we have looked at insist that they are writers whose view of life is informed by a religious belief which is therefore reflected in their writing. This can pose a moral problem for the writer. Bernanos' comment on the ability of literature to corrupt readers hundreds of years after it was written is well known. Green, in his *Journal*, makes an even more telling observation:

> A novel is made of sin like a table is made of wood. Nothing pure comes from our hands. But it is a form of sin which can be useful. I am, of course, talking about novels which are not written for purposes of edification. The morally uplifting novel is usually written by the devil. That is a much more serious case. The damage caused by that sort of literature is incalculable.

The sinful element may make the greater impression on the reader in the first case; in the second, the overt piety may actually alienate him. One has only to try the earnest novels of Luc Estang, for example the trilogy *Charges d'âme* (1949-54) or *Le Bonheur et le Salut* (1961), to see the force of the latter argument.

The aesthetic problem posed is a serious one. How is the reader to be persuaded of the efficacy of metaphysical forces in which he does not necessarily believe? The question is not applicable only to Christian, let alone Catholic, writings. The novels of Dostoievsky, greatly admired by Mauriac and Bernanos, raise the same issue. So do philosophical novels such as Sartre's. If one does not accept the attitude to life embodied in Roquentin (*La Nausée*) he merely seems a pathological case. Indeed, in a certain sense a 'metaphysician in the tangible', as Mauriac called himself, has the advantage that he can use emotive literary effects to transmit his non-rational ideas, whereas the philosopher — and even more so the social theoretician — is obliged to persuade the reader of the truth of their worlds in a rational manner. What is perhaps curious is that so many writers have nonetheless chosen to remain within a realistic mode of presentation. Claudel and the poets are exceptions on this point; so is the Green of *L'Ennemi*, the Bernanos of *Monsieur Ouine*. Otherwise, the writers all accept that it is their job to mirror the world, and then accept the very difficult task of suggesting, behind that world, forces at work without which it is meaningless or inexplicable.

Understandably, symbolism becomes an important part of this undertaking. At its simplest this can involve the mere use of names, although to make the religious implications of *Le Désert de l'amour* hang upon the name of Maria Cross, as Mauriac does, is to overload the device. Nature is a frequent source of symbols of a profounder kind. Both Mauriac and Bernanos use the weather to convey human moods. Heat in *Thérèse Desqueyroux* and *Le Noeud de vipères* accompanies destruction; autumn and its rains, in the latter novel, bring a shedding of material encumbrance and a spiritual purification; spring suggests rebirth. In *Journal d'un curé de campagne* and *Nouvelle histoire de Mouchette*, rain, mist, mud and darkness indicate the moral decay of the world. Similarly, in the later novels of Green there is considerable play with light, dark, and colour. At times this becomes positively emblematic, as with the purity of Joseph Day's white skin and the flaming ardour of his red hair (*Moïra*). At others the inherent ambiguities in Green's presentation of the relationship between carnal and spiritual is emphasised by the changing implications of light — either anguish, desire, evil, or calm, purity and salvation — and dark — the negative world of reality or death's doorway to the afterlife.

As well as this kind of emotive symbolism there is a curious common device to suggest the possible working of Grace. This is the ellipse. As Albert Sonnenfeld has pointed out, it is often what a writer declines to describe which marks the metaphysical climax of a work. This is even true of the end of Claudel's *L'Annonce faite à Marie* (in the stage version) where the saving of Jacques and the intractability of Mara is well conveyed through a somewhat ambiguous use of gesture. Such endings implying an opening on to a new future are by no means confined to metaphysical works, of course. One of the more irritating aspects of Gide's *Les Faux-monnayeurs* is the way in which the author leaves the reader to assume that Bernard will henceforth be able to maintain his new-found liberty within the confines of a family unit which he has chosen to belong to, as opposed to unthinkingly accepted. This is irritating because no indication is given of how it is possible to be authentic in such a context. An open end of this sort can be ambiguous. Mouchette's suicide in Bernanos' *Nouvelle histoire* will only only be looked upon as a step forward if one already accepts the concept of an afterlife. But such an ambiguity is preferable to heavy-handed didacticism of the sort to which Mauriac treats us at the end of *Le Mal*, where, he tells us, he is breaking off at the point at which he should begin describing the workings of Grace, because that drama is not accessible to words. More subtle is the use of the ellipse within the text: the missing pages and erased lines in the curé d'Ambricourt's diary, the broken phrase on which Louis dies in *Le Noeud de vipères*. It is a device used by many writers touching upon things mystical, from Dostoievsky to Graham Greene. Rather than end on the ellipse, the novelist often switches point of view, allowing a clearly partial or inadequate witness to misinterpret, and thereby bring home to the reader the true meaning of the silence. The danger, as with the portrayal of events in such a way that they may have either a psychological or a supernatural explanation (like the curé's vision of the Virgin), is that the reader can justifiably refuse to attribute the meaning which the author manifestly desires.

As a consequence of the ambiguities in the stylistic manipulations on which so much of their would-be mystical effect depends, the realistic novels, aesthetically satisfactory though many of them are, may easily be read without reference to their authors' metaphysical intent. *Thérèse Desqueyroux* may offer a depressing portrait of a world without God, but if we sympathise with the heroine in her attempts to poison her husband and escape from the chains of his family, it is not because we feel that her self-dedication to sin will make her more accessible to God in the future, but because her husband and his family are indescribably awful. The curé d'Ambricourt is undoubtedly an admirable man working for the social and moral improvement of his parishioners. His vision of the Virgin seems as much attributable to his state of health and psychological disturbance as to divine intervention. In maintaining the need for psychological credibility imposed by the realistic novel, the authors have put themselves virtually in the position of a non-believing writer, like Montherlant in *Le Maître de Santiago* and *Port-Royal*, studying the psychological implications of metaphysical attitudes.

This situation is not without secular parallel. It could be said that the absurdity of existence is much more effectively conveyed through the unreal experience of a Beckett play or a Queneau novel than through the psychologically disturbed heroes of the real worlds of *La Nausée* or *L'Etranger*. Much of the use of myth in twentieth-century French theatre is designed to express philosophical concepts without the interference of surface reality but in a more cogent form than the abstract. This is true of Cocteau's attempts to suggest ineffable forces in *Orphée* and *La Machine infernale*, of Giraudoux's matching of absolute and relative in *Ondine* and *Electre*, even of Sartre's exposition of *engagement* in *Les Mouches* and of the inter-relation of individuals in *Huis clos*. For identical reasons, the forces of good and evil obtain a more powerful emotive grip on the reader/audience of the metaphorical worlds of Claudel or in Jean Cayrol's Kafkaesque trilogy *Je vivrai l'amour des autres* than in the mirrors held up to contemporary reality by the Catholic novelists.

CHAPTER 7
Action and Society

> ... acceptance of *any* political discipline seems to be incompatible with literary integrity.
>
> (G. Orwell, *Writers and Leviathan*)

The notion of giving a meaning to existence through action, especially when that action is defined in the limited terms of *Vol de nuit* or *Malatesta*, provides an unsatisfying basis for life, as indeed the heroes of *La Voie royale* and *Les Conquérants* discover. Small wonder then that the adventurer tradition of the inter-war period should swiftly be assimilated into a more positive ethical tradition, that of *committed* action. The association of commitment with literature had been firmly established in the French consciousness in the last decade of the nineteenth century, during the polemics of the Dreyfus Affair. The unbridled indulgence of intellectually disguised passions was given further respectability by the patriotic literature of World War I. Although attempts were made, notably in Charles Péguy's *Notre Jeunesse* (1911) and Julien Benda's *La Trahison des clercs* (1927), to distinguish between defence of abstract values and partisan commitment to individual causes, there was no factual basis for such a distinction. Indeed, when Benda chooses Zola's intervention in the Dreyfus Affair as an example of the disinterested defence of eternal principles, he is picking upon an action which, for many, represented the virtues of impassioned devotion to a specific social cause.

In the inter-war period the idea of commitment became tied to that of political belief, and left-wing political belief at that, an association eventually consecrated in the public mind by Jean-Paul Sartre's *Qu'est-ce que la littérature?* (1947). Of course, much Catholic literature, particularly that of Bernanos, is propagandist in a similar way and faces the same aesthetic problems (see ch 6). There is equally no reason why right-wing political writing should not be as engaged in its passions as that of the Left. Brasillach's *Les Sept Couleurs* is a good example of the eventual fusion of adventurer with group action, and offers an interesting comparison with the early novels of Roger Vailland (particularly given the textual indulgence of both writers in references to Corneille and the heroic ethic of the early seventeeth-century). However, the more clearly defined political causes of the Left, and the insistence in Marxist literary theory on the social functions of writing, meant that *littérature engagée* was identified with such authors as Paul Nizan, Louis Aragon, Paul Eluard, Sartre and Vailland. It is in these writers, then, along with individual works of Malraux and Camus, that we should look for our assessment of the achievements, problems and limitations of the genre. For an appreciation of how some of these problems and limitations have since been transcended, it is important also to look at the work of more recent writers, the dramatists Antoine Adamov and Armand Gatti.

Commitment and the novel
The career of Paul Nizan (1905-40) offers a pattern repeated by many committed writers of his generation both in France and elsewhere — revolt against established social and political values, devotion to communism, gradual disillusionment and withdrawal — although his early death forestalled any trend towards literary formalism of the type detectable in the later

novels of Vailland (and indeed of Aragon). Nizan's early polemics, *Aden-Arabie* (1931) and *Les Chiens de garde* (1932), are typical of the iconoclastic outbursts of the upper-middle-class intellectual youth of his period, for like so many others he was a product of the Lycée Henri IV and the Ecole Normale Supérieure. Of these young revolutionaries, who translated the traditional rebellion of child against parent into that rather more pretentious wholesale rejection of parental values which was to become even more fashionable after the next war, one could say what Orwell said in *Inside the whale* of the public-school-trained English bourgeois intelligentsia of the same period:

> Hunger, hardship, solitude, exile, war, prison, persecution, manual labour — hardly even words. No wonder that the huge tribe known as the 'right left people' found it easy to condone the purge-and-Ogpu side of the Russian régime and the horrors of the first Five-Year Plan. They were so gloriously incapable of understanding what it all meant.

Aden-Arabie denounces intellectual detachment and colonialism in the same breath. *Les Chiens de garde* focuses on the need to throw off the current idealist philosophy, which Nizan sees as a system designed to defend the status quo, and to adopt instead a philosophy of active intervention in life, a specifically proletarian philosophy (whatever that might be) extending the principles of Marx and Lenin. Neither pamphlet is of a kind to appeal to a wide readership. With *Antoine Bloyé* (1933) Nizan took up the novel as vehicle for his beliefs. The alienation is no longer that of a young philosophy graduate but of a railway worker, whose rise into a social twilight on the boundaries of working class and bourgeoisie is accompanied by a growing sense of torment at his own pointlessness. His second novel, *Le Cheval de Troie* (1935), is a more explicitly political work, portraying a Communist cell, a detached and alienated thinker (Lange) who prefigures Sartre's Roquentin, and the conditions of work and pattern of life of an urban working community.

The Zolaesque sense of predetermination dominant in *Antoine Bloyé* is still there in the second novel, heavily interlaced with uplifting comment from the author, but there is a clear avoidance of the black-and-white division of characters into good and bad, after the manner of cowboy films, which will typify socialist-realism proper. In his last completed novel, *La Conspiration* (1938), we find almost a return to the concerns of *Les Chiens de garde*. The central characters, Rosenthal, Laforgue, Bloyé and Pluvinage, are philosophy students who have rejected official French philosophy in favour of Hegel and Marx. However, Nizan undermines their claim to approach social justice via intellectual renewal, and allows their impetus to revolution to disintegrate into adolescent conspiratorial games and self-destruction. Pluvinage, who joins the Party for reasons of personal inadequacy and eventually becomes an informer, embodies an almost melodramatic indictment of the necessary failure of middle-class youth to come to terms with the real problems of the 1930s. In all these novels Nizan copes more effectively with the portrayal of what is wrong with the world, with the delineation of moral climates and intellectual dilemmas, than with the aesthetic difficulties of communicating a positive message in a fictional format.

Quite how hard it is to give weight to a message without interfering with the independence of 'realistic' characters is well illustrated by a committed novel written almost contemporaneously with Nizan's, Malraux's *L'Espoir* (1937). This collage novel about the Spanish Civil War aims to show the inadequacy of individualist action, as represented by the anarchists, in comparison with the disciplined communal action of the communists. The contrast is similar to that between the militants of *Le Cheval de Troie* and the rootless individualists of *La Conspiration*, but the effect is strengthened by having both groups involved in the same events. The novel is built out of no less than 146 short scenes, showing atmospheric action such as the first chaotic night of the uprising in Madrid and the disruption of life in Barcelona, specific incidents such as the storming of a barracks and the bombing of the Toledo Alcazar, and individual dialogue as in Scali's interview with the fascist pilot. These scenes are much more fragmented in the first part of the novel, where emotional conviction in the rightness of their cause brings the Republicans early victory, but cannot forge a unified fighting force. The collapse of the efforts of individualism is marked by the loss of Toledo and the death of the anarchist leader Hernandez. As the communists take over power, in the second section of the novel, with Manuel restoring discipline on the Toledo-Madrid road and Magnin and Scali correspondingly asserting control over the pilots, the scenes begin to block together into more unified focus. Thus the latter part of the second section deals entirely with different aspects of the defence of Madrid, leading up to the repulsion of the fascist attack on the city. In part three, where the focus disintegrates again, there is a thematic unity in the presentation of peasant and soldier uniting to drive back their common enemy. The message of the novel, contrasting individualist disorder and failure with (at an admitted price) communist order and success is implicit in the structural movement of the work.

Malraux's problem is that his literary sensibilities lead him to feature certain elements which run counter to his main thesis. The death of Hernandez in particular is emotively charged in a way that gives its protagonist the status of tragic hero. The propaganda balance of the novel is even more disturbed by the scene, at the climax of part three, of the rescue of the wounded pilots, brought down from the mountain safely as a result of the loyal co-operation of the local peasantry. A bombing mission has ended in mishap for one of the crews: Pujol's plane makes a crash-landing on a mountain side, and the crew are trapped inside. Dramatically staccato arrangements for the rescue are made, and the process itself is emotively evoked in a welter of rich visual images. What has triumphed here is not communist organisation but man's inherent sense of fraternity, a quality unhymned elsewhere in the book and almost at odds with its thesis about necessary submission to an effective hierarchy.

Malraux's technical experiments in *L'Espoir* are far from uniformly successful. The overall journalistic effect, which he claims to have derived from contemporary Soviet writing, has the virtue of immediacy, but necessitates an equally fragmentary response on the part of the reader. At the same time the major characters show a grasp of the higher meaning of the events in hand which militates against our acceptance of their reality. In both respects the novel compares badly with Hemingway's *For Whom the Bell Tolls*. It has, nonetheless, a more satisfactory literary structure than most of the novels of a socialist-realist like Louis Aragon. Without sinking quite as low as André Stil (Stalin Prize in 1952 for *Le Premier Choc*), Aragon often falls into the obvious traps of didactic fiction. His novels belong to the most politically active years of his career. The end of his attachment to surrealism and the assumption of a career as a reporter for the communist paper, *L'Humanité*, coincided with a hiatus in his writing of poetry, apart from the crudely revolutionary *Front rouge* (1932) and the dreadfully prosaic *Hourra l'Oural* (1934), an encomium to the 'new world' of communism. Precisely in this period, 1932-9, Aragon produced the first three in his series of committed novels entitled 'Le Monde réel': *Les Cloches de Bâle* (1934), *Les Beaux Quartiers* (1936) and *Les Voyageurs de l'impériale* (1943, but written in 1939). It is to these (and not to the unreadable six-volume travesty of the propaganda novel *Les Communistes*, with its grotesque misrepresentations of the state of France in 1939-40) that we should look for an understanding of the merits and shortcomings of this type of French writing.

The first thing that strikes one about these novels is how very old fashioned their literary technique is. They take us right back to the didactic manner of the late Zola novels and of Maurice Barrès, a world of caricatures and authorial moralising. *Les Cloches de Bâle* is made up of two independent stories, rather clumsily linked, with a kind of postscript portraying the Congress of the Socialist International at Basle. The focus of each of the stories is on a different woman: the first, Diane, is irrevocably corrupted by the capitalist circles in which she moves; the second, Cathérine, struggles to escape from her bourgeois background but ultimately fails. In the postscript the figure of the Russian communist, Clara Zetkin, is offered as a contrast:

> She is the woman of tomorrow, or rather, let us have the courage to say it, the woman of today. An equal. The woman to whom this book is entirely directed, the woman in whom the problem of woman in society is resolved and left behind.

It is possible, as Aragon himself did in a preface of 1964, to defend the structure of the book as a baroque interplay of related themes, allowing itself great freedom of temporal sequence. It is a great deal less easy to defend its supposed realism. From Wisner the wicked capitalist to Victor the heroic and virtuous taxi-driver the characters are all stereotypes, expounding their values in naïvely formulated speeches. 'When I say *France* it is a simple way of saying *us*, a certain group of common interests,' pronounces Wisner, as he outlines his contribution to French colonial adventures in Morocco. Victor proclaims to Cathérine, demonstrating the sound ethics of his kind:

> Suicide is just running out at the first fence. What is there for a member of the proletariat who is conscious of being a member of the proletariat to be so afraid of that he is willing, against himself, that is against a portion of his class, to resign the game in favour of his opponent, the bourgeoisie, by killing himself?

It is impossible to take this sort of thing seriously. However, individual scenes such as the ill-fated march of the factory hands at Cluze, or the attempts at breaking the taxi-drivers' strike in Paris, are evoked with great passion, and the women themselves are given sufficient depth to make them psychologically interesting if separated from the heavy class-theorising in which the presentation of their lives is embedded.

Les Beaux Quartiers, a more even novel, still exhibits the same basic technical flaws. Its characters again become symbols of the ideas that they embody and its plot is melodramatic to a degree reminiscent of Eugène Sue, or Balzac at his most self-indulgent. The action plays around two main themes: the role of money in the functioning of society, and the contrastive development of two provincial middle-class brothers, Edmond and Armand Barbentane, in the face of the social reality of their day (the eve of World War I). Aragon's dilemma is much the same as Nizan's or Malraux's. The negative facets of his books convince more easily than the positive ones. We believe in the motivation and significance of Edmond's degradation more readily than in Armand's metamorphosis into a good citizen through the act of joining cause with the strikers in the factory where he works.

In *Les Voyageurs de l'Impériale* Aragon seems to concede that his strength lies as a negator. Pierre Mercadier believes in freedom and rejects the conventions and values of his world. Yet his freedom is meaningless and his rejection hollow, since he is as much the victim of money as the protagonists of *Les Beaux Quartiers*. As with the earlier novel Aragon relies a great deal on symbols — the biography of Law (the inventor of the paper money system) which Pierre is writing but will never finish, the act of gambling itself to which he devotes himself. The solitude of such a freedom is emphasised by the failure of Pierre's personal relationships with a succession of very different women, Pauline, Blanche, Francesca, Reine. But, as ever, the author cannot resist unnecessarily rubbing home his message. The news of Pierre's death never reaches his son, who has just been mobilised for the start of the Great War. By its close, the spirit of comradeship engendered by the horrors of war has made the individualism of Pierre obsolete:

> 'The individual. Ah no, Léon, you're joking! Individual indeed!' The day of all the Pierre Mercadiers was definitively over, and even if the impossible had happened and anyone had given a thought to the absurd lives they had once led, how could they have avoided shrugging their shoulders in pity?

As we have seen, the committed novel of the inter-war years covers a broad range of subject matter and setting. There is, however, less significant diversity in the aesthetic approaches of the novelists and little attempt to create a form appropriate to positive political commitment. Sartre, as befits a man who wrote very percipient critiques of other novelists from Mauriac to Faulkner, attempts much more thoroughly to relate the experiences of isolation and of belonging to a group to the actual process of reading the novel. His unfinished tetralogy, *Les Chemins de la liberté*, covers yet another thematic area, since it is largely set in the France of the Phoney War and the Occupation. This offered Sartre the chance to exploit at least one sure way of attracting the reader's sympathy, by using the Resistance as symbol of co-operation. There is, however, relatively little exploration of this, except perhaps in the third volume. Indeed one has only to make a comparison with Vercors' famous portrait of how the nicest Fritz remains indelibly a Fritz (*Le Silence de la mer*, 1942) to see that Sartre's novels are on a quite different plane. His central character, Mathieu, is an analogue of Aragon's Pierre Mercadier, a man whose pursuit of freedom at all costs leads to a false isolation. *L'Age de raison* (1945) studies the philosophical implications of the existentialist predicament for Mathieu and for the homosexual Daniel; the only reference to *engagement* is through the character of Brunet, who has renounced the luxury of so-called free choice in joining the Communist Party and going to fight for the Spanish Republicans. *L'Age de raison*, as befits its subject, is a 'point of view' novel, locked within the heads of its isolated, self-deceiving characters. The sequel, *Le Sursis* (1945), is much more ambitious. The kind of mass consciousness, and rejection of the value of the individual, which Nizan, Malraux and, to a lesser extent, Aragon grasp in isolated scenes, is seen by Sartre as a central modern experience; for him it was, since 1914, society and no longer the individual which constituted the essential 'character' of a realistic novel. The best way of rendering such a picture of society as a whole he found in Dos Passos' *Manhattan Transfer* (1925) and in the *U.S.A.* trilogy, particularly *1919*, published between 1930 and 1935.

In *Le Sursis* Sartre takes the Munich crisis of 1938 and studies the impact of this political event on a vast panorama of characters viewed in constantly intercut flashes and juxtaposed with the interior monologue of unnamed spectators (compare with Dos Passos' Camera Eye), trying to give a definition of 'history' through the totality of its immediate effect on those who participate in it. This enables concealed critique: the juxtaposition of Chamberlain's return from Munich to London with an invalid's attack of diarrhoea has an inevitable effect on the reader's response to the former. The technique also encourages a Marxist view of the relation between individual and the historical process. But, again, it is mainly effective in its revelation of inadequacies, both in Mathieu, Daniel and their circle, and in a broad range of minor characters. This is equally true of the third volume, *La Mort dans l'âme* (1949), where the defeat of the French army is presented in terms of a demoralised chaos akin to that of Saint-Exupéry's *Pilote de guerre*. In both these parts of the tetralogy it is the communist Brunet who alone is fully committed, and this is to some extent a black mark against him, the suggestion being that he has selected the easy option in the face of general metaphysical despair. It is true that Brunet's recruiting activities among the captured French soldiers represent the only really positive action in either novel, and that his one-dimensional character is considerably broadened by his contact with his ambiguous fellow-prisoner Schneider. But the fragments of the uncompleted fourth volume (*La Dernière Chance*) show that Brunet's certainties are to be undermined. Schneider, who is revealed to be (rather like Nizan) an ex-communist disillusioned by the Russo-German pact, persuades Brunet that the Party is not infallible. Brunet temporarily stays faithful to the turnabouts of Party policy, but finally decides to attempt an escape with Schneider from the German camp where they are imprisoned. The 'loyal' Party network which Brunet has set up in the camp settles the fate of the 'traitor' Schneider by giving the escape away to the Germans. Hypocrisy and compromise have triumphed. There is no real *human* solidarity even (or perhaps especially) in the Party.

The tetralogy is quite effective as philosophical literature, but its commitment is inadequate because Sartre's own feelings on politics have shifted. He is more successful, as we shall see, at transferring *engagement* into the dramatic action of the theatre, in the short compass of individual plays, than in sustaining a positive manifesto within the novel. Indeed, the more wedded he becomes in the post-war period to political action, the more he regards literature, especially fictional literature, as an unnecessary distraction from action itself. The post-war development of the literary trends we have so far been examining is more aptly embodied in the work of Roger Vailland (1907–65), who combines the adventurer tradition of Malraux with the uncritical didacticism of Aragon, and yet remains constantly aware, like Sartre, of the aesthetic problems inherent in formulating his message in a fictional context.

The climate in which Vailland had to work was a particularly difficult one. Although there was no official apparatus in France for keeping communist literature as pure in its form as in its doctrine, the party spokesmen, Jean Kanapa and Laurent Casanova, were dedicated to the Stalinist doctrines of socialist-realism. Even Aragon was severely criticised for his novel *Aurélien* (1944) on the grounds that he should not have been writing what is primarily a book about love (but then so are the best bits of his earlier novels) during the war. Vailland himself was suspect. A former member of a minor surrealist group, his interest in eroticism and individualism put him in the tradition of Malraux, an impression heightened by his Resistance novel *Drôle de jeu* (1945), and by the tally of earlier writers who most influenced him — Laclos, Stendhal, Hemingway (together with Corneille and Racine). His movement towards plainly committed literature in *Bon pied, bon oeil* (1950) and *Un jeune homme seul* (1951) is an uncertain one, for the characters who represent the new orthodoxy are often, like Rodrigue in the former and Eugène Favart in the latter, lamentably adolescent and unconvincing in their political passions. However, these novels helped Vailland to qualify for Party membership (in 1952). It is during the next four years (he became disillusioned after the Kruschev revelations about Stalin though he did not hand in his card until 1959) that his two most successful committed novels were written, *Beau Masque* (1954) and *325,000 francs* (1956).

Beau Masque handles the theme of exploitation, particularly of workers by management, as the silk manufacturers of Le Clusot plan a programme of modernisation and redundancy in order to satisfy the demands of American shareholders. In the background are national politics — American intervention to prevent commercial ties between France and China being developed. In the foreground are the struggle for power within the circle of the shareholders, the contrast of would-be class-rebel, Philippe, and communist sympathiser, Beau Masque (the nickname of an Italian immigrant), and the portrait of Pierrette, leader of the workers. The message of the novel, emphasised in the Epilogue, is one of the need for revolutionary solidarity among the workers. Whether, however, the *literary* force of the novel is directed to bringing out that message is a very different matter. The five-part structure (of which Vailland is fond) with an evident climax and confrontation, the relative unity provided by the focus of theme and place, and the fate of Beau Masque, innocent victim of both private passions and public events, all draw one's attention to the tragic and heroic dimensions of the novel rather than to its social message. If *Beau Masque* is an effective novel, it is for reasons unconnected with didacticism.

325,000 francs, more successful in this respect, is an entirely negative book. Its subject is the exploitation of workers in the French plastics industry. But the treatment is such that the focus is as much on an individual relationship, Busard and Marie-Jeanne, as on the political implications of Busard's working career. Busard attempts, by a cleverly designed plan of shift-working with a colleague, to beat the economic dependency to which he is condemned by his job in Morel's plastics factory, and save enough money to set himself up as a café proprietor. His failure is foreshadowed in the cycle race with which the book opens: it is not his skill or understanding that fail him, but some inner insufficiency, the same which makes him subservient to the chilling figure of Marie-Jeanne. At the climax of the action, just short of his goal, Busard loses a hand, very unpleasantly, in the machine he is working. His independence, like his marriage, is predestined to fail. Again Vailland has created a tragic and timeless relationship for which the political dimension is a compelling but subordinate setting.

Commitment and poetry
In the committed novel from Nizan to Vailland, then, there seems to be an inverse relation between political effectiveness and the illusion of reality, such that only the criticism of present society carries with it complete conviction. The

question of whether a non-realistic presentation of positive ideas can be more effective in the novel is one which, for the moment, I will set aside. For the novel is by no means the only vehicle for action which French writers have tried to use. Even poetry, despite Sartre's strictures to the contrary, has been adapted to express a message. The two most significant writers in this field were Aragon and Paul Eluard, both ex-surrealists. The earlier career of committed poetry in twentieth-century France had not been particularly encouraging: one thinks of the mystico-patriotic effusions of Charles Péguy or the jingoism of Déroulède, the poet parodied in Giraudoux's *La Guerre de Troie n'aura pas lieu*. It was the years of the Resistance that gave both Aragon and Eluard a chance to write verse with a broad emotional appeal. There is little in France to parallel the flowering of left-wing poetry in England in the 1930s. But, unlike some of their English counterparts, most socially conscious French poets stayed in Europe to face out the horrors of war, rather than seeking snug refuge in America. It was these horrors of war, and the need to stand out against them, that Aragon sought to transfer into ballad-like verse in *Le Crève-coeur* (1941). In *Brocéliande* (1942), *Le Musée Grevin* (1943) and *En français dans le texte* (1943) he moved into a more satirical vein, whose violence is emphasised by the heavy, chanting, repetitive structures and rhythms, reminiscent of D'Aubigny or Hugo's *Châtiments*. Finally in *La Diane française* (1945) he wrote of victory, bringing together as in some of the earlier poems the images of patriotic and personal love, and putting them in the context of political conviction.

All this poetry is very much limited to its historical context. The few poems that survive, 'Les lilas et les roses' or 'La rose et le réséda' for example, are dependent on an image or images whose effect or meaning transcends the immediate message of the verse. Much of Aragon's post-war poetry, although it continues to intertwine the three kinds of love, for France, Elsa Triolet and communism, makes personal love the focus, and weaves the three strands into a statement about the human condition. The *engagement* is largely an assumption about the personality expressed through the 'voice' of the poem, rather than a didactic aim in itself. The more overtly political the collection, like *Les Yeux et la mémoire*, the more occasional the effect. If the poetry of Aragon is remembered, it will not be for its political message or for the prosaic optimism of the autobiographical *Roman inachevé* (1956) but for the intermittent flashes of musically hypnotic melancholia:

> *Il fera si beau de mourir quand ce sera*
> *Le soir d'enfin mourir d'enfin*
> *D'enfin mon amour d'à mourir le soir d'enfin*
> *Mourir*
>
> *Un soir d'aubépines en fleurs aux confins des parfums et de la nuit*
> *Un soir profond comme la terre de se taire*
> *Un soir si beau que je vais croire jusqu'au bout*
> *Dormir du sommeil de tes bras*
> *Dans le pays sans nom sans éveil et sans rêves*
>
> *Le lieu de nous où toute chose se dénoue*
>
> (*Les Chambres* 1969)

[It will be so beautiful to die when there comes/the evening at last to die at last/to die my love to die the evening at last/to die An evening of hawthorns in flower on the edges of the perfumes and of the night/an evening deep as the earth for falling silent/an evening so fine that I shall believe to the end/I am sleeping in the sleep of your arms/in the nameless, wakeless, dreamless land/our place where all things unravel].

Humanitarian concerns early began to manifest themselves in the work of Paul Eluard (1895–1952), who wandered in and out of the Communist Party but always shared its social ideals. In the 1930s his pronouncements on poetry constantly stress the equality of the poet with his fellow men and his role as a voice for universal experience. It was, however, in his Resistance collections *Poésie et vérité* (1942) and *Au Rendez-*

vous allemand (1944) that he first developed a popular style. Unlike Aragon he never achieved any kind of ballad-like musicality, and the bald rhodomontade of often-anthologised poems like 'Liberté' and 'Courage', today as poetically inspiring as the Romantic clichés of the Greek national anthem, cannot disguise the fact that, admirable though the sentiments were in their historical context, they are much too simplistic to mean anything on a more general level. The post-war poetry of Eluard is more consciously political than that of Aragon. There he only achieves an effective form of expression in his admirable poems on the Greek civil war *Grèce ma rose de raison* (1949), where the violence and harshness of the action is matched by the landscape which provides the basis for many images and settings.

Commitment in the theatre

Committed poetry in France has proved, then, to be more a branch of popular propaganda or an encouragement to the faithful rather than an effective medium of instruction. At its best it often tells us more about the emotional adhesion of the poet to his cause than about the cause itself. A much more fruitful area of literary endeavour has been the theatre. The notion of using the immediacy of audience-impact offered by drama as a way of disseminating ideas was an old-established one, with its own built-in pitfalls. Voltaire's awful tragedies and the social platitudes of Second Empire problem plays had demonstrated some of the difficulties of adapting pre-existing theatrical conventions designed for other purposes. Although the tradition of lavish theatricality in the inter-war years moved away from an emphasis on content, the idea of the problem play had been kept alive by Lenormand, Gabriel Marcel and the early works of Anouilh. It is not surprising, then, to see committed writers attempting to redevelop the genre.

The plays of Sartre and Camus are very instructive examples

of the limitations of didactic realism. Sartre in particular, not a writer known for the quality of his creative imagination, tried to cannibalise existing types of theatre just as much in his political plays as in his more purely philosophical one (the division is in any case an artifical one). *Les Mouches* is a reworked myth, *Les Troyennes* an adaptation of a Euripides play; *Les Mains sales* politicises boulevard crime-drama; *La Putain respectueuse* offers a down-market version of Tennessee Williams crudely interlarded with social satire. Only *Les Séquestrés d'Altona* (1956) has a relatively original form, probably affected by the general evolution of French theatre in the post-war period. The plays of both writers very swiftly sort themselves into two categories: pseudo-realistic 'talk' plays, and works in which the suspension of credulity or the necessary intellectual distance are aided precisely by the non-realistic elements in the plot or form. Just as existentialism is a philosophy technically well adapted to dramatic presentation (see, for example the account of the work of Gabriel Marcel in Chapter 6) because the *act* is its basic element, so political commitment ought to express itself forcefully through stage action. But in practice the dramatist soon faces a dilemma akin to that resolved in opposite directions by Malraux and Hemingway in the novel. Hemingway's heroes are monosyllabic, which is psychologically convincing for adventurers, but leaves the metaphysical implications of their situation unanalysed. Malraux's heroes, for example Tchen in *La Condition humaine*, are quite implausibly self-analytical, which deprives the reader of confidence in the character, and therefore of the problem which the character purports to face. Similarly in *Les Mains sales*, despite the suspense of the action and the problems of morality and Party discipline which it raises, the illusion of reality is broken by the endless speechifying. The drama of Hugo's mission to shoot Hoederer, and the turnabout of Party policy which puts Hugo in the wrong for carrying out its instructions, is in itself insufficient to expose the complexity of the philosophical and political issues raised, but the analysis of those issues kills the tension on which the stage action depends.

The same strictures apply to *La Putain respectueuse* or to a play like Vailland's *Le Colonel Foster plaidera coupable*. The former caricatures the racial problems of the American Deep South, the latter oversimplifies the tension between humanitarian ideals and military training in an American officer during the Korean war. In each case the various characters are one-dimensional representations of a type or a point of view; for example in the former play, Senator Clarke is the embodiment of self-interested hypocrisy and in the latter, Jimmy McAllen represents the unthinking racial and political prejudice of the 'average' American soldier. An extreme extension of this flat type of morality play is Sartre's comedy, *Nekrassov* (1955), where the inherently amusing central situation — a professional confidence-trickster passes himself off as a defecting high-ranking Russian only to find that he is taken too seriously — is used to promote the thesis that opposition to communism is always and by definition wrong. In all these plays the stylisation of ideas is in strong contrast with the apparent intention to represent a slice of some recognisable reality.

Sartre's Greek plays, and much of Camus' dramatic production, are different in kind. As Sartre says in his preface to *Les Troyennes*, the effect (or at least a possible effect) of myth in the theatre is to distance the audience and allow it to bring its intellect to bear on the issues raised, without the necessity for a willing suspension of disbelief imposed by the intrusion of debate into 'realistic' action. The fact that (in part) Egisthe represents the German occupying forces, Clytemnestre Vichy compromise and Electre the Resistance is not, then, a limiting factor on one's response to *Les Mouches*, because we are not encouraged to see psychological depth as a relevant element in the dramatic structure of the piece. Plays like

Camus' *Révolte dans Les Asturies* (corporately written with three student friends) and *L'Etat de siège* approach the advantages of involving the audience intellectually in a more contemporary way, through the conditions of performance. French authors of serious intent were really extraordinarily slow to catch on to expressionist theatre in general and Brechtian techniques in particular, despite the continual process of directorial experiment in the French theatre from Lugné-Poé to Jacques Copeau and the sharp eye for the virtues of artifice in illusionist playwrights like Cocteau, Giraudoux and Anouilh. Camus, however, through his apprenticeship in a communist-based touring company in Algeria in 1935–7, learnt much about the techniques of Reinhardt, Piscator and Brecht. *Révolte dans Les Asturies* is a dramatisation of the miners' revolt in the Asturias in 1934, taken as a symbol of class-conflict and of the complex relation between revolt and revolution. The proscenium arch is done away with and the illusion of recreating an event realistically is rejected. Instead, text, lighting, and sound are intercut in the way later to be associated with workshop theatre in England and France. If the result is unsatisfactory in this work of juvenilia, it is because of imbalance between the elements. The form chosen, as Roger Planchon was later to show with his unconventional productions of Brecht and Gatti, was ideally suited to the propagation of emotionally conceived ideas.

With *L'Etat de siège* (1948) Camus made another attempt to master the theatrical possibilities of a form in which the text is an integral but not the focal part. Like the earlier play this is a drama of revolt, but its political target is the more generalised one (and of course by this stage in Camus' career the un-communist one) of totalitarianism in all forms. Although, or perhaps because, the director was Jean-Louis Barrault, whose work synthesized the various influences of Dullin, Copeau and Artaud, the elaborate allegory of a city struck by Plague, coupled with the weight of a wordy text, caused the work to be a failure. The restrictively explicit socio-political analogies through which the allegory is worked out — city=body politic, plague=fascism — were overloaded by the complex forms of stage expression Barrault chose to clothe them in. At the same time, Camus, while perceiving the value of mime, music, choreography and the other aspects of technical virtuosity, failed to appreciate that they function best as an alternative to a heavily literary text rather than as an accompaniment to it. Camus is, in fact, much more at home in the relatively conventional form of *Les Justes*, an investigation of the limits of political terrorism which takes as its theme the assassination of the Grand Duke Sergei Alexandrovitch by Ivan Kaliayev in 1905. We are back in the world of debate theatre, the focus of the play being the problem of the involvement of the innocent bystander in politically motivated destruction. The status of the text is preserved, and the force of dramatic innovation in holding the audience's attention on the central thesis is no longer explored.

The second wave of committed dramatists, in the 'fifties and 'sixties, harnessed to full effect the non-realistic devices which Camus unsuccessfully investigated. In the work of Adamov and Armand Gatti the epic dimension at which the novelists have been vaguely grasping, in their attempts to portray society rather than the individual, finds an appropriate theatrical form. *Révolte dans les Asturies* is still, in a sense, the rearrangement of recognisably 'real' elements. Adamov's *Le Printemps 71* (1963), a documentary on the Commune, strays a little away from Camus' formula in its use of political allegories inspired by the work of Daumier, the nineteenth-century caricaturist. In other plays, *Paolo Paoli* (1957), *La Politique des restes* (1962), *Sainte-Europe* (1966), the element of fantasy proper asserts itself. In *Paolo Paoli*, for example, the notion of exploitation is embodied in the symbols of feathers and butterflies and their extensive use by the fashion industry at the turn of the century. These natural objects thus perverted into commodities are made matter for barter between representative members of French society for the period 1900–14, who discuss them as functions of human adornment. Between bouts of this obsessive commerce, documentary material from the period is back-projected, showing the way in which the European powers were similarly bartering their colonial dependencies. Whether such material is really ideal for enlarging the proletarian consciousness, as Adamov intended, is something critics have given leave to doubt, since the subject presupposes a fairly intimate knowledge of the Marxist interpretation of the historical situation at the time, as does *Le Printemps 71* of the events of the Commune or *Sainte-Europe* of the political structure and implications of the Common Market. The impact of the dramatic method is, however, undoubted.

A more thorough-going experimenter still is Armand Gatti (1924–). He uses the full range of expressionistic techniques, particularly film projection, music and simultaneous décor, to underline alternations of realism and stylisation, and manipulate the exclusion or inclusion of the audience. Linear narrative disappears almost entirely from his texts, which are confrontations of points of view involving historical and social judgments. The artifice of the presentation is deliberately magnified; an example is *Chant public devant deux chaises électriques* (1964), which uses as its base the Sacco and Vanzetti trial. The play contains the recreation of the Sacco-Vanzetti story as five different plays simultaneously being performed in five different cities, each offering a different interpretation and thereby creating a conflicting commentary on the others. The 'heroes' of the trial are never on stage; material relating to other historic moments of the American class-struggle, the Chicago Five, the Rosenbergs, is incorporated; and the emphasis of the piece is on the attitudes of actors, administrators and spectators in venues from Turin to Los Angeles. One of Gatti's most satisfactory epic works of this type, satisfactory because more focused, is his *Passion du général Franco par les émigrés eux-mêmes* (1972, reworked from a text used for performance at Kassel in Germany in 1967). The play is both a critique of the Francoist system and an exploration of the Spanish mentality, presented via groups of exiles and Francoists, the former all travelling on different journeys; this 'action' is interspersed with symbols, from the cross that links fascism and the church to the prehistoric monsters who represent the fossilised political factions of the Left in Spain. The exchanges within and between groups, which form debate, characterisation of types and lyrical exposition of beliefs, vary sharply between natural interchange and stylised, even poetic, chants and patterned dialogues. There is no narrative development. The play adds up to an elaborate revelation of the complexity of the Spanish situation in the latter days of Franco, seen of course from an openly Marxist point of view. Elaborate constructions like the three plays outlined above need very tightly controlled staging, or they will disintegrate.

Not all Gatti's work is of this kind. Some plays are more obviously polemical in their choice of theme. *Un Homme seul* (1964) is based on a hero of Mao's uprising against the American-supported Kuo Mintang; *Notre tranchée de chaque jour* (1964) deals with an aspect of the Cuban revolution; *V comme Vietnam* (1967) reveals its subject in its title. There are formal variations too. For example, *Les Treize soleils de la Rue Saint-Blaise* (1968) is much more restrained in dramatic structure than the 'epic' works. It presents thirteen pupils, chosen to represent different working and immigrant backgrounds, at an adult evening class, each of whom offers his individual response to a decision to level a large area of the twentieth precinct of Paris in order to build luxury flats. Each pupil becomes the sun rising over his view of the world; they swiftly pass from the broader problems of man and his environment to an interpretation which reflects both specifically on man in his special context (in this case the twentieth precinct) and on the way in which their own backgrounds and occupations determine the realism or fantasy of their responses.

The plays of Gatti, as can be seen from this brief account, are no less simplistic in their view of the world than those of any other propagandist. After all, the view of English history propounded in, say, *Richard III* does not suggest that Shakespeare was overly concerned with a balanced presentation of the anti-Tudor case. What Gatti does very successfully in many of his plays is to soften the black-and-white opposition of values by the complexity of the dramatic texture and the richness of images in the text itself. He also plays down the part given to negation of bourgeois values and tries to find an effective proletarian mythology, as it were. Butch in *La Naissance* (1968) speaks for the author when, in discussing plays as 'conscience in action', he says:

> Sacco and Vanzetti, the American Labour Movement, nobody talks about them. They're just as great and tragic as the princes of the French theatre. We need to rediscover our sense of dignity. It's through our own heroes, brought on to the stage, that we shall succeed in doing so.

Whether the positive aspect of the plays is effective is a matter for individual taste. Dramatically, however, Gatti certainly seems to have found a resolution to many of the problems of earlier committed theatre.

Realism versus stylisation
Gatti's success raises, I think, the question, implicit in my discussion of the plays of Sartre and Camus, of whether a move away from realism in form is not a prerequisite for effective committed writing. Piscator's reservations about plays proletarian in inspiration but naturalist in manner could perfectly well be applied to the novel, especially in the case of Aragon. Nor does the restriction apply solely to Marxist themes. It is noticeable that the most successful didactic works in European

literature of the present century are precisely *not* cast realistically. Orwell's *1984* and Huxley's *Brave New World* adopt the pseudo-realism of predictive fiction; the former's *Animal Farm* is purely allegorical; and Camus' *La Peste* (1947) has links with both forms. None of these novels attempts to transcribe or interpret the world as it is or has been in any naturalistic sense. It might be argued that *La Peste* is primarily a philosophical novel. This is a false distinction in this particular case. With the possible exception of his plays *Caligula* and *Le Malentendu*, none of Camus' work is unequivocally philosophical. *La Peste* in particular deals with the problems of man as a social being in the light of his metaphysical dilemmas, and as such constitutes a positive statement about social action on a generalised plane.

As in *L'Etat de siège* the focus of the story is an outbreak of plague. Camus chooses as his setting the Algerian town of Oran, but he is not interested in the local colour that his choice affords. His reference to it as 'a neutral place' can be extended by the description he gives of it in an earlier essay (1939), *Le Minotaur ou la halte d'Oran*. It is a place in which man is naturally isolated, all the more so if one is a white Frenchman in an Arab world. This isolation is used as symbol both for the limbo of life itself, and for the political enclosure of France after her defeat in 1940. From these two levels of reference, by studying human responses to the predicament, he builds up a set of convincing contrasts between the dangers of individualism and of those who exploit the situation for their own temporary selfish advantage, and the virtues of corporate action prompted by a humanistic concern for the welfare of one's fellows. Although the focus on a narrow area of space and time (the action takes less than a year) and the linear plot, based on the appearance, intensification and abrupt disappearance of the plague, are potentially realistic elements, Camus makes little attempt to exploit them as such. Even the characters are not developd for their psychological interest, despite the sleight-of-hand that allows the narrator to disguise his identity by talking about himself in the third person during the opening part of the book. The meaning of each character emerges from his actions in the context of the plague: Cottard, the black-marketeer, and Rieux, the chief spirit of the medical units formed to combat the disease, are thus at opposite poles — an egotism which endangers one's fellow men, a disinterested co-operation which gives meaning to life. Not only in the actions described but also in modulations of style does Camus convey the emotive attractions of the humanitarian position. The scene in which Rieux and Tarrou go swimming by night is expressed in metaphorical language which creates a sense of unity between man and his environment, and this in turn is reinforced by the spiritual unity of the two men:

> Rieux turned, drew level with his friend, and swam in the same rhythm . . . For some minutes they swam in time with one another, in the same forceful way, alone, far from the world, freed at last from world and plague.

A belief in the value of human togetherness which cannot be rationally sustained (as is only too obvious from Camus' essays or the equally specious arguments in Sartre's *L'Existentialisme est un humanisme*) is here embodied in a part-allegorical action and sustained with a poetic control of style and structure. This is a more subtle weapon than the false naturalism of the socialist-realists.

As I have said before, the precise limits of committed literature are impossible to determine. It would have been easy to include all sorts of works devoted to the exposition of philosophical or religious ideas, regional or national consciousness, or such contemporary issues as feminism and sexual rights. In the French mind, however, *littérature engagée* has always carried with it certain socio-political overtones and certain aesthetic connotations which justify the kind of selection I have made in his chapter. The Anglo-Saxon reader is relatively unused to this sort of literature as a self-consciously separate development. The modern English equivalent of a social view in poetry is represented by the pragmatic morality of the man-in-the-street as propagated by Philip Larkin. French poets, on the contrary, have never accepted that there can be any accommodation between introspection and social consciousness, probably because the class divisions have long been, for historical reasons, equated with political divisions in a way unknown in England before the last decade. Even where there seems to be an overlap between the different cultures, as in the theatre, the comparison can be misleading. The English theatrical tradition represented by John Arden and Joan Littlewood did not come as a solution to a longstanding aesthetic dilemma in the way that the experimental texts of Gatti or the directorial style of Planchon did in France. Perhaps it is ultimately the result of the relative lack of influence of Marxism in British and American intellectual circles that the problem of committed literature has never really crossed the Channel.

CHAPTER 8
National Consciousness

> Since God died we have been trying to set up the material conditions for earthly happiness. We are hardly beginning to glimpse the spiritual conditions (cultural revolutions) that are a prerequisite for such happiness.
>
> (Jacques Godbout)

Everyone knows that there exist entirely independent literatures whose lingustic medium is a particular brand of the English language — American, Australian, Indian, Caribbean and so on. It is easier to forget that French, too, has engendered substantial literatures outside metropolitan France. What is particularly interesting is that both in former colonies and in entirely separate countries like Belgium and Switzerland, for reasons which I shall indicate later, many of these Francophone writers approach the whole problem of man's place in the universe through a scrutiny of their own national roots and cultural identity, such that their work forms an independent category not assimilable under the kind of headings I have been using so far in this book. In the words of Leopold Sédar Senghor, these writers 'are faced more and more, in expressing themselves, with having to express not only their individual realities but also their national, or even in the case of Canada their continental, realities. And when it comes to expressing them effectively in French, it is not clear that it is any easier for whites than for blacks.' Since it is impossible in the space available to consider all possible territories from Mauritius to New Caledonia, I propose to look at representative trends in four areas with distinct traditions of their own, but which each contribute a 'literature of national consciousness': Africa (including the Caribbean), Algeria, Switzerland and Canada.

Africa and the Caribbean
What is called *littérature noire d'expression française* comes from a very widespread area. The French-speaking countries of Africa itself form a block in the west and north-west of the continent: Mauritania, Senegal, Guinea, the Ivory Coast, Mali, Upper Volta, Togo, Niger, Dahomey, Chad, Cameroon, Gabon, the Central African Republic, the two Congos, Ruanda and Burundi. To these can be added Somalia (on the east coast), Madagascar, and the French creole areas of the Caribbean — Haïti, Guadeloupe, Martinique and, on the continent of South America, French Guiana. Although Francophone Africa itself is, therefore, only half as large in area as its English-speaking equivalent, it is twice as densely populated. Furthermore, the cultural policies of France as a colonial power, designed to assimilate the upper level of local society entirely to the standard French model, had a far deeper effect on the development of the intelligentsia than the rather cursory contacts of Anglophone Africa with British cultural traditions. (It would not, I think, have occurred to the British to issue all African schools with a text book which informed the children that their ancestors the Gauls were blond-haired and blue-eyed.) As the native languages of the countries under French rule were distributed in a very fragmentary fashion — there is nothing in West Africa to equal the broad area of the East in which Swahili is understood — French became, like

English in India, an indispensable tool of national consciousness. At the same time it was the ultimate symbol of colonial oppression. It has been, therefore, the first task of Francophone writers in Africa, and the same applies to a lesser extent in the Caribbean countries, to emancipate themselves conceptually from the implications of their linguistic medium.

It was in the effort to do this that two of the foremost writers, Senghor (now the president of Senegal) and Aimé Césaire (from Martinique) evolved the concept of *négritude*, a term first used in the 'thirties in their student review, *L'Etudiant noir*. *Négritude* is a very loosely formulated concept, used by most writers to indicate a certain number of values specific to negro culture of which the rest of humanity should be made aware. Sartre, in his introduction to Senghor's influential *Anthologie de la nouvelle poésie nègre et malgache* (1948), builds up the concept as the basis for an African 'commitment' of a strongly Marxist kind. It is perhaps more useful to see *négritude* as shorthand for the totality of African cultural values and therefore only a basis for a writer's wider aspirations. Other writers have indeed contested the desirability of linking black culture to any specificity, and have, like the Malagasy poet Jacques Rabémananjara, relegated *négritude* to a phase in the decolonisation process.

What is fundamental to African literature is the need to relate to tradition, historical and mythical, and to the religious values which permeate African life — in the sense that the supernatural is assumed to be part and parcel of everyday experience. One of the best ways to approach an appreciation of what this means in literary terms is via the theatre. As yet the novel has hardly established itself as more than a borrowed form, even if it has such distinguished exponents as Camara Laye (Guinea) in his *L'enfant noir* (1953), *Le Regard du roi* (1954) and *Dramouss* (1966). Equally, although there are many interesting collections of short stories, like Birago Diop's *Contes et lavanes* (1963) and Ibrahim Issa's *Grandes eaux noires* (1959), they remain at a largely descriptive level, rather like the 'village' literature which played an important part in the development of prose in nineteenth-century Greece and Spain. Now, although the theatre is in some ways even less developed than the prose genres, it has its roots very obviously in native oral and ceremonial traditions. For the less Europeanised dramatist, the form of the text itself has to take into account the circumstances of possible performance. There are very few theatres, so that performances are often open-air, with the attendant problems of lighting and sound effects; there are very few professional actors or directors and the audience expects to participate — indeed the whole notion of staging is very different from the European one. The writer has to rely on a sense of ritual and the natural incorporation of music and dance into static texts of debate. Although the work of the more consciously literary (and therefore Westernised) writers attempts to overcome some of these limitations, the conditions that generate them inevitably affect all African drama.

As far as the themes of plays go, national consciousness expresses itself most strongly in two forms: 'historical' plays which deal with mythical heroes of the pre-colonial period, and comedies of a satirical type expressing social criticism. Plays which deal with abstractions, rather like morality plays of the medieval period in Europe, are not part of the indigenous tradition, but they do exist. Antoine Letembet-Ambily (Congo Brazz.), for example, has produced *L'Europe inculpée* (published 1971), a play in debate form with biblical reminiscences, in which Japhet, father of Europe, hearing that his daughter has been arraigned before Judge Humanity by Africa, daughter of Cham, exhorts Noah to intervene and stop the trial. Comedy often takes as its theme the marriage system, as in Guillaume Oyono's *Trois prétendants, un mari*, financial skulduggery, and the power of the sorcerer. Guy Menga's *La Marmite de Kota-Mbala* (1969) is a good example of the use of traditional elements to express revolt against the tyranny exercised by custom. The play is set at a period when young people who have irregular sexual relations are thrown into a cauldron of boiling water. King Bintsamou tries to abolish the custom but is stripped of his powers by his council of elders. However a miracle intervenes to save him, and the witch doctor's cauldron is destroyed. The young have acted as an independent force who effect eventual revolution. It is the historical plays, however, which are most forcefully directed to the creation of a sense of black identity. The heroes are often local — Lat-Dior in Senegal, Behanzin in Dahomey (for example, in Jean Pliya's *Kondo le requin*), Radoma II in Madagascar (Jacques Rabémananjara, *Dieux malgaches*). Chaka, a king who lived towards the south at a very early period of African history and was associated with great imperial aspirations, has attracted particular attention, from Senghor's short dramatic poem 'Chaka' (1956) to Seydou Badian's *La Mort de Chaka* (1961, Mali) and Senouro Zinsou's *On joue la comédie* (1972). It is noticeable that all these plays are exceptionally European in form.

In general it can be said of African theatre that it presents a tension between European and native traditions which can only be partially resolved where the two overlap (for example, Brechtian techniques and the native debate formula). What is essentially African in any given text lies in its consciousness of native cultural values (even if it wishes to revolt against them) and its preference for a rhetoric of repetition in which action does not develop, nor are time and place characterised, but various essences (in a metaphysical sense) are defined and celebrated by a process of intensification.

African poetry transcends the limits of *négritude* much more readily than the theatre does, without ceasing to express fundamentally non-European modes of experience. At its most provincial it confines itself to transposing native forms and themes. Flavien Ranaivo (Madagascar) has exploited the forms of the *hain-teny* and the *kahary* (a sort of proverb) in his collections *L'Ombre et le vent* (1947), *Mes chansons de toujours* (1955), and *Retour au bercail* (1962). The result is curiously impersonal, especially in a love poem like 'Vieux thème Merina', of which these are the opening stanzas:

> *Germent les plantes*
> *poussées par les racines,*
> *et je viens jusqu'à vous poussé par mon amour.*
>
> *Aux cimes des grands arbres, chérie,*
> *l'oiseau termine son vol:*
> *mes courses ne s'achèvent que ne sois près de vous.*
>
> *Trébuchent, trébuchent les eaux de Farahantsana, chéri,*
> *elles tombent, elles tombent sans se briser.*
>
> *Mon amour pour vous, chérie,*
> *ressemble à de l'eau sur la grève:*
> *j'attends qu'elle tarisse, il en vient davantage.*

[The plants grow urged up by their roots and I come to you urged on by my love. The bird ends its flight at the tops of the tall trees, my darling: my journeying only finishes when I am close to you. The waters of Farahantsana are swaying, are swaying, my dear, they are falling, they are falling but without breaking. My love for you, my darling, is like the sea on the shore: I wait for it to dry up, and more of it comes.]

Other Malagasy poets, like Régis Rajemisa-Raolison (*Les Fleurs de l'île rouge*, 1948) have followed the same tradition. With a writer like Birago Diop (Senegal) the Africanism lies more simply in the themes and images, as in the ceremonial blessing of the ancestors in 'Viatique' (*Leurres et Lueurs*, 1960). This is the case too with the poems which Francis Bebey (Cameroon) has inserted into the short-story sequence *Embarras et Cie* (1968).

With this relatively descriptive approach to Africanism we can contrast the self-conscious analysis of what it feels like to be an African in David Diop's *Coups de pilon* (1956, Senegal), with its violent hostility to colonialism, contempt for those who accept white civilisation (see 'Le Renégat') and eulogy of the struggle for freedom:

> ...Fils impetueux cet arbre robuste et jeune
> Cet arbre là-bas
> Splendidement seul au milieu de fleurs blanches et fanées
> C'est l'Afrique ton Afrique qui repousse
> Qui repousse patiemment obstinément
> Et dont les fruits ont peu à peu
> L'amère saveur de la liberté.
>
> (Afrique)

[Impetuous son that strong young tree, that tree there, splendidly alone amid the faded white flowers, is Africa growing again, patiently obstinately growing again, and whose fruits gradually acquire the bitter flavour of liberty.]

Influenced by David Diop in his early work, Bernard Dadié (Ivory Coast) has written a much calmer and more lyrical defence of negro values in *Afrique debout* (1950) and *La Ronde des jours*, particularly in the moving 'Je vous remercie mon Dieu de m'avoir créé Noir' of the latter collection, with the sing-song repetitions so characteristic of this poet's later style. The greatest of the analytical poets are, however, two contrasting figures, Senghor, whose expression of *négritude* is so heavily steeped in European forms and images, and Tchicaya U Tam'si (Congo, Brazzaville), whose collection *Arc musical* (1970) sums up the dilemma of his whole generation of African intellectuals committed to the soil and blood of Africa and trapped by the very French language in which they express themselves.

In his first collection, *Chants d'ombres* (1945), Senghor evoked the myths, festivals and customs of Senegal in poems with titles that speak for themselves, like 'Prières aux masques', 'Le totem', Que m'accompagnent kôras et balafong' (types of native musical instrument), but using a verse in which the influence of Saint-John Perse and Claudel is often already evident. His second collection, *Hosties noires* (1948), relates to his experience in the French army and as prisoner of war: the ideas of the fight for liberty and the place of negroes fighting for the French cause inevitably inspired poems in which exile, solidarity and the nature of freedom are all raised, particularly 'Camp 1940', 'Prière des tirailleurs sénégalais' and 'Lettre à un prisonnier'. *Chants pour Naëtt*, later incorporated into *Nocturnes* (1961), expressed his feelings for Africa in terms of the woman he loves. But this love is now coupled with a feeling, first expressed in *Hosties noires*, of his own importance as poet-seer and spokesman of his race, a function which comes to the fore in the section 'Epîtres à la princesse' of *Ethiopiques* (1956). In the 'Elégies' which are the main new contribution to *Nocturnes*, he uses his privileged role to express a faith in the role of the African within the community of nations which constitutes humanity as a whole. Thus at the climax of 'Elégie des eaux' the unequal justice that falls on man is unequal within nations rather than between them:

> *Seigneur, entendez bien ma voix. PLEUVE! il pleut*
> *Et vous avez ouvert de votre bras de foudre les cataractes du pardon*
> *Il pleut sur New York sur Ndiongolor sur Ndialakhar*
> ...
> *Pleut sur le Sahara et sur le Middle-West, sur le désert sur les terres à blé sur les terres à riz*
> *Sur les têtes de chaume sur les têtes de laine*
> *Et renaît la vie couleur de présence.*

[Lord, hark well to my voice. Rain! it is raining and you have opened the cataracts of pardon with your arm of thunder. It is raining on New York on Ndiongolor on Ndialakhar . . . raining on the Sahara and on the Middle West on the desert on the wheat-lands on the rice-fields on the heads of straw on the heads of wool. And life is reborn the colour of presence.]

U Tam'si began his literary career with the collection *Le Mauvais Sang* (1955) from which African consciousness is notably absent. In *Feu de brousse* (1957) both the manner and matter of his poetry moved toward that of his two main collections, *A triche coeur* (1960) and *Epitomé* (1962). There is none of the affirmation of a poetic mission or the concrete evocation of specific contexts which marks the poetry of Senghor. U Tam'si seems to have been influenced by the French surrealists, and by Aimé Césaire in particular. His volumes of poetry form total units in which a background of memories — the exploitation of the Congo by the colonial powers and the political upheavals with their attendant violence — is overlaid with recurring images and phrases. He employs three main symbols: the tree, the sea, and the Passion of Christ. The first two are put to unexpected uses: for example, the sea denotes pollution rather than purification, whilst the Passion of Christ becomes associated with the humiliation of the negro, especially in poems like 'Le contempteur' and 'Au sommaire d'une passion' (*Epitomé*), a humiliation that will carry its own redemptive power. Having to some extent come to terms with his racial consciousness in these poems, U Tam'si moves on, in *Arc musical*, to a much more analytical style, in which, using the vehicle of imaginary voyages, he expresses his problems, fears and aspirations in a more universal form. If he belongs to a humiliated race, there is still hope for the future:

> Quand l'homme sera plus féal à l'homme
> la femme plus attentive à la lune
> l'enfant docile à la caresse du père
> mes mains décalquant une aube
> la vie réinventera mon corps
> et ma mémoire soudain de silex
> ne pétrira plus l'argile du crime
> sur le dos d'aucun de mes frères.

[When man will be faithful to man/woman more attentive to the moon/ the child submissive to the father's caress/my hands taking a tracing of a dawn/life will reinvent my body/and my memory suddenly of flint/will no longer mould the clay of crime/on the back of any of my brothers.]

The insoluble problem remains the cultural one — the paradox of expressing a negro identity in a non-negro medium.

It is interesting to make a brief comparison of these different ways in which black Africa has expressed its search for identity in literary form with the Francophone literature of the West Indies. There the writing is more violent and racist, and yet less able to emancipate itself from the metropolitan French tradition because its African roots are 'lost'. There can only be a limited worth in exploring ancestral values as such, although the yearning for Africa itself is a fundamental theme. In Haïti, for example, it is possible to trace three clear phases — what is called *l'indigénisme*, a movement associated with Jean Price-Mars (1876-1969) and producing a largely descriptive, if sometimes surreal, exoticism of local colour; an association of folklore and political themes, as in the poetry of Jacques Roumain, for example, *Bois d'ébène* (1938); and militant anti-Western pro-African literature of the sort associated with the novels of Jacques Stephen Alexis and the poetry of René Depestre (see *Un Arc-en-ciel pour l'Occident chrétien*, 1967). It is noticeable that voodoo in its cultural and philosophical manifestations plays an important role in the expression of the Haitian identity in many of these writers.

It is to Martinique that we must look for the major Caribbean centre of black literature in French. The switch from *indigénisme* to Africanism occurred slightly earlier there; it can be remarked in René Maran's novel *Batouala* which received the Prix Goncourt in 1921. And already with Etienne Lero (1909-39) strong European influences — Rimbaud, Lautréamont, Breton — were imported into Martiniquais poetry. This then was the cultural background which influenced the development of the best known of the black writers after Senghor — Aimé Césaire.

Césaire's concept of *négritude* is far more polemical than Senghor's. In the words of his famous definition in *Cahier d'un retour au pays natal* (first full edition, Cuba 1943):

Ma négritude n'est pas une taie d'eau morte sur l'oeil mort de la terre
Ma négritude n'est ni une tour ni une cathédrale
elle plonge dans la chair rouge du sol
elle plonge dans la chair ardente du ciel

[My *négritude* is not a fleck of stagnant water on the dead eye of the earth/ My *négritude* is neither tower nor cathedral/it goes deep into the red flesh of the ground/it goes deep into the burning flesh of the sky].

Négritude is for him an act, an act of revolt. It was natural for him to associate with surrealism, a movement of social and cultural revolt itself. What is interesting in a collection like *Les Armes miraculeuses* (1946) is how consistently the imagery reflects violence: the vocabulary of blood, blows and weapons dominates. Gradually the disconnections of syntax and image give way in his later verse to a more conventional *engagement* as in *Ferrements* (1960). However, his militancy has been more effectively expressed in his three anti-colonialist plays, *Et les chiens se taisaient* (1956), *La Tragédie du roi Christophe* (1963) and *Une Saison au Congo* (1967). The second of these is similar in conception to the African Chaka plays, but the political implications of its theme are extended much further. Through the story of the rise and fall of Henri Christophe, who proclaimed himself king of the western part of the island after the revolution, Césaire explores the relationship of power to political justice. Christophe is made to stand for the aspirations of the people as against the compromise and manipulation of the politicians. As such the author's criticisms are addressed not merely to Martinique or the Caribbean states but more specifically to Africa itself:

> It's time to bring to their senses those negroes who think that revolution is just a matter of taking the place of the Whites and continuing to play the White man in his stead, on the backs of the negroes I mean.

Césaire is implicitly arraigning the corruption and exploitation rife in some newly independent régimes in Africa. The result of revolution must not be domination of black by black. Events in Africa in the fifteen and more years since the play was written have confirmed the truth of what Césaire says in it.

It has been, of course, impossible to do more here than outline the main aspects of *littérature noire d'expression française*. Such an account does no justice to the substantial regional differences within Africa itself, especially the divergent influences of Islam and Christianity. It would be possible too to say much about the Marxist tendencies of many novelists, or the problems of creating realist literature for a society hedged in with important metaphysical preconceptions about the nature of reality. In particular I have treated rather summarily the debate over the use of French at all, and the strong opposition of those who believe that an oral culture based on native languages is much more important to African development than what they regard as a spurious version of colonial culture. This is not a simple political opposition: radical spirits such as Jaques Stephen Alexis (Haïti) are perfectly content with their linguistic medium. Nor is the question merely a matter of general principle. It has legitimately been pointed out that the relationship between the ordinary African people and traditional culture is entirely overturned by the introduction of written texts, be they in native or European languages. However, although these various issues complicate the picture I have given, it should at least be clear that a consciousness, both descriptive and analytical, of African roots and culture plays a primary part in the works of Francophone negro literature today.

Algeria
The situation in North Africa is comparable, particularly in Algeria, with that in the rest of Francophone Africa and the Caribbean; Morocco and Tunisia, merely protectorates, were never exposed to the same degree of Gallicisation. There are however significant differences both political and cultural. In

the first place written literary traditions already existed in Algeria in classical Arabic, together with oral traditions in the popular dialects, so that there was no *de facto* case for a *lingua franca*. In the second, the incorporation of Algeria into the metropolitan political structure and its forcible withdrawal, together with the militant nature of contemporary Arab nationalism, has made the status of French culture in North Africa more contentious than south of the Sahara. Paradoxically, the first wave of Algerian writers are all white. Taking their example from Robert Randau (1873-1946) the European intelligentsia of the province set about establishing their cultural independence from metropolitan France. But their novels, stories and poems were 'Algerian' only in their local colour and their determination to define the white community in terms of a moral code much more violent and sensual than that of contemporary Europe. Randau's own *Les Colons* (1907) is a typical work. With the so-called School of Algiers, established in the wake of the victory of the Popular Front in the French elections of 1936, a more progressive literary movement came into being: it is the period of Camus' *Noces* (1938) and Emmanuel Roblès *L'Action* (1938). In the 'fifties and 'sixties the writers of this school, which included Gabriel Audisio, Jules Roy, Jean Pelegri and Roger Curel, expressed a more liberal view of native Algerian aspirations which influenced the formation of French public opinion.

Already, however, in the immediate post-war period, partly as a response to the granting of French nationality to the native population in 1947, an ethnic literature looking for roots in the Arab past and in Berber customs was developing. Three sorts of literature develop, more or less in chronological sequence: the descriptive, where, as in Mouloud Mammeri's *La Colline oubliée*, the values of village life are examined, or the psychological tensions between the two cultures are evoked, as in the works of Marguerite Taos-Amrouche; the nationalist, as embodied in the anti-colonial novels of Mohammed Dib, *La*

Grande Maison (1952), *L'Incendie* (1954) and *Le Métier à tisser* (1957), the curious symbolic fiction of Yacine Kateb and the revolutionary poetry of the half-French Henri Kréa; and the social (affirmatory or critical), as exemplified in the post-independence period by the novels of Nabile Farès and poetry of Bachir Hadj Ali. The critic Ghani Merad has described this literature as 'a vast quest for a personality, the search for a self rooted in history and projected toward a better future, the hope for a national "we" '. Although there is a certain *parti-pris* about this definition, it does in general suggest the themes and manner of the writers concerned.

The fundamental theme is the loss of identity and the sense of cultural alienation which arise from the very fact of colonisation, an alienation which later reappears in a different form among French-speaking Algerians as a result of the arabisation policy of Ben Bella and Boumedienne. As the heroine of Marguerite Taos-Amrouche's novel, *La Rue des Tambourins* (1960), puts it:

> As far back in my memory as I can go, I discover the inconsolable pain of being unable to take a part in the world around me, of always being 'marginal'.

In Mouloud Feraoun's *La Terre et le sang* (1953) Amer-ou-Kaci comes back, after several years as an immigrant worker in Paris and the north of France, to his native village with his French wife, and has to face the problems of reconciling his old and his new life. Feraoun's following novel, *Les Chemins qui montent* (1957), makes its young hero, also newly returned, denounce in more bitter terms the inner contradictions of his existence and the limitations of the traditional life-style. At a different social level the same tensions exist in the heroes of Malek Haddad, such as the doctor in *L'Elève et la leçon* (1960). Such a division reflects itself sometimes within the more personal voice of lyric poetry too, particularly in the sense of inherent alienation produced by the language itself. As

Boualem Khalfa beautifully expresses it in 'Préface' (*Certitudes*, 1962):

> *Je n'ai pas de portée*
> *pour les notes qui naissent en moi*
> *on m'a donné des mots sans âme*
> *des mots aux yeux de chien battu*
> *. . .*
> *touristes perdus sous les voûtes d'un souk*
> *et qui soudain*
> *pris d'angoisse*
> *se sentent désespérément seuls*
> *en pays étranger*
> *étranger même quand il sourit*
> *surtout quand il sourit*
> *Je pense en Algérien*
> *et j'écris en Français*
> *des mots qui ne disent pas tout*

[I have no compass for the notes which are born in me/I have been given soulless words/words with the look of a beaten dog . . . tourists lost under the vaulted roofs of a *souk*/and which suddenly/seized with anguish/feel desperately alone/in a foreign land/foreign even when it smiles/especially when it smiles/I think as an Algerian/and I write as a Frenchman/words which do not say everything].

The second major theme of Algerian literature is the concept of liberation. On a physical level this inspires the poetry of Henri Kréa, very much 'occasional', bred of a given political moment. Kréa uses simplistic rhetoric reminiscent of Aragon:

> *Alger la Rouge*
> *Tu es plus que jamais vivante*
> *Car tu es plus qu'un symbole*
> *Tu es Vie tu es Liberté*

[Algiers the Red/you are more alive than ever/for you are more than a symbol/you are Life you are Liberty].

Anna Greki's committed poetry, like *Algérie, capitale Alger* (1963), is more effective because its themes of love, fraternity, imprisonment and confidence in the national destiny are more elaborately inter-related and are expressed in a more forceful imagistic language. But none of this poetry compares in literary interest with the mystical symbolism of Yacine Kateb's novel *Nedjma*, in which the figure of the woman Nedjma, her wanderings and destiny, also represent Algeria, the reference to ancestral myth and history forming both her regretted past and her future goal. This kind of lyrical writing in which chronological perspective and narrative line are subordinate to other facets is also used in the critical novels of the post-Independence era, when the failure of society to live up to revolutionary expectations becomes the central theme. Nabile Farès' *Yahia, pas de chance* (1970) and *Un passager de l'Occident* (1971), Rachid Boudjedra's *La Répudiation* (1969) and *L'Insolation* (1972) are the most important examples. Boudjedra's novels in particular function through multivalent images both political and psychological in import, in which violence, repression and castration are the key elements.

Algerian literature has found its voice, as the example of Boudjedra suggests, not merely because of particular themes, but because it has brought to bear an Arab consciousness of literary form which is very different in kind from French norms. The novels of Kateb, Farès, Djebar often include passages in verse; they ignore conventional chronology and allow abrupt shifts of both time and space. Even characterisation shows an 'Eastern' preference for studying emotive responses at the expense of recording external characteristics or intellectual activity. How long it will preserve this tradition is difficult to say. Unlike the African ex-colonies Algeria has reduced French to a second language, and is encouraging the development (still as yet vestigial) of an Arabic literature. It is already relatively difficult to publish in French in Algeria, but there is still a flourishing tradition published abroad. It remains to be seen how long the Francophone voice of North Africa will continue to be a living cultural force.

Switzerland

For obvious reasons the expression of national consciousness in Swiss literature is very different in its origins and its expression from the same phenomenon in African, Caribbean or Algerian writing. French is the language of just under a fifth of the Swiss people: three existing cantons, Vaud, Geneva and Neuchatel, and the nascent canton of Jura are entirely Francophone, and three further cantons, Fribourg, Valais and Berne, are bilingual. This relatively small proportion of French speakers creates a double identity crisis within what is called *littérature romande*, provoked by the shadow of German-Swiss culture on the one hand and of metropolitan France on the other. It has been the custom to absorb successful Swiss writers, from Blaise Cendrars to Robert Pinget, under the heading 'French'. Even C.F. Ramuz (1878–1947), who is credited with giving modern *romande* culture both status and self-confidence, is usually treated by French critics as an appendage of their own provincial novel as produced by writers like André Chamson, Maurice Genevoix and Henri Bosco. Yet Ramuz' novels, such as *La Grande peur dans la montagne*, *Derborence* and *Le Garçon savoyard*, are typical of a traditional strain of Swiss writing, metaphysical in implication but looking to the countryside and the people of the Vaud and Valais regions for the themes and poetic effects which they embody. So, although the Swiss search for cultural identity is relatively free from the political impulses which dominate much African and Algerian writing, it is nonetheless an influential factor in the form that modern literature takes.

Initially Swiss consciousness took the form of a certain *indigénisme*; although as Jacques Chessex has pointed out there is no local folklore or mythology to speak of, a mystique of the countryside itself provides the exotic focus. This descriptive literature has its descendants today in the sentimentally rural novels of Maurice Zermatten, for example, *La Montagne sans étoiles*, *Pays sans chemin*, in works in which the traditions and history of a region are the centre of interest, such as Alice Rivaz' *L'Alphabet du matin* (1969), and in a continuing tradition of nature poetry of which Alice Heinzelmann's *Saisons* (1971) is a good example. More significantly, it is linked with the Protestant introspective ethos through the notion of isolation and solitude, first as the implicit background to psychological novels — Monique Saint-Hélier's *Bois-mort* (1934) is an early example — then increasingly as an observation on the human condition, as in the poetry of Gustave Roud (1897-1976). Jean-Pierre Monnier in *La Clarté de la nuit* examines the problem through the characteristically Swiss image of the spiritual struggles of a pastor in a remote district. (Other contemporary 'pastor' novels, in the wake of Gide's *Symphonie pastorale*, are Yves Velan's interior monologue *Je* and Jacques Chessex' *La Confession du pasteur Burg*.) In Monnier's later novels the idea that the landscape is part of the transcription of human experience is extended to more overtly social themes; thus in *L'Arbre un jour* (1971) the scenery and climate of the Jura are an essential part of the problem of human communication as explored in the context of a group of unemployed cutting down forest trees. The same phenomenon occurs in the modern Swedish novel — like Stig Claesson's study of depopulation in the north in *Vem älskar Yngve Frej?*

Social and religious commitment are more frequent subjects for Swiss literature than politics; Anne Cunéo, for example, has written two powerful feminist novels, *Mortelle maladie* (1969) and *Poussière du réveil* (1972). Admittedly the theatre, not a genre well developed despite the socialist-idealist activities of the Théâtre du Jorat in the first half of the century, has produced a committed tradition influenced initially by Sartre, Camus and the directorial work of Jean Vilar and Jean-Louis Barrault. Its themes are sometimes Swiss, as in Henri Debluë's *Force de loi* (1959) based on the last death-sentence passed in a Swiss canton. More often such plays reflect the traditional obsessions of the Left: the work of Walter Weideli, comparable in themes and techniques with that of Adamov and Gatti, includes *Eclatant soleil de l'injustice* which treats the Sacco and Vanzetti affair as the basis for a moral commentary on the inadequacy of human justice in a bourgeois world. However, a more authentically Swiss commitment can be found in the novels and poetry of Maurice Chappaz and in those of Jacques Chessex.

Chappaz started his writing career with lyrical evocations of the scenery in the Rhone valley, in both prose and verse, for example, *Verdures de la nuit* (1945). Into these subjective descriptions of the natural cycle, already laced with religious images, he began to introduce the contrastive world of man's destructive 'creation'. The four-part poem-cycle *Le Valais au gosier de grive* (1960) starts on an ominous note:

> Le Valais de bois est à l'agonie.
> Le Valais qui est la seule parcelle de l'Eden,
> dans une fente de neige
> entre les siècles dormants
> hostie intacte et fraîche
> Valais de l'abîme!
> Aux joues brunes, aux reins de forêts bleues,
> . . .
> Légion de collines, de calvaires,
> de pics, de vallées de Josaphat;
> et le lit du fleuve
> taciturne.

[The wooded Valais is in its death throes./The Valais which is the only scrap of Eden,/in a pocket of snow/between the sleeping centuries/bread of the Eucharist intact and fresh

Valais of the abyss!/Brown-cheeked, with the small of your back forested in blue . . .

Legion of hills, of Calvaries,/of peaks and valleys of Jehosaphat;/and the bed of the river/taciturn.]

The following poems evoke the beauty, strength and simplicity of the countryside and develop the Catholic implications of the image 'the great peasant Christs' as a definition of man's native role in this setting. Then, at the end of the first section, the modern world intrudes, with hints of its sickness and false wisdom. The second section of the cycle paints the destruction of God's creation by mines, dams, depopulation, and its replacement by Man's:

> *Beauté des bassins de Babel:*
> *algèbre pure,*
> *digestions des étoiles comme un kilo de cérises*
> *. . .*

[Beauty of the pools of Babel: pure algebra, the stars gobbled down like a kilo of cherries . . .].

Man himself is transformed; only the few, particularly the poet, keep the landscape alive within them — 'It is within the human being/that the cherry and apple trees awake again.' The poem becomes a meditation on the poet's identity as man and artist in the face of the spiritual and physical crisis posed in the Valais by the modern world. It closes, in the single poem of the fourth section, on a bitter description of a society in which money is 'the new original sin' turning the earth into 'orchards of electric wires'. Yet there is a vision of rebirth, still dominated by the thread of religious images, ending in an assertion of the poet's own status as a divine intermediary:

> *Réjouissez-vous,*
> *le Jourdain coule à travers moi*
> *et le Seigneur a renouvelé l'alliance*
> *avec son pays préféré.*

[Rejoice, the Jordan flows through me and the Lord has renewed his marriage with his favourite land.]

The *Chant de la Grande-Dixence* (1965) expresses similar themes, focused on the building of the Grande-Dixence dam and hydro-electric plant.

The satirical side of Chappaz's vision comes over more forcibly in his prose. *Les Maquereaux des cimes blanches* (1976), a pamphlet attacking financial speculation and its effects on the countryside, is the natural development of the indignation which had castigated '. . . those bishops of commerce/with eyes like marrow seeds' in *Le Valais au gosier de grive*. More startling is the novel *Le Match Valais-Judée* (1968) in which God organises a contest at Sion in the Valais to celebrate two thousand years of Catholicism. The two teams, local saints and celebrities on the one side, biblical figures on the other, set to with a will, creating a scene which has justly been called Rabelaisian and is pictorially reminiscent of the lighter aspects of Breughel. But when God comes down to look at the world, he is appalled at the desecration and commercialism. He decrees that the Devil must be caught at once, and the world may then go on for another thousand years. This battle for the soul of mankind, expressed through the image of the Valais, creates a powerful myth for which Chappaz's atemporal images and language are a fitting medium. The novel is outstanding as an example of how regional consciousness can be the basis for a universally valid statement about the human condition.

Jacques Chessex expresses his Swiss identity somewhat differently. One could more aptly in his case talk about a distinct Swiss sensibility, rather than national consciousness. His interest lies with people rather than places. Lacking Chappaz's metaphysical dimension he is typical of the Protestant tradition in his concern with self-knowledge and the problem of human isolation. In particular his book of prose sketches, *Portrait des Vaudois* (1969), illustrates his search for the identity of his own generation in the traditions, history, moods and scenery of his environment. In his novel *L'Ogre*, which won the Prix Goncourt in 1973, he is not merely painting the psychology of his central character, Jean Calmet, a teacher in his late thirties whose tyrannical father obsesses him even after death, but developing an Ogre myth through which the whole of Swiss society is attacked. The devouring of tender flesh is a recurrent image, applicable to the intolerant M. Grapp, director of Jean's school, who drives out his rebellious pupils with a whip, applicable too to the destructive power of bourgeois morality. The younger generation has the strength to combat its ogres, a strength symbolised in the sexuality of Thérèse and Marc. Jean's impotence is sexual, intellectual and spiritual. The same sort of attack on Swiss values is developed in *L'Ardent Royaume* (1975), but in his poems, *Élégie soleil du regret* (1976) and the short studies, *Le Séjour des morts* (1977), a more fragmented and uncertain response to life emerges. In the stories, obsessive themes of irregular sexuality surface, now less obviously in the context of society's hypocrisy. Death is ever-present — accidental, suicide, during an abortion in 'Le Fort', even simulated in 'Te Deum' (just as when Marc and Isabelle are photographed playing dead in *L'Ogre*). The poems also reduce the themes of his earlier work to fragments: the ogre-father image in 'Tyran', oppressive morality in 'Hiver', solitude in 'Impénétrables'. In these later works Chessex' desperation about his own identity has absorbed all his vision of the world around him. The tone is summed up in the poem 'Le beau canal', where he contrasts himself with the serenity and certainty of La Fontaine.

> Et j'eusse aussi peut-être rencontré
> La perfection dans ma vie et dans mes songes écrits
> A mon tour calme et heureux dans cette éternité
> Où ne m'eussent pas déchiré les anges
> Vengeurs de ma saison et du paysage
> Pleins de souci de mon pas précaire
> Jaloux de cette eau pure dans le vert.

[And I should also perhaps have met/perfection in my life and in my written dreams/in my turn calm and happy in this eternity/where I would not have been torn apart by the angels/avenging my season and landscape/full of concern for my precarious step/jealous of this pure water in the green grass.]

As we can see, many Swiss writers of today find that their awareness of being Swiss is an important basis for both the investigation of the self and the expression of universal problems. It is interesting that the Swiss-French have taken longer to orientate themselves in this respect than their German-speaking counterparts. What Max Frisch saw as 'the great good-fortune of being the son of a small country' was the freedom to work outwards from immediate experience to a universal dimension. Perhaps Jean-Pierre Monnier is right in attributing this difference between the two sectors of Switzerland to the forcible severance from metropolitan German culture inflicted on the Swiss-Germans by the rise of the Nazis and the events of World War II. There is no doubt, however, that it is now in their immediate world that those Swiss-French writers who have something new to say on a general human plane find their finest source of inspiration. As Monnier puts it in *L'Age ingrat du roman:* '. . . it is to it [ie, the land] that we owe our struggles, our departures and returns, our brief certainties and our eternal questions. Of course, it is not enough to describe it. Thanks to the highest virtues of the imagination we must also learn to leave it behind, but in the hope of finding it again, this time above us.'

Quebec
The situation in French-speaking Canada — which can be more or less identified with the province of Quebec — is different again. At one level it is as though the struggles between the Jura and the canton of Berne (of which the former until very recently has formed a part) were raised to national status. But the proximity of America and the status of English as a world language, together with a social conservatism which considerably widened the gap between Quebec and France in the period 1930-60, have made the problem of relations with the metropolitan culture less relevant and the difficulties of retaining a separate identity from the alien culture much

greater. Hence the present existence of two quite different types of literary identity: the desire to mark one's separateness from Anglophone North American literature by integrating oneself to some degree into metropolitan French culture, and the desire to create a literature which exclusively reflects the forms and values of Quebec in its peculiar situation.

The development of *littérature québécoise* has followed a clear chronological pattern. François-Xavier Garneau's *Histoire du Canada* (1845-8) was the inspiration for a literary nationalism of an historical and picturesque sort. From the 1860s, with the periodicals *Les Soirées canadiennes* and *Le Foyer canadien*, a folklore movement got under way, leading to an *indigénisme* heavily influenced by the conservative moralising of the Canadian Catholic church. Until World War II, fiction in particular worked under these constraints. The novel of the pioneer spirit, such as Louis Hémon's *Maria Chapdelaine* (1916) and Félix-Antoine Savard's more mystical reworking of Hémon's themes in *Menaud, maître-draveur* (1937), presents a study of national types, the clash of rural and urban society, the confrontation between past and present and the need for man to face up to the call of the great open spaces. Gradually the idealising tendencies of this sort of work give way to a more detached appraisal of rural realities. *Trente arpents* (1938) by Ringuet (pen-name of Louis-Philippe Panneton) suggests with Zolaesque fatality the decline of the agricultural community and the loss of cultural identity. This sociological form of novel quickly absorbs a broader area of Canadian life, taking in the urban realities of Quebec and Montreal both descriptively, as in Roger Lemelin's *Au pied de la Pente douce* (1944), and critically, as in Gabrielle Roy's Prix-Femina-winning *Bonheur d'occasion* (1945). The latter is a good illustration of the growing sophistication of the French-Canadian novel at this period: the portrait of the Saint-Henri district of Montreal is integrated into a social study of women workers, a psychological study of Rose-Anna

Lacasse and her daughter Florentine, and a more general analysis of the repercussions of war. With *Bonheur d'occasion*, thematically and stylistically the synthesis of national and wider interests begins to be achieved.

French-Canadian poetry developed in a less steady fashion. No one now would read for pleasure the imitations of Lamartine and Hugo with which the nineteenth century abounded, and though the aestheticist verse of Paul Morin (1889-1963) and René Chopin (1885-1953) has its charm, there is nothing specifically Canadian about it. Of these earlier generations only Alfred Desrochers interested himself directly in Canadian types and scenes, in *L'Offrande aux vierges folles* and *A l'ombre de l'Orford*, but his verse is unadventurously Parnassian in its manufacture. The major figures of the period were both lost to literature while still young: Emile Nelligan went mad at twenty, having written some effective poems in which the accents of Baudelaire, Verlaine, symbolism and the decadents were applied to the themes of Gide's *Cahiers d'André Walter*; Saint-Denys-Garneau died at thirty-one, but not before revolutionising the techniques of Canadian poetry by the syntactic and prosodic innovations of *Regards et jeux dans l'espace* (1937) and the work posthumously published under the title *Les Solitudes*. It is with the work of Alain Grandbois that the individualism of these poets begins to work itself more consistently into both a Canadian and a universal context. Grandbois has something of the Blaise Cendrars about him: an inveterate traveller, he became involved in the Chinese Revolution and the Spanish Civil War without any revolutionary commitment to either. Though thematically his poems present a broad attempt to define and surpass the limits of the human condition, the insistence on vast, overpoweringly monotonous space, on wind, cold and heat in their greatest intensity, reflects a sensibility formed by the Canadian environment. Grandbois' major collections are *Iles de la nuit* (1944), *Rivages de l'homme* (1948) and *L'Etoile pourpre* (1957).

The period following World War II has been marked by growing political awareness and an accompanying emancipation from traditional literary techniques. The *Editions de l'Hexagone*, founded in 1953, has played a conscious role in this development; the individual alienation of the poet was to be put at the service of the group alienation of the French-speaking society to which he belonged. The theme of founding and belonging to a 'country' was now used in a way very different from the exoticism and pioneering patriotism of the Savard–Desrochers tradition. This is not to say that good folklore writers do not still exist, but the general trend has been to absorb the images of Quebec as a physical and historical entity and to incorporate them into more individual or metaphysical statements. Gatien Lapointe, in his collections *Jour malaisé* (1953) and *Otages de la joie* and his *Ode au Saint-Laurent* (1963), expresses the doubts of modern man, the problem of solitude, through images of the physical world, at times achieving a symbolism clearly valid on individual, political and universal levels together, as in 'Le chevalier de neige'. In his *Poèmes de l'Amérique étrangère* (1958) Michel van Schendel explores alienation through what he sees as the inherent foreign-ness of the French-Canadian in his own country, unless he can assimilate its space and history. With the growth of political consciousness in Quebec this type of poetry takes on a more affirmative tone. Jean Guy Pilon, much of whose poetry depends on variations of water imagery as the title of his collected work *Comme eau retenue* suggests, has moved further than van Schendel or Lapointe into a poetry of Lyrical committment, as in *Recours au pays* (1961):

> . . .
> Je suis d'un pays qui est comme une tache sous le pôle,
>   comme un fait divers, comme un film sans images.
>
> Comment réussir à dompter les espaces et les saisons, la
>   forêt et le froid? Comment y reconnaître mon visage?

NATIONAL CONSCIOUSNESS

> Ce pays n'a pas de maîtresse: il s'est improvisé. Tout
> pourrait y naître; tout peut y mourir.

[I am from a country which is like a stain beneath the pole,/like a trivial news item, like a film without pictures./How can one succeed in taming the spaces and seasons, the/forest and cold? How can I recognise my face there?/This country has no mistress: it has improvised itself. Anything/could be born there; anything can die there.]

The periodical *Liberté*, launched by L'Hexagone in 1959, took a lead in this politicisation. Two of its major contributors, Yves Préfontaine and Gaston Miron, are violently separatist. Their poetry, however, expresses revolution not directly, in the Aragon tradition, but through the violence and turmoil of language and image: nightmare landscapes in Préfontaine's *Boréal* and *Pays sans parole*, paradox and verbal disjunction in Miron's *L'Homme rapaillé* (1970). In 1963 another periodical, *Parti pris*, became the intellectual organ of the separatists, attempting to replace the old-style nationalism of the right wing and to undermine the pan-Canadianism of the Left. The poets associated with *Parti pris* are more traditionally committed in tone and more tied to a poetically fragmented reality, as, for example, Jacques Brault in *Mémoire* (1965) and *La Poésie ce matin* (1971). The leading poet of the movement, Paul Chamberland, has moved from the political rhetoric of *Terre Québec* (1964) to work that places his political and cultural aspirations more firmly in the context of modern man's metaphysical predicament, in *Eclats de la pierre noire d'où rejaillit ma vie* (1972).

The contemporary novel, together with the slowly developing French-Canadian theatre, has also evolved towards the expression of a political national consciousness. Yves Thériault's work started with the *Contes pour un homme seul* (1944) in which the celebration of a region which is both part of the real Canada and a transposition of it outside conventional time and space is carried out in a way reminiscent of C.F. Ramuz and the Giono of *Le Chant du monde*. Thériault's major novel, *Agaguk* (1958), extends to its ultimate the theme of human solitude, seen in all his works as an inherent function of human psychology rather than a product of environment. In the figure of the Eskimo hero man's instinctive patterns are laid bare without any suggestion that there is less psychological complexity simply because there is less civilisation. Indeed in *Ashini* and *Tayaout, fils d'Agaguk* the message is that natural man, the Amerindians of the former or the Eskimos of the latter, has power to carve a meaning out of life which has been lost by the decadent and hypocritical civilisation of the colonising 'whites'. Jacques Ferron has also looked to the Indian and to other non-Western traditions in his two collections of short stories, *Contes du pays incertain* (1962) and *Contes anglais et autres* (1964), where oral tradition, self-conscious fictionality and the fable all determine the special tone of the narratives. Writers associated with *Parti pris* or the periodicals which have succeeded it have seen the French-Canadians themselves as the colonised, but accept the notion of their culture as a debased one, of which *'joual'*, Montreal lower-class French, is the symbol. Hence Chamberland's belief that *joual* is a necessary vehicle for the literary expression of the cultural and social oppression which has given birth to such a linguistic form. In the novel Laurent Girouard's portrait of subhuman degradation, *La Ville inhumaine* (1964), adopts *joual* for this purpose; in the theatre Michel Tremblay uses it to express the same sense of dehumanisation in *Les Belles-soeurs* (1965), in which the 'action' is essentially verbal, focusing on the rather disconnected monologues of fifteen women who are sticking on gift stamps. In *La Duchesse de Langeais* Tremblay goes on to attack the pretence of virility which characterises French Canada, political impotence and social charade here being transferred into the metaphor of transvestism. Such metaphorical portrayal of political issues occurs in the novel too, for example, thinly disguised in the detective-story-formula anti-novels of Hubert Aquin, *Prochain épisode, Trou de mémoire* and *Les Ambassadeurs*.

It would be wrong, however, to suppose that national consciousness is only represented where political and social images of this sort are present. Some of the best modern *littérature québécoise* identifies itself by a Canadian literary sensibility rather than through a limited range of themes. Apart from those of the younger generation who enthusiastically espoused American pop culture and sexual liberation (entertainingly known as the Californicators) and the much less readable admirers of the Parisian *Tel Quel* group, there are serious writers of the last thirty years who have expressed their psychological and metaphysical dilemmas without reference to separatism. Fernand Ouellette, whose poems are informed by a consciousness of the nuclear age and consequently full of ambiguous images of light, heat and explosion, is a good example. Sylvain Garneau (1930-53) was another: his two collections *Objets trouvés* (1951) and *Les Trouble-fête* (1952) evoke man's detachment from and fascination with the objective world, and a brooding awareness of death and yet the temporary power of youth to bring a moment of gaiety. Among the novelists, Anne Hébert is particularly interesting because in her *Les Chambres de bois* (1958) she seeks to explore the nature of emotion and of contact between man and world on a poetic level, closely relating the first two sections to her own poem cycle, *Le Tombeau des rois*. Similarly, in his *L'Aquarium* (1962) Jacques Godbout, also a poet before he took to prose, has created a poetic structure to communicate the theme of *ennui* in the setting of a cosmopolitan group caught in a tropical country at the beginning of the rainy season and in a period of political ferment. The story line is, though a little odd, banal enough. The interest lies in the idea of psychological rebirth, this time that of the narrator, a Canadian artist, who gradually acquires the strength of character of the dead man whose body lies in the quicksands within sight of the house where the group are marooned. The narrative develops in a kind of psychological time, the gradual revelation of the dead man's character coinciding with the process of renewal in the narrator, so that the rains end, the revolution breaks and the narrator escapes, only when the picture of the dead man is complete.

Godbout's more recent novels, *Le Couteau sur la table*, *Salut Galarneau* and *D'Amour P.Q.*, move gradually towards a more overtly Canadian vision of society and a reflection of the place of the artist in that society, thus confirming his stated view that the novel is for him a tool of knowledge and an approach to life. A similar attitude to his medium, though leading to a very different kind of novel, is shown by the last of the writers I can mention here, Claude Jasmin. Jasmin's novels are theatrical in the same way that Godbout's are poetic: theatrical in the double sense of a cinematic action and a fascination with role playing. Violence occurs or is implied in all of them. The narrator of *Et puis tout est silence* lies trapped in the ruins of a barn-cum-summer theatre; the hero of *La Corde au cou* is to pay the penalty for murdering Suzanne; *Ethel et le terroriste*, launched by a murder, reflects throughout on the psychology of violence. The novels jump back and forth in time, showing the twisting and turning of characters caught in the 'destinies' defined by them at the outset of the plot. Like the modern world in which they are contained the heroes move further and faster from novel to novel, but they cannot escape their own emptiness, the emptiness which has drawn them into the destined act around which the narrative is built.

The novels of Jasmin and Godbout have been called *nouveaux romans*. Yet this is evidently only shorthand for saying that their meaning is partly or wholly defined by their form, a statement broadly true of Anne Hébert's prose also. None of these writers is interested in the intellectual games of a Nathalie Sarraute or a Robbe-Grillet. Like Aquin, their experimentalism is intended to express a particular sensibility

— not in this case primarily political but reflecting the conditions of contemporary man in an individual fashion. The themes of the two groups are by no means discrete: alienation, oppression, violence, the need for rebirth are simply the common source of disparate images. All their works are distinctively French-Canadian, but in slightly different ways. Since 1960, in the novel and poetry and to a lesser extent the theatre, French-Canadian literature has been finding it relatively easy to maintain a clear distinction from American or English literature in its forms. At the same time many writers have carried that distinction over into themes, maintaining their distance from the preoccupations of metropolitan France by a new kind of 'nationalist' literature. The future is therefore very much dependent, as some of these writers have publicly stated, on the political evolution of Quebec.

West Africa, Algeria, Switzerland, Canada: in each area a Francophone literature exists, but in each the production of that literature is defined by a different set of political and cultural factors. Very little of the work is narrowly nationalistic. It absorbs into itself many of the major preoccupations of modern man; it acknowledges the major aesthetic issues of other contemporary literatures. Nonetheless a wide range of very different writers from Senghor to Yacine Kateb, from Maurice Chappaz to Jacques Godbout, have seen their national identity as being the filter which must colour their expression of all other issues. In this sense it is fair to treat the disparate phenomena of non-metropolitan Francophone literatures as together creating a contribution to modern literature for which there is no parallel in France itself. In 1979 even the French themselves seem to have realised this. Not only was the Prix Goncourt awarded to the French-Canadian Antonine Maillet for *Pelagie-la-Charette*, a *Roots*-style epic about the ten thousand French immigrants deported to the USA after the British victory in Canada, but the runners-up were also non-metropolitan (one Caribbean, one Mauritian).

CHAPTER 9
The Literature of Literature

> All art is a surrogate for the individual imaginations of its audience.
> (John Fowles, *Daniel Martin*)

In France the alternation of ideas and form as the preoccupation of the literary artist is a phenomenon which goes back to the early nineteenth century. One can talk of the socially concerned Romantics as being replaced by the art for art's sake generation of the 1850s, of the moralists of the Catholic revival in the 1880s giving way to the aestheticists of the modernist movement after 1910, in the same way that the literature of action and commitment of the 1930s and 1940s yielded up its popularity to the dehumanised *nouveau roman* in the 1950s and 1960s. It is, however, a little misleading to accept these divisions between thought and form at their surface value. Just as art for art has its own idealist implications, so the formalists of the present century can be shown to be making their own contribution to the philosophical definition of the human condition. It is also, in the present century, misleading to draw too sharp a distinction between different periods, for the process of experimentation has been a constant one, leading towards a greater self-consciousness in literature, as dramatists and novelists began to explore and exploit the artifice inherent in the literary act. Even politically committed writers such as Vailland and Aragon have devoted attention to the problems of the writer as subject for fiction, Vailland in *La Fête*, Aragon in *La Mise à mort* and *Blanche ou l'oubli*.

As far as the novel goes, most major European innovators of the early part of the century were concerned primarily with developing techniques appropriate to their new vision of the world. In this they were less far from their predecessors than might be supposed. The function attributed to the novel in the nineteenth century had been descriptive and analytical, the recording of human institutions and psychology in a way that is at the same time an instruction and an entertainment. The assumption was that there are quantifiable objects, human nature, moral values, social structures, which the novelist will observe, dissect and present to the reader in palatable form. For such time as the world was thought to present a stable system of determinable values, this approach to the novel caused no problems. An impersonal narration implied the objectivity of the portrait. In so far as the writer felt the need to manipulate the reader's response to that portrait he could do so by direct intervention, by symbols and other forms of literary patterning or by a mixture of both. But already in Flaubert the seeds of a crisis are sown. The character of other people is unknowable, language deceptive, reality a relative term exposed to the distortion of the individual consciousness.

This crisis of language translates itself into poetry via the modernist movement and the surrealists, into the novel via Joyce and Virginia Woolf. When the latter writes:

> Life is a luminous halo, a semi-transparent envelope surrounding us from the beginning of consciousness to the end. Is not the task of the novelist to convey this varying, this unknown and uncircumscribed spirit, whatever aberration or complexity it may display, with as little mixture of the alien and external as possible?

she is proposing that the novelist stand back from the

incomprehensible processes of modern life and simply record details as they impinge on the individual consciousness. Reality ceases to have a meaning except as the incidental material from which the individual creates an independent aesthetic construct. Equally important is the psychological crisis. The notion of a human nature which exists for the novelist to analyse is undermined by the presentation of the human personality in Freudian and post-Freudian psychology. The rounded character, the psychological problem cease to be a reflection of the world around us. The logical conclusion deduced from this state of affairs is that literature cannot reflect the world outside *at all*. The world it creates is self-referential. Hence Alain Robbe-Grillet's assertion in *Pour un nouveau roman* (1963) that '. . . the true writer has nothing to say. He has merely a way of saying it'.

The self-conscious novel
The key influences for the development of the self-conscious novel in France have been Proust and Gide. In the former case the influence is at times difficult to appreciate, because it depends on very French exegeses of the text, such as Georges Poulet's *L'Espace proustien*, in which the conventional chronology of the novel expressed in the idea of *recherche* is suppressed altogether and the text represented as entirely existing in a Bergsonian psychological time, a series of independent images welded together by the artistic persona of the narrator. In fact there is nothing self-referential about Proust's thesis that art gives meaning to life. It is just that later writers have become mesmerised by the fact that this equation between art and life is symbolised in the sleight-of-hand by which it is implied that the novel *A la recherche* is the novel that Marcel will write (in mirror image) in response to the aesthetic principles deduced during the narrative. Gide's *Les Faux-monnayeurs*, on the other hand, only makes full sense as a reflection on the nature of literary form. Gide's approach to

the novel derives initially from a desire to represent the formlessness of reality: hence his objections to the closed system of significant relationships represented by the plot and to the notion of a privileged narrative observer.

What Gide is reacting against is clear from *Les Caves du Vatican*. This *sotie*, as he calls it, makes fun of the realistic novel with its portraiture of family relationships and cross-sections of different social milieux; it apes the didactic novel by presenting the conversion of the free-thinker, Anthime, and in inverse direction the aesthetic conversion of the novelist, Julius de Baraglioul (both later lapsing); there is a picaresque element in the tale, with Lafcadio as the adventuring hero; and finally a stratum of detective story in Protos' gang's duping of the Catholic faithful and Amédée's consequent attempts to unmask the kidnapping of the Pope. More important than the general parody of certain types of novel is the way in which *Les Caves* exaggerates the extent to which its characters are trapped within the system imposed by the traditional novel. Anthime and Julius are determined by set formulas, thus preventing them from having any meaningful three-dimensional existence. Even Lafcadio eventually falls back into the same sort of trap, representing a philosophical concept which prevents him from acting independently in any way. All Gide has done is to make this idea of the inauthenticity of human behaviour as portrayed in the traditional novel more overt by burlesquing it. Characters, events, themes, ideas are all beautifully structured to present a completely hollow world empty of meaning because its extreme 'systematicness' bears precisely no relationship to the randomness of reality. It is the function of Julius as novelist to comment on the very way in which Gide is writing *Les Caves*: he imagines a story conceived as an anti-system, with as its plot the actions which Lafcadio lives out; but when the crime he has imagined takes place, he refuses to believe in it as proof of his new theories, and returns instead to his old literary manner. In a sense he is right: for

Lafcadio the crime should have determined his freedom from the falsification of the system of Western society and bourgeois life — instead he becomes totally enmeshed in the system by falling under Protos' control, and is only released by an accident. System and reality are incompatible, system and the novel are only too compatible.

Gide wants the world of his own novels to be knowable only via the subjective responses to it of the various characters. It is not, however, possible for an author to renounce total control over the creatures of his text. At most the author can disclaim omniscience and attempt to install the reader in a position superior to his own. As Gide puts it in the *Journal des Faux-monnayeurs*:

> I should like these events to appear marginally distorted in the narrative they will make of them: a certain interest derives for the reader from the fact of having to *reconstruct*.

As the word *reconstruct* implies, the reader does not really take on the role of creator, because the novelist has planted the evidence of which he pretends ignorance. To put this artifice at one further remove Gide resorts to the inclusion in *Les Faux-monnayeurs* of a novelist writing a novel about events from which Gide's own novel is constructed, and called by the same title. The artistic process of writing can be discussed inside the attempt to put that theory into practice. Technically the structuring of reality which is inevitable on the author's part becomes determined by Edouard the fictional author rather than Gide the author of the real novel. The events, characters and so on are then the autobiographical fodder, the author's projection of his own possibilities; the limitations on their development are in part a function of Edouard the novelist's response to them — Edouard's theory of the novel being, as Gide makes plain, an inadequate one, for Edouard will never complete his novel.

Edouard's association with the novel presents, then, the same duality as is posed by Gide's theory of the novel: subjective involvement and artistic detachment. He is subjectively involved in his role as a plot reagent: he is uncle to Georges and Olivier, used to be intimate with Laura (whom his other nephew, Vincent, met by chance in a sanatorium), La Pérouse was his old music teacher and the Azais-Vedels his old landlords. His relationship with his nephew Olivier, contrasted with Olivier's other homosexual *affaire* with the other author in the book, Passavant, is of central importance. However, Edouard is also a detached observer, judging events from the outside, as the novelist seeking to reshape reality. At certain points he even intervenes in life in the interests of art as he sees it, for example, when he takes Boris to the Vedel school. He is then very put out by Boris' suicide because it does not fit the pattern of the novel as he predicts it. It is easy to suppose that because Edouard has preconceptions, they limit his ability to allow events to dictate the course of his novel, as he theoretically wants them to. Yet if we look into the second section, at Edouard's long discourse on the novel, its inner contradictions are exactly those of the theory which Gide propounds in his lectures on Dostoievsky. What is happening is that mutually incompatible forms of novel presentation are combined with theorising, itself ironically presented, to form a novel whose very artifice implies that systematisation is a function of the literary act and has nothing to do with the real world on which the 'matter' of the narrative is in some degree a comment.

One point which has to be made clear, for it is important for the way in which we read individual novels, is that the ideas of psychological time, reader participation and self-reflective literature are not specifically tied to any one view of the world or of the novel. They all imply a rejection of the knowability of outside reality and of the appropriateness of earlier forms of fictional presentation. One has only to compare Giono's *Les*

Ames fortes (1949) with Robert Pinget's *Autour de Mortin* to see how two writers of entirely different allegiances can exploit very similar techniques. *Les Ames fortes* deals with all the problems of space, time, and narrative perspective in one by adopting dialogue as its exclusive medium. Within this framework of present narration Giono creates a complex experience of past time, in which the same chronological area is gone over a number of times from different spatial perspectives (ie, by different characters or through shifts of memory within the same character). The novel superficially takes place entirely in reader time, and the inaccessability, the unverifiability, of the facts to which it relates is emphasised by the fact that both reader and characters, trapped in the eternal present sequence of the dialogue, are too far away in time to do more than hypothesise. The plot of the novel is, in fact, extremely complex if one takes into account not the superficial plot, which is the conversation between several village women who are holding the traditional vigil over a dead friend, but the subject of their conversation, which gradually becomes centred on the past life of the oldest of them, Thérèse, who takes over the main voice of the dialogue, while the various other women intervene to contradict and modify Thérèse's version from hearsay. *Autour de Mortin* is nominally the script for a radio play, but there is nothing to distinguish it formally from a novel in dialogue. Its three sections represent, firstly two people, possibly private detectives, watching an unidentified man through a keyhole, until they are obliged to intervene in what may be a suicide attempt, secondly a series of interviews about a writer, Alexandre Mortin, given by acquaintances and relatives more than ten years after his death, and thirdly some confused notes which appear to be those lost by Johann, Mortin's one-time manservant (the nature of his post is obscure). As in *Les Ames fortes* the distance in time between the present tense of the dialogue and the events of the chief character's life obliges both reader and participants in the dialogue to reconstruct, without any real criteria for evaluating the hypotheses.

Can one make any obvious distinction between the themes and forms of the two works? It is true that the dialogue in *Les Ames fortes* becomes concealed monologue as the elderly Thérèse offers the accounts of her relationship with Firmin and the Numances; but this allows for the ambiguity of autobiographical discourse and the difficulty of assessing how far a person knows even themself. At first Thérèse pictures her husband as an easy-going type who falls for her and elopes with her. Gradually this changes into the picture of a rather stupid man whom she manipulates by such devices as withholding her sexual favours. So that Thérèse's account, which is in other ways flattering to herself, gradually alters the weight of the husband–wife relationship until she appears the greater force for evil of the two. Whereas her companions' account from the outset makes Thérèse a silly young girl caught in an infatuation for a ruthless and coarse man who uses her in his machinations against the Numances. This account, which is fundamentally hostile to Thérèse in other respects, exonerates her of plotting the destruction of her benefactors and places the blame with Firmin. In each account a proportion of the facts overlaps; indeed it is noticeable that Thérèse's second version of life at the inn at Châtillon absorbs some of the alternative versions previously offered. But this absorption of previously given elements is not of itself a guarantee of truthfulness. It may reflect role-playing, myth-making, or simply the defective memory of an elderly lady. Since there is no irony in the presentation by which the reader might determine the gap between what the character says and the 'truth', he or she can only rely on the indications furnished by the accumulated common denominators, of which the most substantial is undoubtedly the climactic, calm admission that she deliberately manoeuvred to bring about the death of her husband, and that she enjoyed it. But is that pleasure explained by a hatred inspired by Firmin's role in the Nuance affair? Or is it the logical extension of Thérèse's account of her own behaviour? And does the confession correspond to a reality? The coincidence of versions does not guarantee fact, the coincidence of fact would not help us understand motivation.

Much the same problems arise in assessing the life of Alexandre Mortin. The significance of the keyhole passage is far from clear: the reader assumes that it concerns Mortin, and certain 'facts' overlap with information that crops up later in interviews, ie, that he walked around the house naked and that his niece had him under surveillance. The eight interviews progressively confuse matters. Did Mortin drink? What were his relations with Johann, with his niece, with Jacques Karas? Even the originality of Mortin's work on his friend Mortier is called into doubt. As each new character contributes his views, it becomes plain that we are learning more about the personalities of the speakers, especially the interviewer, than about Mortin. Memory is really an act of imagination (compare with Pinget's later novel, *Cette voix*, 1975). Just as in *Les Ames fortes*, there is very little value in the reader making hypotheses beyond a certain point because the writer has deliberately created a defective structure.

Both works provide a comment on identity, memory and communication. If there are significant differences they are these. Firstly that Giono implies that whatever else is in doubt, there was a conflict of essences between Thérèse and her husband and the Numances:

> Whilst the Firmins were plotting on the one side, the Numances were plotting on the other. Sheep and lambs, it was all the same . . . There was even a savagery on the Numance side which the Firmins were far from expecting.

Though the speaker is merely advancing an hypothesis, that the characters are examples of the will to power taken to opposite extremes and outside any sort of conventional psychological realism, the title of the novel and the coherence of the notion of the *âme forte* with the common elements in the different accounts suggest a potential if ungraspable reality. In the case of Mortin nothing could be less true. As Pinget's earlier monologue about the same character, *L'Hypothèse* (1964), suggests, there is no connection between literature and fact. More significantly, perhaps, by making his absent figure a writer, Pinget has drawn attention to the relationship, or non-relationship, of the autobiographical facts to the writer's texts. By the end it is clear that Mortin was probably unknowable in his lifetime and certainly cannot be reconstructed from the biased and faulty memories of those who claim to have known him. By implication the reader should stick to considering the texts of a writer without reference to his personality. Except that here of course we have a writer who, being himself fictional, has produced no texts. The centre of the play is doubly hollow. These points aside it is clear that the two works use similar techniques to make overlapping points, though put in the wider context of the respective work of Giono and Pinget they can be made to add up to something rather different.

The nouveau roman
Pinget belongs, in fact, to the recent wave of French writers for whom literature is supposed to be inward looking rather than a reflection of the world outside. The so-called *nouveaux romanciers*, writing mainly since 1950, are a very disparate group who are more clearly defined by their rejection of nineteenth-century realist techniques and their interest in Dostoievsky, Proust and Gide than by any common programme of stylistic or thematic innovation. Nor in my opinion can one talk about the work of any given writer as itself conforming to a single pattern. If we take for example Nathalie Sarraute's *Tropismes* (enlarged edition 1957) and Robbe-Grillet's *La Jalousie* (also 1957) it is plain that these works do

relate to identifiable psychological mechanisms outside the world of literature. *Tropismes*, a series of short texts exploring a number of related psychological phenomena, attempts to isolate the minute mental movements which lie at the origin of each human feeling or act and to show how these psychic ripples relate to the surface world of human interchange. The sketches therefore deal with psychological generality rather than the artificial construction of fictional personality. In a world of social convention, like that of the middle-class women taking tea in the tenth sketch, certain people will have instinctive perceptions of the threatening chaos (a brand of the absurd) which lies behind the masks. At the extreme point of awareness is the woman, in number five, to whom going to the bathroom seems 'an abrupt leap into the void, an act full of audacity', whereas in number sixteen the elderly couple in the café have had all their lifetime to construct a myth of reality. The resulting text is no less an interpretation of an external reality than *La Nausée* (the first edition of *Tropismes* appeared, interestingly enough, in 1939).

With *La Jalousie* the case is equally clear. Robbe-Grillet places the entire perception of events within the consciousness of a single character, but without giving that character an 'I' voice or the distance from self that accompanies such a voice. What the character is experiencing is a pathological state of jealousy. This really does not square with two of the statements in the author's essay 'Sur quelques notions périmées' (1957), to wit, that the novel can no longer have a central psychological study and that the artificiality of invention implied in the literary act should exclude the possibility of relating back to external reality at all. *La Jalousie* is certainly about a hole in time and about filling it with fiction, but the whole is a psychological reality. *A*, the narrator's wife, and Franck, a friend and possibly her lover, go on a business-cum-shopping trip into town, and are away longer than planned, ostensibly because the car breaks down. Into this absence the narrator projects a series of possibilities created out of minor aspects of reality but all probably figments of his jealous imagination. The entire time scale of the novel is the psychological time of the husband's mind, through which reality and fiction are filtered, indistinguishable to the reader. The exterior world as it impinges on the husband's consciousness becomes of great importance both because of its unyielding indifference to his inner state and because of the indications of that state which one gains from measuring the changes in his perceptions. In other words the techniques of the novel are being marshalled, albeit extremely skilfully, to recreate a common-or-garden psychological condition without having recourse to analysis from outside.

If *Tropismes* and *La Jalousie* can be read as a new form of psychological fiction, other works by Sarraute and Robbe-Grillet clearly cannot. Though in the former's *Portrait d'un inconnu* and *Martereau* the elusiveness of identity provides the central theme, in *Les Fruits d'or* the focus has started to shift towards the literary object. In *Entre la vie et la mort* the subject matter of the novel itself is the process of literary creation, by a writer who is given implicit general status: the fragmented material of the writer's life, from memories of his first train ride, of a teacher at his school, of his parents' reaction to the publication of his first book, to more literary chit-chat of the kind in *Les Fruits d'or*, is ambiguously both part of the creation of the writer and of his book; like Pinget's Mortin the writer only exists through his text, though the text has an undeniable and inextricable relationship with the experiences of its writer — what Proust referred to as 'consequently the only life really lived'.

Robbe-Grillet's novels remove the overt reference to fiction, but self-consciously suggest that they are composed of the parts of a conventional novel which will not fit together. *Les Gommes* for example relies on the pre-existence of the detective story as a genre. A man, Wallas, investigates a murder and eventually discovers the murderer to be himself. Into this potentially linear plot are inserted switches of time-sequence, and imaginary events that develop the *potential* of a situation. The switches of time result from the fact that within different psychologies the same phenomena stand in different relationship to one another. Yet at the same time it is possible to talk of real time as being entirely suspended during the process of the narrative. Wallas' watch has stopped at 7.30, the time when Dupont is supposed to have been murdered. Once the murder has been 'completed' at the close of the book, the watch is going again. The illusion of psychological realism which clings to the character of Wallas is undermined by the insistence on the world of the novel as constructed out of reality but existing in its own non-chronological time. This kind of approach to fiction is intensified in *Dans le labyrinthe*, where a soldier is wandering through a town after the defeat of his regiment, trying to return a box containing some apparently unimportant objects to the next-of-kin of a dead comrade. The material of the novel adds up to nothing more than a number of obsessions, unresolved except in so far as the initial narrator, the soldier, is dead by the end of the book, his narration taken over by the doctor who was caring for him. The labyrinth is an image of the soldier's wanderings, but also of the creative process of both author and reader. Like *Les Gommes* the novel is a jigsaw puzzle in which the pieces are deliberately made not to fit.

Such novels as these perform two functions. Firstly they stand with respect to *La Nausée* as the plays of Beckett or Ionesco do to those of Camus: they embody the existentialist position instead of merely propounding it. To borrow a neat phrase from Victor Brombert: 'These fictional anti-fictions negate philosophy in a philosophical manner.' The downgrading of plot, the fragmentation of psychology, the importance of objects and the colouring given to objects by the observing eye are essential elements of the text. Then, more radically, some of the novels undermine accepted conventions of writing as such, creating impossible tasks for the reader and destroying his confidence in the validity of critical judgment, just as his confidence in clichés and conventional views of reality are undermined by the material of the novels. There is a problem here. As happens with Ionesco and Beckett too, the reductive process leads either to a new set of conventions congealing or to silence. It is noticeable that Robbe-Grillet, between *La Maison de rendez-vous* (1965) and *Souvenirs du triangle d'or* (1978), confined himself almost entirely to making films, and that there is no real development in the form or ideas of the work of Nathalie Sarraute. These same limitations are apparent to a lesser degree in the work of Claude Simon, which shows a greater range of material and a significant development of style, but is equally static in its preoccupations.

Simon's novels are about time. They are dramatisations of the tension between the eternal present of existence and the awareness of chronological sequence into which that present is swallowed up. Each moment of experience is changed by the act of perceiving it, changed again by the act of remembering it, further deformed if any attempt is made to write it down. The secondary images through which these statements about time are made are constant: sexual obsession, love of nature, fascination with visual art, rejection of social convention and conservative forces, whether they be such inanimates as the power of money or human institutions like the army. With his fourth novel, *Le Vent*, Simon found a style appropriate to his themes. The description of the central character, a Dostoievskian 'idiot' who is exploited by the world around him, has to be reconstituted from the fragmentary account of the schoolmaster narrator. Yet, rather like Pinget's dead characters whose identity is deformed by the memory of others, Simon's character cannot be reconstituted; language itself distorts the attempt. *Le Vent*, however, still bears traces of a plot: an event like the theft of the jewels carries significance. With *La Route des Flandres* (1960) the action is more clearly absorbed into the psychology but the themes are the same. The defeat of the French at the battle of the Meuse in 1940 as transmitted through the memory of George, the narrator, becomes the disintegration of the world itself and the collapse of the power of memory to reconstruct that world. The dimension added in later novels is simply that of the self-consciousness of art itself in the attempt to transcribe reality. Thus *La Bataille de Pharsale* (1969) starts in the writer's study, and introduces a number of images which are themselves the story, there being no central thread: the battlefield where Caesar defeated Pompey, graffiti in the plaster of a farmhouse wall, an abandoned combine harvester, the battle on the Meuse again. Quotations are introduced from other authors — Caesar, Apuleius, Proust; erotic material is repeated word for word. What grows out of the various juxtapositions is an association of sexuality and death, time destroying love like everything else. *Triptyque* (1973) takes the process further, reducing its fragmented parallel 'events', a circus, a woman disembowelling a rabbit, a drunken stag party on the eve of a wedding, various barren sexual acts — adolescent masturbation, a couple in a barn committing *fellatio, coitus interruptus et al* — to the status of scraps of film, film in the making or static pictures. Yet one never feels in Simon's case as one does in Robbe-Grillet's that the fiction has become gratuitous: the work remains a monument to the vanity of man, and as such a reflection on the human condition.

Ironically the *nouveau romancier* with the most to express has been the one who has written the least fiction — Michel Butor. Butor's reputation as a novelist rests on four works published between 1954 and 1960: *Passage de milan, L'Emploi du temps, La Modification, Degrés*. Although the four novels show an increasing concern with the problem of writing, just as happens with Sarraute and Simon, they are neither escapist in the Robbe-Grillet manner nor as agonisedly pessimistic as Simon. One can even speak of a didactic purpose, a desire to 'change life', in the Rimbaud formula which Butor quotes with approval as the only possible aim for literature. Like Rimbaud, Butor sees the potentially liberating force of art as not prescriptive but inherent in the form of a work and the reader's response to it. The novelist's task is therefore both to interpret and to form reality:

> The novelist is the man who perceives that a structure is in the process of delineating itself in everything around him and who will pursue the structure, encourage its growth, perfect and study it up to the moment when it becomes legible to all.

Passage de milan begins the process of inter-relating writing and change but it is in *L'Emploi du temps* that the role of writing is rather more explicitly incorporated into the action of the novel. The central character, Jacques Revel, is spending a year in a northern English town, Bleston, for his firm. The text of the novel is his diary, five chapters representing the last five months of his stay; the previous seven have been a nightmare in that the city is meaningless to the outsider, off-putting in its ugliness and monotony, indifferent to human aspirations and values. What Revel does is to attempt to master this alienness by imposing the order of his own consciousness upon it, an order not merely geographical (whence the constant reference to maps) but in a broad sense psychological, as represented by the stained-glass window of Cain and Abel in the Old Cathedral and the eighteen Theseus tapestries in the Bleston museum. Murder and the labyrinth are indeed the obvious images for the insoluble riddles which the miniature universe of the city proposes. Revel's analyses do not answer questions about reality — was George Burton's accident really attempted murder? They do constitute a retrospective digestion of his past in Bleston in which the mythical strands, the journey, the issueless exploration, fratricide, parricide are also linked with the idea of cleansing via destruction. As Revel begins to understand himself via this retrospective assimilation, so the reader digests the relationship between the microcosm of the novel and the macrocosm of the real world.

La Modification hardly needs reading at the same level of abstraction as the earlier novels, even if the hero, it is suggested, will write a book about his experiences, thus transforming himself from a typewriter salesman — a representative of the everyday mechanics of language — to an artist. It is not, however, like *La Jalousie*, a disguised version of a conventional novel. The hero's experience does have a broader philosophical implication. At the simplest level the rather transparent device of having the narrator address himself, and therefore the reader, as *you* implies a generalisation in the meaning of the action. More importantly, the action itself is a metaphor of self-realisation. The narrator's journey between Paris, where his wife and family live, and Rome where he has a mistress, takes place in psychological time and space in so far as the new time and vision he gains from it and its incorporation into his remembered past are more important than the superficial reality of travelling. The modification that results is one of plans: he will not give up his intention and return to his family. It is also a more radical psychological modification which allows him to get his past into perspective, like the abbé in *Passage de milan*.

With *Degrés* we reach the ultimate in the *literature of literature* without losing any of Butor's didactic purpose. Jean Revel's attempt to investigate in depth the city of Bleston is already hampered by the difficulties of even reconstituting a meaning for his own actions there in the seven months of his stay prior to the act of writing. Pierre Vernier's ambition to chronicle a complete class in his school is correspondingly more difficult to realise, involving as it does the family and private life of thirty-one boys, not to mention the other masters who teach them. What Vernier inevitably discovers is that the truth of his account is transformed by its passage through his mind; it becomes 'instantly and fatally a lie'. Though he will not complete his task, it is to be carried on by others. If the ultimate realism and complete integration of space and time sought by Vernier are impossible, because the new world of the literary object is a distorting mirror, the attempt is a necessary one and revealing both for the individual and for man as a whole.

New mythologies expanded
Butor can be seen to share certain of the thematic and formal obsessions of the other *nouveaux romanciers*, particularly the detective story format, the obsession with time, and the concern with the nature of the relationship between writing and the real world. However, he distinguishes himself from them by the part he attributes in his novels to myth. I have already mentioned some of the mythological dimensions to *L'Emploi du temps*. In his essay, 'Le roman et la poésie', Butor emphasises the dangers to a society of losing contact with its mythological roots, for myth has a cleansing ritual function. In this he allies himself with a substantial movement of contemporary writers whose literary manner is very various, Julien Gracq and Michel Tournier for example, and also reveals a connection with at least one writer of what has been called the *nouveau nouveau roman*, J.M.G. LeClézio.

The 'new new novel' is really nothing of the kind. Much of it derives independently from the work of Maurice Blanchot and the linguistic and social philosophy associated with the periodical *Tel Quel*. Blanchot's novels illustrate what he has called 'the realisation by literature of its unreality', an unreality dependent on the deceptiveness of words, the absurdity of asking 'who is speaking?, what is happening, when and where?' about a collection of disembodied symbols on a piece of paper. At most one could say of a novel like *Thomas l'obscur*

(1941, a second version 1950) that it contains a consciousness trying to give itself reality. The negation of literature is completed by a writer like Philippe Sollers, the mouthpiece of *Tel Quel*. This periodical, founded in 1960, has become linked with the isolated French linguistic school which detaches words from any referential meaning in the concrete world. The conventional communicative function of language is then condemned as a bourgeois conspiracy:

> . . . the real is defined, in given historical circumstances, as what the majority, through those in power, and for specific economic reasons, is obliged to hold as real. This reality, moreover, is not manifest anywhere but in language, and the language of a society, its myths, is what it decides its reality to be. (Sollers, *Logiques*)

For Sollers, who began his writing career with a couple of traditional psychological novels and a more obviously experimental work, *Le Parc*, in which past, present, dream and reality are integrated, a literary work is not a structure but a process. Works like *Drame* (1965) and *Nombres* (1968) therefore fall into the same critical category as a certain sort of surrealism. If you entirely accept the philosophical, linguistic and political principles on which they are written, they are exemplary. If not, they are pointless collections of words.

LeClézio, though in some ways the most violently iconoclastic of writers in his theoretical pronouncements, has little in common with Blanchot or Sollers. While he accepts, in *Les Géants* (1973), that language is a weapon of society for the suppression of individuality, an ultimate form of aggression, he believes nonetheless that it is possible for an author to work his language over until it expresses what is unique to him. The literature of literature becomes, as has the act of criticism for Roland Barthes in *Fragments d'un discours amoureux*, an autobiographical statement, connecting in LeClézio's case via mythical reference to a universal human framework. From *Le Procès-verbal* (1963) to *Voyages de l'autre côté* (1975) archetypes abound, from Western, Central American and Indian tradition in particular. The first novel has a central character called Adam Pollo, Adam the first man and A. Pollo, Apollo the Greek sun-god; the boy obsessed with death in the last of the nine stories of *La Fièvre* is called Joseph Charon; François Besson in *Le Deluge* is an Oedipus transcript. *Voyages* represents a sustained exercise in mythical reference. It begins with the description of a pre-human world where all is under water and concludes with a description of the world as stone, inhabited only by snakes. The central narrative contains a series of journeys, imaginary developments which have their source in the contemplation of everyday objects, an olive tree, rain, a bat, reflections on water. LeClézio's aim here is to show that communication between men should be achieved via the elements — water, wind, flames in particular. The imaginary journeys, which have to avoid the sleeping giants of the man-made world (carrying on part of the symbolism of *Les Géants*) are guided by a mother-goddess figure, Najanaja, who teaches her companions how to integrate themselves with objects. The themes of all LeClézio's novels, alienation, metaphysical anguish, flight, sexual obsession, the sterility of man's creations, the nature and function of art, all find a resolution in this final myth — final in the sense that it is difficult to see where his work can develop next.

It would seem that French novelists have largely renounced the more abstruse and navel-contemplating forms of fictional meditation on the literary act that were fashionable in the 1960s, and are now leaving this to autobiography, a natural development for those who have seen the only connection between writing and reality as the process of reflecting the writer's consciousness. Those who find phenomenology an inadequate account of existence and Jacques Derrida's *De la Grammatologie* an unsound conception of the nature of language may find themselves in considerable sympathy with Jean-Pierre Monnier, the Swiss novelist and critic, when he protests in *L'Age ingrat du roman* that post-war French trends in the novel represent an essentially pessimistic formalism:

> ... revolt and despair are merely words emptied of their content if they do not leave open ways by which revenge may be taken. Unhappiness consists in the conception of unhappiness one forges by persisting in believing that unhappiness is an irrevocable condition, by resigning oneself to it ... by affirming that today all speech is inauthentic, all action useless, all communication impossible, in other words by acceding to Claude Simon's astonishing principle, 'The only way to avoid being alone any longer is to give up thinking.'

Quite obviously it is not inherent in literary experimentation that such an impasse should be reached. Even the 'novel within a novel' motif as used by Gide or Butor can communicate substantial matter which reflects upon the world outside the text. When the technical manipulation takes the form that it does in Queneau, Michel Tournier or LeClézio, it is a necessary part of the expression of a genuine attempt to confront major human issues. It is noticeable that nowhere is the novel less self-consciously new in its forms than in Algeria or Canada, where the urgency of everyday problems does not allow the writer the luxury of the kind of cultural auto-eroticism represented by the most hermetic of the metropolitan writers. Why are there no Yacine Katebs or Hubert Aquins in France itself, adapting experimental forms to overtly social ends? Possible answers might dwell on the sociological differences of the cultural environment. This would hardly account, however, for the absence of a parallel to Cathérine Colomb, the Swiss equivalent, on a surreal level, to Ivy Compton-Burnett.

Cathérine Colomb (1899-1965) published three major novels, linked in both themes and forms, *Chateaux en enfance*, *Les Esprits de la terre* and *Le Temps des anges*. The expulsion of plot and characterisation has not led to the treatment of writing as an object of study in itself. The problems of time, space, memory and their inter-relations, of isolation, exploitation and the conventions of a society (including its language) are explored for their own sake. In *Les Esprits de la terre* the kernel of action reflects a typically Compton-Burnett situation of family hostility: César, we can deduce from fragments of text, has been shouldered out of his share of the family inheritance by his younger brothers Eugène and Adolphe, and more specifically by Eugène's domineering wife, the ominous Madame. Somewhere behind the splintered mirror of the novel's time scale, in which past and present coexist with César's dream world, can be glimpsed the pattern of his existence, as he is shunted every six months from Eugène's curious chateau (only one tower surviving) among the vineyards at Fraidaigue on the shores of Lake Leman to La Maison d'En Haut, where Adolphe and Mélanie live. It is misleading to transcribe even the shreds of a plot in this way, because this totally misrepresents the way in which the images and language of the novel work. Man's inhumanity to man, the rapaciousness of the landed bourgeoisie, nostalgia for childhood, the anguish of solitude are themes reflected throughout the novel: by the Rims, poor relations confined to the stables at Fraidaigue, by Madame's shattering of César's plans for matrimony, by the young men who always fail to ask for the hand of Isabelle and César's attempts (or desires?) to murder Madame and his nephew Abraham. The same elements recur in different patterns, evolving only towards César's death. The childhood of Eugène, Adolphe, César, and their sister Zoe, who has escaped the world by going (or pretending to go) mad, represents a point which César disassociates from the present. He comes to the conclusion that nothing stops him from gaining '. . . the misty country of the children [ie, his brothers and sister], leaving this fragment of time the way you leave a fragment of space, falling vertically instead of always progressing horizontally'. At one level it is a romantic escape. At another, violence within and between people, expressed in action and suppressed in dreams, has finally triumphed on an

Earth which the meek seem unlikely to inherit. The novel contains a profound vision in which psychological and social implications are as integrally incorporated as metaphysical ones, all elements being embodied in the kaleidoscopic structure.

The view of life offered by Cathérine Colomb may not be one which her potential readers are inclined to share, any more than would be the case with Gracq or Tournier, let alone LeClézio. There is no doubt however that these writers have side-stepped or gone beyond the phenomenological and linguistic obsessions of certain *nouveaux romans*. (I would stress that one can best speak of the limitations of individual texts rather than the work of writers as a whole.) It seems that France may be in the middle of one of the periodic swings of emphasis from form back to content, and that the main value of the work of Robbe-Grillet and Claude Simon may prove to have been that they provoked radical reassessment of the potential of non-traditional novel techniques in subsequent writers with rather more to say. The new ingredient of the metropolitan novel seems to be its concern with mythology — not the reworking of previous literary structures which was so popular with dramatists in the 1920–40 period and has produced interesting reflections on identity and role playing in more recent texts such as Jean-Jacques Varujean's *La Ville en haut de la colline*, but an investigation of the significance, in human existence, of elemental forces, often interpreted in the light of non-Western traditions. It was necessary to sweep away many preconceptions about plot, character, time and space before the novel could freely explore the new ground. All that is slightly surprising is that it should have taken until now for writers to think of doing it. After all, *Tristram Shandy* and *Jacques le fataliste* did the spadework two hundred years ago.

Epilogue

As I suggested at the beginning of this study, it is easy to see in what way modern French writers have remained preoccupied with problems and ideas which have their roots in the nineteenth or late eighteenth centuries. The metaphysical and social ideals of the Romantics and their concern with the problem of self-knowledge are merely modified, extended or made more extreme, in surrealism, existentialism and *littérature engagée*. Just as the rational values of eighteenth-century philosophy, found wanting, were supplanted by the metaphysical aspirations of the generation of 1800–30, so the 'scientific' convictions of the turn of the present century were overturned by an anti-rationalist trend that surfaces in modernist poetry, in Giraudoux and Giono, Queneau and Samuel Beckett. Equally, the nineteenth-century division between solipsists and those who wanted collectively valid solutions (Stendhal, Rimbaud, Huysmans, versus Balzac, Hugo, Léon Bloy) is precisely mirrored in the contrast between Mauriac, Bernanos, Malraux, Camus and Gatti, and the individualists like Gide, Montherlant and Michel Tournier. One could even say that the insouciant *ennui* of a Laforgue turns up in the novels of a Marguerite Duras, the metaphysical anguish of Nerval, Baudelaire and Mallarmé in the plays of Ionesco or the novels of Claude Simon.

There is, for all this, a distinct modern sensibility in French literature which marks a definite development of the old preoccupations, if not a significant departure from them. It can be explained with reference to political events — the Great War, the *Front populaire*, Vichy, De Gaulle — or to cultural watersheds — Bergson, the *Ballets russes*, cubism, Proust — though neither method does more than highlight the importance of individual thematic and formal innovation. At their most extreme, Nervalian mistrust in the evidence of the senses and Flaubertian concern for the corrupting power of language have become the basis for an almost hysterical denial of the significance of the human mind itself. In their more restrained forms they have bred a greater sensitivity to the ambiguity of the relationships between thought and expression, representation and reality. Traditional concepts of poetic structure and diction, of stage illusion, of plot, characterisation and temporal sequence have all been subverted to reflect man's disintegrating faith in his perceptions of both the world around him and of himself, a mistrust as evident in metaphysicians like Bernanos and Cayrol as in Sartre or Nathalie Sarraute. Even in more conventionally didactic literature it has become accepted that the structure of a work necessarily determines the nature of its message; Catholic novelists seek ways of making the divine seem aesthetically inevitable; political playwrights attempt to command the aesthetic assent of their audience. In consequence, as the century progresses, an ever-increasing participation in the creative process is demanded of reader or spectator.

The growth of interest in formal experiment has been accompanied by a rejection of rational processes, as I said above. Yet, by a paradox that seems to have no parallel, in England at least, the greater the contempt a writer shows for reason and intellectual values, the less concession he or she makes to the literary conventions accepted by the ordinary reader. Even Julien Gracq and Michel Tournier are only in a comparative sense more accessible than Pinget and Claude

Simon. There is no less a mutual contempt between artist and society in France today than there was a hundred years ago. From an article in the *Bulletin du livre* in 1961 it can be seen that of aesthetically significant writers of the period only Saint-Exupéry has had three works in the top twenty 'bestsellers of the century'; by topping the million sales mark his *Vol de nuit* achieved equal status with *Tin Tin* and stayed slightly ahead of the French translation of *Gone with the Wind*. There is no reason to suppose that the attempts of *Tel Quel* and the school of Roland Barthes to present themselves as the dedicated enemies of bourgeois values have made their works any more acceptable to the average Renault worker than those of Claudel or Marguerite Yourcenar. French literature remains the most intellectually anti-intellectual in Europe.

Predicting the future of a culture is an activity somewhere between astrology and long-range weather forecasting in accuracy. The social and cultural variables in modern society are too numerous to list. The growing instability of Western society makes it improbable that the problems of human identity and social commitment which have exercised the minds of French writers for two centuries will become less pressing. On the other hand the reaction against a defeatist and self-indulgent formalism which denies even the transitional values of communication will doubtless continue, creating a situation where, on that critical Wall Street for which Auden and Macneice expressed their contempt, stocks in Robbe-Grillet are weak. All that is certain is that French literature will continue to develop in ways quite distinct from those of the Anglo-Saxon world, and Francophile *litterati* to murmur, in the tradition of Sterne, that, 'They order this matter . . . better in France.'

Further Reading

Political and social history
Cahm, E. *Politics and Society in Contemporary France* (London, 1972)
Cobban, A. *A History of Modern France*, vol 3 (London, 1965)
Zeldin, T. *France 1848–1945*, vol 2 (Oxford, 1977)

Literary history
Bruézière, M *Histoire descriptive de la littérature contemporaine* (2 vols, Paris, 1975)
Cruickshank, J. (ed.) *French Literature and its background*, vol VI (Oxford, 1970)

Intellectual and cultural background
Bradbury, M. and McFarlane, J. *Modernism* (London, 1976)
Caute, D. *Communism and the French Intellectuals 1914–1960* (London, 1964)
Coutrot, A. and Dreyfus, F. *Les Forces religieuses dans la société française* (Paris, 1966)
Gray, C. *Cubist Aesthetic Theories* (Baltimore, 1961)
Kochno, B. *Diaghilev and the Ballets Russes*, trans. A. Foulke (London, 1971)
Macquarrie, J. *Existentialism* (London, 1973)
Nadeau, M. *The History of Surrealism*, trans. R. Howard (London, 1973)
Peyrefitte, R. *Des Français* (Paris, 1970)
Prost, A. *Histoire de l'enseignement en France 1800–1967* (Paris, 1968)
Smith, C. *Contemporary French Philosophy* (London, 1964)

Aspects of literature
Adereth, M. *Commitment in Modern French Literature* (London, 1967)

Blair, D. *African Literature in French* (Cambridge, 1976)
Brombert, V. *The Intellectual Hero: Studies in the French Novel 1880–1955* (Philadelphia, 1961)
Caws, M. *The Inner Theatre of Recent French Poetry* (New Jersey, 1972)
Cruickshank, J. (ed.) *The Novelist as Philosopher: Studies in French Fiction 1935–1960* (London, 1962)
Esslin, M. *The Theatre of the Absurd* (London, 1962)
Fletcher, J. (ed.) *Forces in Modern French Drama: Studies in Variations on the Permitted Lie* (London, 1972)
Flower, J. *Writers and Politics in Modern France (1909–1961)* (London, 1977)
Gouze, R. *Les Bêtes à Goncourt: un demi-siècle de batailles littéraires* (Paris, 1973)
Guicharnaud, J. *Modern French Theatre from Giraudoux to Genet* (New Haven, 1967)
Heath, S. *The Nouveau Roman: A Study in the Practice of Writing* (London, 1972)
Hobson, Sir H. *French Theatre since 1880* (London, 1978)
Lejeune, P. *L'Autobiographie en France* (Paris, 1971)
Lehan, R. *A Dangerous Crossing: French Literary Existentialism and the Modern American Novel* (Carbondale and Edwardsville, 1973)
Mailhot, L. *La Littérature québécoise* (Paris, 1974)
O'Flaherty, K. *The Novel in France 1945–1965: A General Survey* (Cork, 1973)
Pondrom, C. *The Road from Paris: French Influence on English Poetry 1900–1920* (Cambridge, 1974)
Reck, R. *Literature and Responsibility: The French Novelist in the Twentieth Century* (Baton Rouge, 1969)
Sayre, R. *Solitude in Society: A Sociological Study in French Literature* (Cambridge, Massachusetts, 1978)
Warwick, J. *The Long Journey: Literary Themes of French Canada* (Toronto, 1968)

Index

Adamov, Antoine, 202, 220-1, 245
Alain, 84-5, 92, 99
Alain-Fournier, 86-8, 100-1, 108
Alexis, Jacques Stephen, 236, 238
Alquié, Ferdinand, 133-4
Anouilh, Jean, 46, 98, 100, 159-61, 165, 177, 216, 219
Apollinaire, Guillaume, 11, 28, 30-5, 37-41, 43, 46-7, 49-50, 136
Aquin, Hubert, 255-6, 278
Aragon, Louis, 134-6, 202-3, 206-12, 214-16, 223, 241, 253, 259
Arden, John, 226
Arrabal, Ferdinand, 155
Artaud, Antonin, 137, 165, 219
Audisio, Gabriel, 239
Auric, Georges, 45-6

Bachir Hadj Ali, 240
Badian, Seydou, 231
Bakst, Léon, 28
Ballets russes, 28, 50, 69, 282
Balzac, Honoré de, 208, 281
Barbusse, Henri, 110
Barrault, Jean-Louis, 219-20, 244
Barrès, Maurice, 48, 71, 110, 207
Barrie, James, 86
Barthes, Roland, 81, 276, 283
Baudelaire, Charles, 6-7, 31, 48, 86, 251, 281
Bazin, Hervé, 133
Bebey, Francis, 232
Beckett, Samuel, 134, 156-8, 200, 270-1, 281
Benda, Julien, 201-2
Bergson, Henri, 9-11, 21-2, 27, 31, 46-7, 82, 95, 133, 178-9, 282
Bernanos, Georges, 178, 191-9, 202, 281-2
Binet, Alfred, 83
Blaise, Marie-Claire, 108
Blanchot, Maurice, 275-6
Blondel, Maurice, 179
Bloy, Léon, 192, 281
Bonnefoy, Yves, 12
Borel, Jacques, 108
Bosco, Henri, 243
Boudjedra, Rachid, 242
Bourniquel, Camille, 108
Braque, Georges, 30
Brasillach, Robert, 100-1, 124, 130, 202
Brault, Jacques, 253
Brecht, Bertold, 219, 231
Breton, André, 11, 134-7, 165, 236
Butor, Michel, 272-5, 278

Camus, Albert, 150-5, 161, 177, 196, 200, 202, 216, 218-20, 223-5, 239, 244, 270, 281
Cayrol, Jean, 200, 282

Céline, Louis-Ferdinand, 74-9, 111, 147
Cendrars, Blaise, 11, 22-8, 30-2, 36-7, 41, 43, 46-9, 135-6, 243, 251
Césaire, Aimé, 229, 235-8
Cesbron, Gilbert, 179
Cézanne, Paul, 11
Chamberland, Paul, 253-4
Chamson, André, 243
Chappaz, Maurice, 245-7, 257
Char, René, 135
Chateaubriant, Alphonse de, 182
Chessex, Jacques, 243-5, 247-8
Chopin, René, 251
Claesson, Stig, *Vem älskar Yngve Frej?*, 244
Claudel, Paul, 182-4, 190, 197-8, 200, 234, 283
Clough, Arthur Hugh, 46
Cocteau, Jean, 8, 11, 24, 28-30, 36, 40-7, 49, 84, 94-102, 104, 108, 136-8, 177, 200, 219
Colette, 54
Colomb, Cathérine, 278-80
Compton-Burnett, Ivy, 278-9
Copeau, Jacques, 219
Cunéo, Anne, 244
Curel, Roger, 239

Dadié, Bernard, 233
Dahlberg, Edward, 106
Debluë, Henri, 244
Debussy, Claude, 28-9
Delaunay, Robert, 27-8
Depestre, René, 236
Déroulède, Paul, 214
Derrida, Jacques, 277
Desnos, Robert, 135
Desrochers, Alfred, 251-2
Diaghilev, Sergei, 28-9, 46
Dib, Mohammed, 239
Diop, Birago, 229, 232-3
Diop, David, 232
Dolin, Anton, 29
Dorgelès, Roland, 110
Dos Passos, John, 210
Dostoievsky, Feodor, 197, 199, 263, 267, 271
Dreyfus Affair, the, 69-71, 201
Drieu la Rochelle, Pierre, 110-11, 113, 124, 130-1, 147, 181
Dufy, Raoul, 45
Duhamel, Georges, 110, 146
Dullin, Charles, 219
Dupanloup, Bishop, 83
Duras, Marguerite, 158-9, 281

Eliot, T.S., 12, 15, 24, 35, 46, 49, 124
Eluard, Paul, 135, 202, 214-16
Emmanuel, Pierre, 184-5

Estang, Luc, 197

Farès, Nabile, 240-2
Farrell, James T., 106
Feraoun, Mouloud, 240
Ferron, Jacques, 254
Firbank, Ronald, 50, 90
Fitzgerald, Scott, 94
Flaubert, Gustave, 6, 259
Fowles, John, 258
France, Anatole, 69, 71
Frisch, Max, 249

Garneau, François-Xavier, 250
Garneau, Sylvain, 255
Gatti, Armand, 202, 219-23, 226, 245, 281
Gauguin, Paul, 11
Gautier, Théophile, 8
Genet, Jean, 158
Genevoix, Maurice, 243
Gide, André, 7, 9-11, 18-23, 46-50, 52-62, 69, 73, 85, 89, 102, 106-8, 133, 180, 198, 244, 251, 260-3, 267, 278, 281
Giono, Jean, 8, 110, 124-31, 158, 263-7, 281
Giraudoux, Jean, 106, 115, 134, 138-46, 147, 153, 159, 161, 165, 168, 171, 177, 200, 214, 219, 281
Girouard, Laurent, 254
Godbout, Jacques, 227, 255-7
Golding, William, 96, 105
Gorz, André, 79-81
Gracq, Julien, 159, 165-70, 176-7, 275, 280, 282
Grandbois, Alain, 251
Green, Julien, 81, 90, 187-92, 194-8
Greene, Graham, 199
Greki, Anna, 241
Gris, Juan, 30

Haddad, Malek, 240
Hahn, Reynaldo, 29
Hartley, L.P., 105
Hébert, Anne, 255-6
Heinzelmann, Alice, 244
Hemingway, Ernest, 101, 206, 212, 217
Hémon, Louis, 250
Hugo, Victor, 7, 83, 168, 190, 214, 251, 281
Huxley, Aldous, 94, 132, 224
Huysmans, J-K., 281

Ionesco, Eugène, 145-6, 154-5, 270-1, 281
Issa, Ibrahim, 229

Jacob, Max, 30, 43, 136
Jarry, Alfred, 11, 136
Jasmin, Claude, 256
Jouve, Pierre-Jean, 184-5
Joyce, James, 105, 259

Kateb, Yacine, 240, 242, 257, 278
Kerouac, Jack, 105
Khalfa, Boualem, 241
Kréa, Henri, 240-1

Laclos, Choderlos de, 212

Lacretelle, Jacques de, 6
Laforgue, Jules, 23, 31, 34, 281
Lamartine, Alphonse de, 251
Lapointe, Gatien, 252
Larbaud, Valery, 11, 23-5, 31, 46-7, 89-93, 99-101, 108
Larkin, Philip, 109, 226
La Tour du Pin, Patrice de, 183-4
Laye, Camara, 229
Le Clézio, J.M.G., 275-8, 280
Leconte de Lisle, 17
Leiris, Michel, 74, 77-80
Lemelin, Roger, 250
Lero, Etienne, 236
Letembet-Ambily, Antoine, 230
Littlewood, Joan, 226
Luze, Hubert de, 108

Maillet, Antonine, 257
Mallarmé, Stephane, 8-9, 11, 14, 18, 29, 31, 36, 281
Malraux, André, 28, 101, 111, 116-21, 124-125, 130-1, 151, 196, 201-2, 204-6, 208, 210-12, 217, 281
Mammeri, Mouloud, 239
Maran, René, 236
Marcel, Gabriel, 138, 179-82, 216-17
Marinetti, Filippo, 31
Maritain, Jacques, 178-9, 196
Martin du Gard, Roger, 105, 146
Massine, Leonide, 44
Matisse, Henri, 30
Mauriac, François, 178-9, 185-7, 191-2, 195, 197, 199, 281
Mendousse, P., 83
Menga, Guy, 230-1
Merleau-Ponty, Maurice, 133
Middleton Murry, John, 47
Milhaud, Darius, 29, 44-6
Miron, Gaston, 253
Monnier, Jean-Pierre, 244, 249, 277-8
Montherlant, Henry de, 8, 28, 82, 84-5, 97, 101-4, 108, 110, 121-4, 130-1, 199, 201, 281
Morand, Paul, 147
Morin, Paul, 251
Murdoch, Iris, 104-5

Nelligan, Emile, 251
Nerval, Gérard, 9, 281
Nijinsky, Vaslav, 29, 136
Nimier, Roger, 108, 170
Nizan, Paul, 202-4, 208, 210, 213

Orwell, George, 201, 203, 224
Ouellette, Fernand, 255
Owen, Wilfred, 38
Oyono, Guillaume, 230

Pascal, Blaise, 12, 61
Péguy, Charles, 110, 201, 214
Pelegri, Jean, 239
Péret, Benjamin, 135, 165
Peyrefitte, Roger, 102-3
Picasso, Pablo, 29-30, 43-4

287

Pilon, Jean-Guy, 252-3
Pinget, Robert, 243, 264-7, 269, 271, 282
Piscator, Erwin, 219, 223
Planchon, Roger, 219, 226
Pliya, Jean, 231
Poe, Edgar A., 6, 165
Politis, Kosmas, *Eroica,* 86
Ponge, Francis, 158
Poulenc, Francis, 44-6
Pound, Ezra, 13, 35, 49-50
Préfontaine, Yves, 253
Prévert, Jacques, 158, 161
Price-Mars, Jean, 236
Proust, Marcel, 7, 11, 29, 58-60, 62-74, 79-80, 106, 108, 260, 267, 272, 282
Psichari, Ernest, 110

Queneau, Raymond, 105-6, 134, 159, 161-5, 177, 200, 278, 281

Rabémananjara, Jacques, 229, 231
Radiguet, Raymond, 8, 11, 94-5
Rajemisa-Raolison, Régis, 232
Ramuz, C.F., 243, 253
Ranaivo, Flavien, 231-2
Randau, Robert, 239
Redon, Odilon, 11
Reinhardt, Max, 219
Renard, Jules, 84
Rimbaud, Artur, 7, 43, 48, 86, 94, 165, 236, 273, 281
Ringuet, 250
Rivaz, Alice, 244
Robbe-Grillet, Alain, 256, 260, 267-73, 280, 283
Roblès, Emmanuel, 239
Rochefort, Christiane, 108
Rolland, Romain, 105
Romains, Jules, 27, 105, 110
Roud, Gustave, 244
Roumain, Jacques, 236
Rousseau, Jean-Jacques, 53, 80-2
Roy, Gabrielle, 250-1
Roy, Jules, 239
Royère, Jean, 53

Sacco and Vanzetti, 221, 245
Sachs, Maurice, 74, 90, 108
Sagan, Françoise, 108, 181,
Saint-Denys-Garneau, Hector, 251
Saint-Exupéry, Antoine de, 111-16, 121, 124-125, 130-1, 201, 210, 283
Saint-Hélier, Monique, 244
Saint-John Perse, 8, 124-5, 130-1, 171, 234
Salacrou, Armand, 159-60
Salinger, J.D., 105
Salmon, André, 30
Sangnier, Marc, 179
Sarraute, Nathalie, 256, 267-9, 271, 273, 282
Sartre, Jean-Paul, 11, 67, 79, 111, 123, 133, 138, 140, 146-50, 153-5, 161, 164-5, 170, 177, 180-1, 196-7, 200, 202-3, 209-11, 214, 216-18, 223, 225, 244, 268, 270, 282

Satie, Eric, 29, 43-4
Savard, Félix-Antoine, 250, 252
Seferis, George, 12
Senghor, Léopold Sédar, 227, 229, 231, 233-236, 257
Shakespeare, *Romeo and Juliet,* 140, 189
  Richard III, 223
  Hamlet, 143
Simon, Claude, 271-3, 280-3
Six, Les, 44-5
Sollers, Philippe, 276
Soupault, Philippe, 135-6
Spender, Stephen, 101-2
Stein, Gertrude, 30, 52, 81
Stendhal, 53, 81, 103, 212, 281
Sterne, Laurence, 280, 283
Stevens, Wallace, 50
Stil, André, 206
Stravinsky, Igor, 29
Sue, Eugène, 208

Taos-Amrouche, Marguerite, 239-40
Thériault, Yves, 253-4
Tournier, Michel, 100, 106, 159, 170-77, 275, 278, 280-2
Tremblay, Michel, 254
Twain, Mark, 105
Tzara, Tristan, 134-5

U Tam'si, Tchicaya, 233-5

Vailland, Roger, 202-3, 211-13, 218, 259
Valéry, Paul, 10-18, 21-2, 24, 35, 43, 46-7, 49, 53
Vallès, Jules, 84
van Schendel, Michel, 252
Van Vechten, Carl, 50
Varujean, Jean-Jacques, 280
Velan, Yves, 244
Vercors, Pierre, 209
Verhaeren, Emile, 27
Verlaine, Paul, 94, 251
Verne, Jules, 171, 176
Vilar, Jean, 244
Visan, Tancrède de, 47
Vitrac, Roger, 136-7

Wagner, Richard, 72
Weideli, Walter, 245
Whitman, Walt, 23, 105
Wilde, Oscar, 62
Williams, Tennessee, 217
Williams, William Carlos, 30, 49
Wittig, Monique, 108
Woolf, Virginia, 104, 147, 259
Wordsworth, William, 73

Yeats, W.B., 11
Yourcenar, Marguerite, 133-4, 283

Zermatten, Maurice, 243-4
Zinsou, Senavo, 231
Zola, Emile, 201, 204, 207, 250